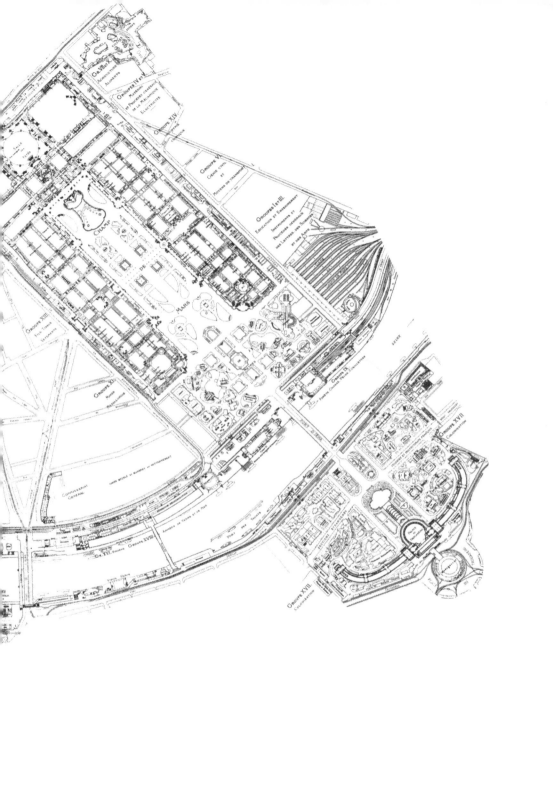

Binet's monumental entrance gate to the Place de la Concorde, with La Parisienne surmounting it

PARIS 1900

The eastern portion of the Quai des Nations

Italy   Turkey   United States   Austria   Bosnia   Hungary   Great Britain

The western portion of the Quai des Nations

Belgium   Norway   Germany   Spain   Monaco   Sweden   Greece   Serbia

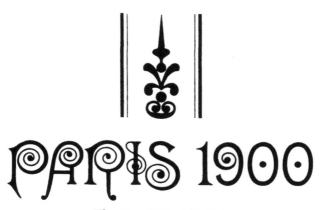

PARIS 1900

The Great World's Fair

Richard D. Mandell

University of Toronto Press

Preface • The impression given by the Exposition of 1900 can only be imagined by one who has toured and tried to glean some message from a large local fair or a world's fair. Typically at a large exhibition there are surging crowds, hawkers, flapping banners, and garish colours everywhere. In addition to the gaiety and the spendthrift atmosphere, the observer can sense about him a pervading rivalry as new products strive for his approbation, and businessmen, sleek representatives of great corporations, or hucksters of vulgar entertainment, vie for his cash.

The colours, noises, and crowds may mask purposeful competitions within a fair. The nineteenth-century exhibitions were occasions for the awarding of excellence by means of eagerly sought medals, ribbons, and richly engraved certificates of merit. The awards (or lack of them) could make or break an artist, craftsman, or inventor who offered his unique skills for judgement by the international juries. The expositions launched or ended careers, made or destroyed fortunes, and established or weakened the reputations of great firms. In all the large universal expositions nations too joined in expensive and earnest, though bloodless, battles for prestige.

The following long essay really has two purposes: one will be stated emphatically here and then neglected until the bibliography; the other will occupy the bulk of the discussion and is, in fact, described in the title of the book. I am eager to direct the attention of historians to the larger international exhibitions or world's fairs, particularly the nineteenth-century ones. I know that traditional problems (the Dreyfus Affair, for the Exposition of 1900) can be newly illuminated by such fresh sources of light. I also feel that the expositions themselves, being international and universal, are revelational, multi-sensuous summations of our culture at a particular period of time. Many, perhaps even all, of these great manifestations of our past deserve careful description, evocation, and analysis.

My discussion of the Exposition of 1900 will be an extended (though by no means as extended as it might be) illustration to support my espousal of the larger neglected topic. Paris 1900 was unusual in several ways. It was so very large, and its immensity extended to the number of visitors, exhibitors, prizes given, and the actual area covered. Then, too, its year and location naturally brought quite different results than those of its predecessors and followers. But other fairs were as fascinating, as rich, and can teach us as much about our past. In fact, an examination of each of the great expositions could offer a sort of comprehensive, though variously distorted, flash picture of world civilization at its particular epoch.

The nineteenth-century expositions, like the later ones, delighted their observers, but offered more and were less slickly organized than recent world's fairs. They were great events for the political, scholarly, and literary élites of the world. Each of those fairs was itself the occasion for demonstrating several preoccupations of the intellectuals of its age. Examples were the courageous and often amended schemes to classify the geometrically expanding fund of scientific and technical knowledge. Other efforts were the scholarly and technical congresses and the attempts to promote universal education. Most of all, the fairs themselves were manifestations of the positivists' faith in material and scientific progress as panaceas for all man's ills.

The impressions of a twentieth-century tourist at a world's fair are likely to be far paler than were those of a visitor at one sixty or more years ago. We of the mid-twentieth century all favour standardized clothing and rational architecture. Even at a great modern fair, such as the Universal Exposition in Brussels in 1958, one could distinguish the various nationalities by the cut of their trousers or the pointedness of their shoes, for in our vitamin-fed, mode-conscious world everyone looks and dresses almost alike.

· In 1900 only the rich resembled one another. At that time, it was still expected that the bourgeoisie of each nation would dress distinctively. Peasants flocked to Paris in 1900 and wore their festive national costumes. This diversity of clothing was seen against the jewel colours—iridescent purples, deep greens, and sultry oranges and reds—that were the rage at the end of the century. These tones enlivened façades, banners, frescos, arches, columns, fountains, and arbours, and were just the two-dimensional aspect of a spectacle that changed constantly in sensuous intensity and in levels of intellectual appeal. For most observers during the summer of 1900, the dazzling, shifting, and ultimately chaotic impression of the exposition was stirring beyond all expectation, for in 1900 there were no movies or other amusements that could even feebly compete with that miracle in total effect. The novelist Paul Morand has recalled the Exposition of 1900 in Paris as

. . . a new and ephemeral city hidden in the centre of the other, a whole quarter of Paris in fancy dress, a ball, where the buildings were the masqueraders. To our childish eyes it was a marvel, a coloured picture book, a cave filled by strangers with treasure.[1]

An exposition's size can be gauged by its attendance (the usual indicator of grandeur), the number of exhibitors, its extent of geographical representation, its comprehensiveness, its over-all cost, and the total area it covers. By all these standards, except for the last two, the Exposition of 1900 was the greatest of all time. In attendance, its closest competitors have been the ones in Brussels in 1958 and in New York in 1964–65. Brussels attracted 41,454,412 visitors; attendance in New York for two years was 51,607,307. Total admissions for *one* year at the exposition in Paris were 50,860,801. The Exposition of 1900 probably was the largest and most ambitious international gathering for any purpose ever. All the great nations tried to offer the pick of their art and industry for the judgement of the millions of visitors. Many of the remotest regions of the world were represented in the colonial exhibits. In one major respect, this world's fair will never be equalled: it was the last time anyone tried to include *all* of man's activity in one display. The pace of technical and artistic innovation since then has made inconceivable any plan for assembling the evidence of man's creativity in one exhibit, however immense. That last festival of amusement and education, co-operation and competition, chauvinism and internationalism, could only be planned during a time that still had faith in optimistic philosophical systems, hopes for social reform, joy in expanding material wealth, and confidence in the moral benefits of art.

A large part of this book will be an extended aside on the political history of an important period of the French Third Republic. The French universal expositions were not only larger and more comprehensive than those that took place elsewhere, they were projects of the government itself. Elsewhere they were (and still are) usually arranged and financed by businessmen, assisted perhaps by governmental subsidies or guarantees. France in the nineteenth century could not entrust anything so important to businessmen. I shall examine some of the political debates that took place during the planning stages of the Exposition of 1900. Most of one chapter will examine in detail the last months of the Dreyfus Affair. As a rough indication of the importance of the subject, it will be seen that to Frenchmen the Fair of 1900, since then almost forgotten, was a more serious and compelling matter than the Affair which has endlessly been of current interest. In other parts of the discussion that are properly political, I shall deal with the impact of the Exposition of 1900 on two further matters of enduring interest to political historians: French diplomacy, particularly relations with Germany before the war of 1914; and the changes in French nationalism as a result of the more general internal recognition that France had declined greatly as a world power during the course of the nineteenth century.

Any world's fair is complex, certainly so complex as to be unknowable as a whole. One can recall the difficulty of describing a large party to an uninvited acquaintance of the guests. Does the narrator describe the past party chronologically, by individuals (their dress, states of sobriety, amorousness, moods, relationships to the host and to each other), or by groups (the "ins," the "outs," the young, the old, the boisterous, the introverted, those striving for attention, those not needing it)? Can or should the narrator tell his listener how much the festivities cost? What are the standards for judging whether this complicated party was a success? Many will agree on certain aspects of the party and disagree on many others. Parties (and world's fairs) can be rich experiences; they can mask ambition, be stepping-stones to triumph or disaster. They can succeed or fail, live indelibly in the minds of the participants (or in history) or be immediately forgotten.

A long chapter will survey the actual contents of the Exposition of 1900. The choice of what to include was not made arbitrarily; though perhaps in a cursory form, I have tried to cover the whole exposition spatially, by nations, and chronologically. Since my discussion is for today's readers, I shall make only passing reference to such things as ballooning and hook-and-ladder competitions, which were considered important news at the time. On the other hand, the second revived Olympic Games will be discussed at considerably more length, though they received almost no attention in 1900. The relatively extensive descriptions of decorative art and architecture are, I believe, in balance with the "tone" of the whole show. A paramount intention of the exposition's organizers was to offer a visual feast. In their eagerness to surpass the visual impact of previous expositions, the designers of 1900 may have inadvertently contributed to the eroding of the consensus that supported the vast productions of nineteenth-century eclecticism. The outpouring of books on Art Nouveau frequently suggests that the Exposition of 1900 offered the apotheosis of this style. But no recent writer has investigated what kind of Art Nouveau was actually at the fair. I wish to set the record straight.

This exposition's place in time, its size, and its ambitions will require the discussion of some traditional historical problems. Peaceful idealism and selfish nationalism, pervading and conflicting motives of the organizers and participators in 1900, will receive considerable attention. By definition the Exposition of 1900 was a *fin de siècle* event *par excellence*. Since it was attended and observed by many intellectuals, I feel the exposition can be viewed as a weathervane indicating certain currents in *fin de siècle* thought. Other writers have analyzed the ideology of major figures during these years, which, for European intellectual history at least, are at last beginning to form a coherent "period." I have deliberately chosen to emphasize four figures who represent a fairly wide spread of national reactions. All were very close to the actual contents and events of the Exposition of 1900. There were many others, less close, less concerned, who might have been examined in depth.

The lack of available surveys of world's fairs has made the inclusion of a lengthy Introduction advisable. This chapter consists of a history of international exhibitions through 1889. An explanation of the issues, content, and results of the Exposition of 1900 demands a discussion of this fair's debts to exhibitions that took place earlier in the century, particularly to its predecessor and competitor, the Exposition of 1889.

The extensive Bibliography again illustrates the twofold intention of this book, to demonstrate the variety and richness of the sources that deal with this one exposition and then, hopefully, to point the way for future historians of world's fairs. Very little reliable secondary literature on the great expositions exists, yet there are vast amounts of extant materials that could be the bases for the writing of useful histories. With the exception of the Crystal Palace Exhibition of 1851 (the Exhibition of 1862 in London was bigger, but has been totally forgotten) there is no well-rounded survey of any world's fair. Some fairs are known only by minor side issues or by anecdotes: Vienna 1873 (Japanese art in Europe), Philadelphia 1876 (the telephone), Chicago 1893 (Louis Sullivan's condemnation of the "White City"), Paris 1889 (the Eiffel Tower). Many great international exhibitions have been almost totally forgotten. This oblivion is especially to be regretted in the case of a noble, carefully thought-out, and influential exposition, such as Frédéric

Le Play's in 1867 in Paris. The World's Columbian Exposition of 1893 in Chicago began an era of distinct intellectual activity in the American Middle West. Historians, a conservative breed, have perhaps avoided examining the world's fairs because they are so difficult to classify. The problem will remain, but this book will be helpful if it clears up some mysteries about the availability and relevance of the bibliography of international exhibitions.

After 1900 the whole international exhibition movement changed. The aims of the exhibitions became narrower, less political. The changes could be largely attributed to the loss of interest in fairs by the French governments and the emboldening of the businessmen's organization, the Comité français des expositions à l'étranger, discussed in the Conclusion. Sources for a study of the rationalization of the movement and then of the revival of ambitious expositions in the 1930's and again after World War II will also be found in the second section of the Bibliography.

There may be some unnecessary confusion about terminology. In accepted usage in Great Britain, a fair is small, an exhibition is large. Exhibitions may be local, national, or international; they may also be special or universal. The French term *exposition* has passed into English, particularly into American usage. Almost all the complications can be attributed to the Americans, who embraced the French word at the same time that they transferred the last half of "state fair" to much larger international exhibitions and called them "world's fairs." I will continue the practice of previous American writers on this subject and use "world's fair" (now the most common American usage), "international exhibition" (the usual English term), and "universal exposition" almost interchangeably.

Comparisons of currency and standards of value for different periods are always difficult. However, it will be helpful to the reader if he assumes that the purchasing power of the franc in France during the period here considered was very roughly the same as that of the present-day dollar in North America.

I must thank many people for their encouragement and suggestions. Richard Herr of the University of California at Berkeley was wisely restraining and critical at the inception of this work. John C. Cairns, of the University of Toronto, whom I heeded, suggested reorganizations and areas for strengthening the manuscript. The encouragement and corrections of David L. Landes of Harvard University were greatly elating and emboldening. I am extremely grateful for the generous and strikingly lucid comments of James Sheehan of Northwestern University, one of the most rigorous intellectuals and subtlest wits I know. Katherine Homes, Peter Larmour, Hugh Parry, Gunther Sieburth, Thomas Marchant, John Yolton, and others were kind enough to read and comment on early versions of the manuscript. Barbara Hill offered especially valuable suggestions. My gratitude to all these persons is deeply felt.

This project is based upon a great deal of library research. I was fortunate to be encouraged and given bibliographical assistance by M. H. Marty, retired librarian of the Chambre de Commerce de Paris. I am grateful to the staffs of the Center for Research Libraries in Chicago, the library at the University of California at Berkeley, the New York Public Library, the Widener Library at Harvard University, and the Library of Congress. I was able to carry out research in Paris at the Bibliothèque municipale, the library of the Chambre de Commerce, the Bibliothèque nationale, the Bibliothèque Forney, and the Archives of the Ministry of Foreign Affairs; in London at the British Museum; and in Brussels at the Royal Library. Librarians at all these institutions were unusually gracious, possibly because of their awareness of the long neglect of such fascinating materials. The University of California at Berkeley and York University in Toronto gave me grants that paid for travel and microfilms. My greatest debt of gratitude is to my wife for her patience, encouragement, and good humour from the very beginning of the project.

Contents

ix Preface

3 Introduction: Exhibitions in the
Nineteenth Century

25 Origins and Opposition

52 Preparations

62 At the Fair

89 The Affair and the Fair: Politics
and the Exposition

104 Was it a Success?

118 Conclusion: The End of an Era

122 Bibliography

141 Notes

167 Index

PARIS 1900

Introduction: Exhibitions in the Nineteenth Century • Even in primitive markets purchasers and sellers mix business and pleasure. People come to the market place from great or small distances not only to trade, but to see and be seen. To one who observes the periodic markets in India or Mexico, it is clear that the bustle and gaiety of a town on market day is quite different from the atmosphere of an A & P, a Macy's, or a Selfridge's. The animation of the people, the noise, the variety of regional goods and regional costumes give a temporary market or fair a *Stimmung* and an excitement that transcend its economic purpose. For market day or week, for a state fair, for a national exhibition, or for one of the universal expositions or world's fairs, one hopes for smiling crowds, bracing weather. Indeed, many things besides trade goods are on display. As we shall see, exhibitions can serve many purposes. In the large exhibitions the didactic intentions of their organizers, national prestige, and international politics may even cause commerce to be only the occasion for the display as a whole.

There were fairs in the ancient Middle East. The mediaeval trade fairs were important in the revival of commerce, intellectual life, and political stability in Europe. Since fairs brought some wealth to the areas where they flourished, petty rulers competed as hosts by offering legal protection or tax exemptions to traders and visitors. Later, as territorial units became larger and the power of the state greater, princes promoted fairs for political purposes. Parochial states and national economic policies are not inconsistent with a thrilling exhibition, provided the sovereign area covers a variety of crafts and regional specialties. But with the rise of the state, the cosmopolitanism of the fairs naturally declined.

In the early eighteenth century a new kind of exhibition came into being in Paris. This was the public art show sponsored frequently by Louis XIV and staged by his Académie des Beaux-Arts. The "salons," as they came to be called, were annual affairs by the end of the century. Public art displays (really the revival of a Graeco-Roman custom) also spread to other European capitals. These exhibitions of painting and sculpture were always well attended. Among their multiple intentions were the promotion of sales for the artists, the improvement of public taste, increased competition for excellence, and the strengthening of the national reputation for artistic creativity.

The first public industrial displays had similar purposes. In 1760 the Royal Society of Arts in London purchased the prize-winning models of agricultural tools, cranes, windmills, and sawmills from a recent competition. The Society then hired a warehouse for a public display to last two weeks. However, its popularity convinced them to extend the show for three more weeks.[1] This exhibition occurred when there was in England a fresh and intense interest in mechanical contrivances and their possible use for profit. Independently of the art shows, the small industrial exhibits also began to be staged on the continent. By the end of the eighteenth century, then, several European states considered it wise to encourage inventors and artists by public displays of their work and by awarding prizes and decorations such as medals and elaborately engraved certificates of merit. However, there was always a rigid caste division between the *arts libéraux* and the *arts utiles*. Inventors had far less prestige than painters or sculptors.

In 1797 the French national warehouses of Gobelin, Sèvres, and Savonnerie were overstocked because of the English blockade of the continent. The commissioner in charge of these factories received permission from the Minister of the Interior, François de Neufchâteau, to hold a public display of these goods at the then empty château at St. Cloud.[2] This sales promotion worked well, partly because there were accompanying band concerts and a lottery with some of the displayed goods as prizes. A similar bazaar was held the next year.

These sales-*cum*-entertainment were successful and popular. Neufchâteau quickly planned a much larger exhibit that would benefit French industry generally. On August 28, 1798, he circulated a proclamation calling for a "public exhibition of the products of French industry" to be held in Paris during the five complementary days of the year VI (September 17–21, 1798). The proclamation ended:

The French have astonished Europe with the rapidity of their manœuvres in war; they must rush into commercial ventures, and the arts of peace with the same eagerness.[3]

The great painter Jacques Louis David designed the temporary façades that sheltered the exhibits. There were parades, speeches, and music at the opening. Balls honored important exhibitors and observers.[4] Though there were just 110 exhibitors, and little time for elaborate preparations, this exhibition was significant in several ways. The products of industry had never before received honours usually due to the fine arts. Eleven exhibitors won gold medals; eighteen others had their names publicly proclaimed. The prestige of the manufacturers and that of the government were thus deftly intertwined.

This first national industrial exhibition, which publicized the arts of peace at home, was also part of the long struggle against England. By encouraging technological competition within France, François de Neufchâteau intended this exhibition and its hoped-for successors to raise the level of French technology above that of England. He also planned to expand French commerce on the continent by demonstrating the excellence of French goods to foreign observers.

Neufchâteau wanted to make the exhibitions annual, but the distractions of war delayed the next one until 1801.[5] This also took place at the Louvre (then called the Palais national des Arts et des Sciences). In its duration, the number of exhibitors, and the number of awards, this exhibition was about double the size of its predecessor. A longer period of preparation permitted the assembling of exhibits from thirty-eight departments. The government attempted this time to persuade artists to exhibit with the industrialists. All but David refused.

A third national industrial exhibition in 1804 was much larger. The holding of the fourth one in 1806 showed that they had become part of Napoléon's economic and political policy. This exhibition had nearly a thousand exhibitors. In 1806 the artists had a separate section and were no longer reluctant to exhibit with manufacturers. For ease in viewing and judging, the exhibits were divided by class into mechanical arts, chemical arts, fine arts, and textiles.

As the Napoleonic exhibitions attracted growing numbers of foreign visitors and became larger in terms of area covered, the numbers of displays and awards also increased. It seemed that each exhibition *had* to surpass its predecessor in order to maintain an atmosphere of novelty and avoid the dreaded accusation *déjà vu*. With the Exhibition of 1804, the criteria for awarding prizes became broader; luxury articles could now win prizes. Previously the juries, consisting mostly of teachers of technology, had rewarded products "likely to become objects of mass production and commerce."[6]

The decline of Napoléon delayed the fifth exhibition until 1819, under the Restoration. It was open for thirty-five days in August and September. Louis XVIII used the occasion for displays of royal pomp, especially at the ceremonies for awarding prizes. This exposition introduced the awarding of the *Légion d'honneur* as a prize to industrialists. The last days of the exhibition were a harvest of high decorations for manufacturers, artists, and the organizing bureaucrats. The state thereby encouraged outstanding performances by some of its most talented men, who in turn became intensely concerned for the success of their exhibition and developed a craving for future ones.

The French exhibitions continued to evolve with the sixth (1823) and the seventh (1827); each of these exhibitions had about 1,600 exhibitors. The seventh did not surpass the sixth greatly in number of exhibitors, perhaps because some manufacturers were hesitant to display their goods to foreign visitors (and domestic competitors) for fear of losing trade secrets. These later exhibitions occupied the Ecole Polytechnique, much of the Ecole des Ponts et Chaussées and the Esplanade des Invalides.

The July Monarchy continued and expanded the exhibitions. There were about 2,400 exhibitors in the Exhibition of 1834. In an effort to make the great variety of the displays of the Exhibition of 1839 more manageable and rational, the former simple fourfold classification was replaced by an eightfold one. The categories were Fabrics, Metals and Minerals, Agricultural Utensils, Precision and Musical Instruments, Chemicals, Fine Arts, Ceramics, and Miscellaneous. This new systematization (and later ones as well) was evidence of the efforts of nineteenth-century intellectuals to organize and keep logical and comprehensible the increasing creativity of Europe's scholars, artists, scientists, and technicians.

The Exhibition of 1839 was nearly 40 per cent larger than its predecessor. The one that followed it, in 1844 (a five-year interval seemed established by then), was yet larger, and had spread out to cover the park grounds near the Champs Elysées. These later exhibitors were also occasions for the national government to make surveys of the conditions

[1] TOP   *View of the Esplanade des Invalides*
[2] CENTRE   *A panoramic view of the Exposition*
[3] BOTTOM   *A view of the inaugural procession on the Pont d'Iéna*

[4] TOP   *The Pont Alexandre III and two of its monumental pillars*

[5] BOTTOM   *Part of the area known as "Vieux Paris" which recreated
the mediaeval city*

[6] TOP *The Palais du Génie Civil*

[7] BOTTOM *The Palais lumineux on the Champs de Mars*

[8] *A certificate of award with characteristic allegories*

[9] *A jury-member's badge*

[10] *A commemorative plaque*

[11] *A prize medal*

[12] TOP   *A cancelled admission ticket*

[13] CENTRE   *A "bon": a certificate which was sold before the opening
and was redeemable for admission tickets*

[14] BOTTOM   *The Théâtre Loïe Fuller on the Cours-la-Reine*

[17] TOP *The pavilion of the Parisian department store, Printemps*

[18] CENTRE *One of the tents set up for the mammoth "Banquet of the Mayors"*

[19] BOTTOM *The mayors of Finistère at the great Banquet*

of the economy, and the surveys were published as parts of the official reports.[7]

The last French national exhibition was the largest. The Second Republic, proclaimed in the Revolution of 1848, saw the monarchy's preparations to completion. This large exhibition now included agriculture and was the Exhibition of Agricultural and Industrical Products. Despite a serious economic depression, the National Assembly voted 600,000 francs to pay for the exhibition. Outstanding were large exhibits of steam engines and, for the first time, colonial displays from Algeria, Réunion, Pondichéry, and Guadaloupe.

As early as 1834 there had been requests that foreigners be permitted to display their goods in Paris:

Why are our Expositions still so restricted? Why are they not planned on a truly large and liberal scale? Why are we afraid to open our exhibition halls to the manufacturers we call foreign: the Belgian, the English, the Swiss, the Germans? How beautiful, how rich a European Exposition could be! What a source of knowledge it would be for everyone![8]

That indispensable requirement, novelty, encouraged later discussion and this kind of proposal actually received a serious hearing before the Exhibition of 1849. French artists and manufacturers, it was claimed, would not only learn by foreign example, but would surely benefit because the larger foreign attendance would lead to the increased purchase of French specialties outside France.[9]

Until 1819 these industrial exhibits were exclusively French. But foreign observers carried the idea home and organized imitations. There were industrial fairs in Ghent in 1820, Tournai in 1824, and Haarlem in 1825. The Netherlands collaborated in a large exhibition in Brussels in 1830; the Zollverein had a big exhibition in Berlin in 1834. By the 1840's there were frequent national industrial exhibits. Some rivalled the size and comprehensiveness of those taking place in France. But whereas the organizers of these other exhibitions were private individuals, the French ones were always directed by the state. All French governments thought them too important to be entrusted to ordinary citizens. Elsewhere the organizers of exhibitions might lobby for subsidies, but the exhibitions were run for the benefit of the displayers, not for politicians or bureaucrats, nor for the prestige of the nation as a whole.

The later French national exhibitions had drawn especially large numbers of British visitors to Paris. In the mid-1840's pressure for a grand and comprehensive British national exhibition became strong within the Royal Society of Arts, which had staged British exhibitions since 1760. In 1849 orderly, science-favouring Prince Albert was president of the Society of Arts. In that year the Prince convinced a few prominent members of the Society, and then some manufacturers and politicians, that a large exhibit planned for 1851 in Hyde Park should be made yet larger, and international.

Albert was sure that such a meeting would lessen international hostility by demonstrating the similarity of men's interests everywhere. He further believed that comparison, particularly with the more elegant French models, would improve English design of manufactured articles. Some British manufacturers who felt that business was good enough opposed Albert. Stronger opposition came from Englishmen who were against a motley gathering in principle. In the House of Commons one member claimed,

It is the greatest trash, the greatest fraud, the greatest imposition ever attempted to be palmed upon the people of this country. The object of its promoters is to introduce amongst us foreign stuff of every description—live and dead stock—without regard to quantity or quality. It is meant to bring down prices in this Country, and to pave the way for the establishment of the cheap and nasty trumpery system. . . . All the bad characters at present scattered over the country will be attracted to Hyde Park. . . . That being the case, I would advise persons residing near the park to keep a sharp lookout after their silver forks and spoons and servant maids. . . . Let [the English] beware of mantraps and spring-guns—they will have all their food robbed—they will have a piebald generation, half black and half white. . . .[10]

Memories of the revolutions of 1848 were still fresh. Alarmists feared disguised foreign revolutionaries would arouse the English rabble to slaughter Victoria and the aristocracy and then proclaim a red republic.

Albert succeeded in obtaining only a small subsidy from Parliament. Heretofore, admission to exhibitions had been free. This one was paid for by private capitalists who were to be reimbursed, if all went well, by the entrance fees.

The whole exhibition was housed in one iron and glass building which, as Englishmen boasted, was "bigger than St. Peter's." The architect, Joseph Paxton, had until that date built only a few greenhouses for wealthy patrons. As Paxton was proud to state, he had designed a building that could be put up like a bedstead. Construction, which preserved many of the trees and fountains of Hyde Park by encompassing them, took just seventeen weeks.[11]

The plate glass roof and walls of the building sheltered an unprecedented display of Europe's artistic and industrial accomplishments. The exhibition, which attracted 6 million visitors, was four times larger than the French exhibition of 1849. The airy spaciousness of the building gave a lustre of magic to all the objects that it embraced. The exhilarated millions who strolled the miles of galleries among greenery, flags, machinery, art works, amid visitors from all over the world, might well believe that they were witnessing the birth of an age of inconceivable progress and tranquillity. For despite the fears of many members of the ruling class, the exhibition caused no acts of violence in London that year; all the prophets of insurrection appeared rather foolish as the exhibition closed.[12]

The peaceful success of the Crystal Palace Exhibition was important in the great increase in international contacts among people with similar interests during the rest of the century. Its method of choosing juries, half highly respected citizens of the host nation, half chosen by foreign governments, was followed thereafter. Scholarship, technology, social welfare, philanthropy, and sport were no longer contained within national boundaries. After 1851 a major purpose of expositions was to encourage the *international* application of the arts and sciences to industry, to education, and to society in general.

The Exhibition of 1851 was a memorable triumph for Albert, the Society of Arts, and the nation that was host. The most tangible benefit to the Society of Arts was a substantial profit. This it invested in land in South Kensington, the income from which even today finances the Victoria and Albert Museum and a continuing series of scholarships for English art students.[13] Hope for similar gain was the spur for most of the exhibition's imitators. The organizers for the second and larger British international Exhibition of 1862 debated long on how to dispose of their surplus, which, regrettably, never materialized.

One of the first imitators of the Crystal Palace Exhibition was a so-called "international exhibition" in New York in 1853. This was a small affair organized by Horace Greeley, and was really an expansion of a previously planned national industrial exhibit. But invitations were sent all over the world, and the main building, erected on the site of the New York Public Library, looked like a greenhouse. Dublin also held an international exhibition in 1853. A large German exhibition in Munich in 1854 included only the German states, but it had a *Glaspalast*.

News of the British triumph was most closely followed in France, where admiration was alloyed with bitterness. For had not the English stolen a march? The French had, it is true, participated enthusiastically in 1851. Theirs were the largest and (almost everyone admitted this) the most tasteful foreign exhibits. A large group of French workers was sent to the exhibition at government expense. Louis Napoléon himself visited the exhibition and later gave a great party in Paris for its British organizers. His government began a careful report of the exhibition and its importance; it had reached the eighth volume when the project was abandoned in 1873.

The next of the French quinquennial exhibitions was scheduled for 1854. Preparations were under way when Louis Napoléon (by then Napoléon III, for the Second Empire had been proclaimed in the meantime) decided to make this exhibition an international one. This innovation, plus the Crimean War, necessitated a year's postponement. It was clear that this exposition (called an *exposition universelle* to suggest its coverage) would be much grander than the national exhibitions. The Emperor's cousin, Prince Napoléon, was the chief administrator of the enterprise and wrote the official reports.[14]

To make this exposition larger than the Crystal Palace Exhibition Napoléon made the universal exposition outstanding by other means. French patriots were put out that the British had emphasized the products of industry and had not permitted a display of painting in 1851. The public proclamation that began official preparations accordingly stated that the arts were as important as industry. The large exhibition building, called the Palais de l'Industrie, was a kind of Crystal Palace with added stone neo-classical decoration. This permanent building, however, was not spacious enough for the show as it developed, and the exposition flowed out into several other buildings and the grounds near the focal great hall.

In the Crystal Palace there had been no posted selling prices. In this, the first French international exhibition, all objects had to have price tags. This innovation demonstrated French confidence in their own technology, and the industrial competitiveness of the event as well. The whole occasion, however, was planned to channel competition toward peaceful progress.

This was the first French exposition to charge admission. The charges were one franc for all days except Sunday, which at first cost five francs and was later reduced to two. The admission system was designed to discourage the mob on the days tacitly agreed to be most attractive to the upper classes. However, large groups of working men were occasionally admitted free.[15] A widely publicized part of the exposition was devoted to the display of cheap products designed for household (especially kitchen) use, and intended to ease the lot of the workingman and the housewife.

This new class was part of the greatly expanded classification scheme designed by the great engineer and Saint-Simonian, Frédéric Le Play, early in his career.[16] The new classification was designed to allow the incorporation of almost any likely innovation from any of the world's regions. As an ostensibly infinitely expandable and adaptable scheme, it was a precursor of the universal decimal classifications designed later in the century. Le Play's system acknowledged that the expositions had indeed become international and universal.

Probably the most heavily attended parts of the exposition were the international art shows. Government patronage of art, dependent upon advice from experts drawn from the conservative national academies, banned the French painting of protest and rebellion. On the other hand, the English pre-Raphaelites had their first large public display in Paris in 1855.[17]

Though attendance at the Exposition of 1855 was slightly lower than at its English competitor, the attendance figure was, of course, much higher than that of any previous French exhibition. More than double the number of Frenchmen exhibited their products of manufacture or art than had done so six years before.

Managing the affair could not have been a very cheerful experience. In his official report Prince Napoléon warned that it was evil for an exposition to compete with its predecessors. Spurious novelty would be unmasked by the public. The demand for ever greater size had to stop somewhere. A universal exposition was so complex that it was impossible to organize well, and the difficulties rapidly multiplied with greater size. The delayed opening of his own exposition led Prince Napoléon to believe that the proper scheduling of such an effort was nearly hopeless. He warned that members of the juries, despite their acknowledged integrity, were under irresistible pressure from their nationals and erred, with consequent international resentment, in favour of these nationals. He also discouraged the use of expositions for political purposes. Instead of heterogeneous *entrepôts*, the Prince proposed that exhibitions be limited to certain kinds of machinery or art and that only the *cognoscenti* be invited to observe. The ignorant crowd, gawking, uncomprehending, should be otherwise amused.

Prince Napoléon's advice made little impression. Despite a loss of 8 million francs, disappointment at the late completion of the fair and its exhibits, and the bitterness of the losers in the awards system, suggestions for the abandonment of exhibitions were scarcely considered. Besides being a political and intellectual victory, the Exposition of 1855 was viewed by many Frenchmen as a brilliant episode in a proud French tradition.

The next universal exposition was in Paris in 1867. It deserves special attention because of its idealism, its relative freedom from political overtones, and the warmth with which it was remembered afterwards. The chief administrator and chronicler in 1867 was Frédéric Le Play, who caused the architecture to be arranged to suit his classification of 1855.[18] The exposition took place mostly within a great elliptical iron and glass building with raised galleries for spectators. The hall had a grid arrangement within it, each nation having a wedge of the ellipse. Products that were similar could be seen by an elliptical tour. The whole display was an encyclopaedic conception constructed in space. Though temporary, Le Play's project, called later "la merveille du genre," was analogous to the monumental and contemporaneous encyclopaedias assembled by European scholars and sold in great numbers during these years.

Like the nineteenth-century encyclopaedists, Le Play and Jules Simon (another Saint-Simonian who guided the preparations) planned to exclude nothing. They felt that a demonstration of man's works could only ennoble him. As a rule for the organizers Simon proposed:

The very poorest student in the poorest school, the most incapable, the most ignorant, the least gifted, is, after all, a man and since he is a man, he has the capacity to recognize the truth, to understand and to live by it.[19]

In 1867 the exhibition accordingly emphasized educational and social matters. It also featured, as much as was possible, demonstrations of machinery in motion and sequential displays showing products in the stages of manufacture. Visitors' galleries, demonstrations of technical processes, graphs, guided tours—all these were intended to increase the exposition's educational value.

Previous exhibitions had been criticized because, though they showed the products of labour, labour itself was not on view. So in 1867 special attention was paid to the workingman. There were displays of old tools and new ones in an exhibit called the "History of Labour." There were, besides, restaurants with low prices for workers, free trips to the exposition, and free medical care for labourers while they were there. In Paris that year 67,000 workers, 40,000 of whom were foreigners, occupied free lodgings at the exposition.

The Exposition of 1867 had more than its share of "firsts." It had the first display of aluminum, the first distillation of petroleum, and the first demonstrations of many chemicals, among them phenol, important in the history of antisepsis. This was also the first exposition to have national pavilions for the headquarters of the foreign participants. Besides, there were exotic restaurants with ethnic music, spicy dishes, and waitresses in national costumes. The wider embrace of this exposition also took in gardens, an amusement park, and, for the first time, sideshows of a type familiar to carnival goers. Le Play had unsuccessfully resisted pressure for commercial *attractions*, as they were called. The taste of some of the entertainment, notably the freaks and semi-nude dancers, conflicted with the lofty aims of the exposition as a whole.

Long afterwards Frenchmen remembered that eighteen monarchs visited Paris in 1867, including Wilhelm of Prussia, who was accompanied by Otto von Bismarck and General Helmuth von Moltke, Chief of Staff of the Prussian army. Owing to France's recent diplomatic fiascos in Mexico, Luxembourg, and in the Austro-Prussian War, diplomatic tension was high in Paris that summer. Pierre de la Gorce has noted that in a *funeste* period, when Napoléon's whole political system was decaying, the year 1867 stood out as the brilliant *année de l'exposition*.[20]

Its exalted tone, its excellent administration, its idealism caused this exposition to be long remembered despite the somewhat intruding circus atmosphere. Yet, here again, administering it all must have been a disillusioning experience, for Le Play, like Prince Napoléon, left a testament in which he attacked the idea of temporary exhibitions. Instead, he proposed permanent expositions, such as today's technical museums, for serious observers.[21]

Notwithstanding their selfless concern with culture and progress, the expositions of 1855 and 1867 served several of Napoléon III's conflicting purposes well. With them the Emperor could advance the cause of international idealism while narrowly promoting French prestige and material interests. They were salutary occasions for Napoléon III and Baron Georges Eugène Haussmann to beautify Paris and maintain its preeminence as a world capital and world resort. To some extent, the expositions also allied the Imperial government with businessmen by providing manufacturers with a government-financed platform for the display of their wares to an international clientele. They also continued to hold the enthusiasm of influential Frenchmen by dangling before them decorations, medals, and lavishly coloured certificates of merit, all of which were given out liberally after 1855 and 1867.

The next French exposition had a political urgency and seriousness that Napoléon III had at least attempted to mask in his expositions.[22] The defensive, apprehensive deputies of the young Third Republic had, in the seventies, to produce an exposition that was grander than those of the Second Empire, and to prove to Europe that France was recovering from the wounds of the Franco-Prussian War.[23] They succeeded. Attendance, the most closely watched statistical index in 1878, was 16 million, more than twice that of the Exposition of 1867.

The expositions continued to be the occasions for demonstrating advances in technology and, so to speak, for placing them on the market. In 1878 there were the first demonstrations of a primitive phonograph, rubber tires, and typewriters. Photography was already advanced and had a large section to itself. A popular success was a tidy Japanese farm which indirectly increased the rage for oriental art objects. Though not at the exposition proper, a café near the Opéra nightly demonstrated a new sensation, electric light.

The Exposition of 1878 added the classifications of medicine, hygiene, and public assistance. It also included many sequential exhibits illustrating the history of technology and of science. Continuing the tendency of the expositions to concern themselves more and more with cultural matters, this was the first to devote great space and effort to international scholarly, diplomatic, and scientific congresses. The huge Trocadéro Palace (razed for the Exposition of 1937) with its long colonnaded arms reaching for the Seine, was built especially to house these parts of the exposition. Scholars, diplomats, bureaucrats—all came for international meetings on statistics, weights and measures, postal regulations, copyright legislation, and other matters. There were also meetings of social workers to exchange information on methods for helping the blind.[24]

Though many Frenchmen, even those who supported this exposition, deplored the fact that its origin and purposes were not as altruistic as those of Napoléon III, they were still proud that the young Third Republic had proven itself capable of such a task. Few dared to cavil over the gap between income and expenses which made this exhibition one of the great money losers of all time. Less than half its cost was recovered; deficits had to be paid out of the national budget. The Exposition of 1867 had been financed partly by a private corporation of guarantee. This Exposition of 1878 was, from the beginning, felt to be too serious to entrust to private hands and it almost always remained above criticism. A severe critic of expositions later wrote,

[The Exposition of 1878] was useful, it was indispensable for demonstrating to an astonished Europe France's vitality and energy, her progress after defeats which many had thought beyond our abilities to repair. Perhaps we should have stopped there.[25]

An unexpected dividend to the Republic was the exposition's role in calming France after seven months of political insecurity following the *seize mai* crisis of 1877. For a period of four years after the 1871 settlement of the Franco-Prussian War, France had been ruled by a conservative National Assembly and an aristocratic executive. This provisional republic's president, first elected in 1873 for a term of seven years, was the former Marshal Patrice de MacMahon, the Duke of Magenta. MacMahon conceived of himself as a preserver of the upper classes and the church. During the time that the Right he protected was breaking up into squabbling Legitimists, Orleanists, and Bonapartists, prosperity and peace helped the republican Left to gain strength in the Chamber of Deputies established by the new constitution of 1875.

While the new buildings for the exposition were rising in Paris, the increasingly confident Left controlled the Chamber and thus the budget. They confronted the stiff, almost anti-republican autocrat who was entrenched in the presidency. After much uncertainty the inevitable crisis came on May 16, 1877, when MacMahon dismissed a cabinet headed by the Left republican, and therefore unco-operative, Jules Simon. The later preparations for the first great republican international exposition were gloomily overcast by seven months of fears of massive administrative purges, coups d'état, and even another war with Germany. Finally, in

December 1877, MacMahon capitulated to the republican principle that cabinet ministers were responsible to the majority of the Chamber. The Third Republic was launched on a long period of needed calm:

The great tranquillizer was the Paris Exhibition. In 1878 all ranks of society were determined that the Exhibition should outshine the imperial festival. Party differences were sunk. . . .[26]

As a remarkable political boon and as a device to demonstrate recovery and material prosperity in the face of foreign disrespect, the Exposition of 1878 set an example, perhaps, for politicians.

After 1851 international exhibitions also became common elsewhere. Large ones were held in London in 1862, in Vienna in 1873, and in Philadelphia in 1876.[27] Though the idealism and internationalism of the Crystal Palace Exhibition were present in all of these, none of them rivalled the Exhibition of 1851 in cultural impact, or the three expositions in Paris in variety and international participation.

Smaller exhibitions all over the world blithely took on the adjective "international." One in Moscow tried to interest foreigners in Russian mineral resources. Among many striking displays was a diorama of stuffed Siberian dogs pulling a sled over papier-mâché snow, the whole scene illuminated by light filtered through blue glass. There were surprisingly large international expositions in Sydney in the summer (there) of 1878–79 and in Melbourne in the summer of 1880–81. A small, so-called "international exhibition" was even held in Calcutta in 1883–84.[28]

By the 1880's it appeared that the world community had adopted a new kind of quasi-educational amusement that served the purposes of industrialists, artists, scholars, entertainers, and politicians alike. The exhibitions were all occasions for displaying technical and artistic innovations. The Bessemer process for making steel was first shown in London in 1862. Japanese art was first seen on a large scale in Paris in 1867 and created a sensation at the Vienna Exposition of 1873. The awards system was a powerful incentive for excellence for all kinds of producers and even led to a clandestine market (centred in Paris) of counterfeit lush certificates of merit. Only recently have the manufacturers of American office furniture and some patent medicines dropped from their advertising the attesting seals garnered at the fairs. Some great French wines and Mexican rums still bear the proud stamps, "Paris 1878" or "St. Louis 1876." The expositions also stimulated whole nations by forcing upon their citizens more accurate gauges of their own natural and human resources and those of their rivals. All of these expositions were made possible by widespread international idealism among educated, politically powerful men. Sceptics who predicted violence as a result of close contacts between people of different nations were refuted. The evolution of universal expositions or world's fairs was certain to continue in the direction of greater size and comprehensiveness. In terms of size, in any case, all previous exhibitions were dwarfed by the brilliant Exposition of 1889 in Paris.

A periodicity of eleven years, suggested by the spacing of the expositions of 1855, 1867, and 1878, made the next one happily coincide with the hundredth anniversary of the Revolution. Preliminary studies guessed that the Exposition of 1889 would cost about 43 million francs. The state was to pay a subsidy of 17 million francs and the city of Paris 8 million. The financial deficit in 1878 led the deputies to insist that part of the risk of this show be assumed by private banks. An "Association of Guarantee," authorized by government decree, was to furnish the other 18 million francs.

The bankers who raised these 18 millions were to be reimbursed by selling booklets of prepaid tickets of admission called *bons*. An additional attraction was the serial numbering of the booklets with provisions for lotteries to be held until 1964. In addition, the colonies offered subsidies. Algeria gave 350,000 francs, Tunisia donated 510,000 francs, and the others gave sums ranging from 20,000 to 5,000 francs.[29]

The Exposition of 1889 eventually cost 46,500,000 francs. Of this sum, 6,817,000 francs was a special credit to pay bonuses to civil servants in Paris who earned less than 2,500 francs per year. It was believed that these people would suffer most from temporarily inflated prices caused by the influx of carefree tourists.

Called *l'Exposition tricolorée*, 1889 marked "a date holy to French patriotism."[30] Since its declared purpose was to celebrate *quatre-vingt-neuf*, it consequently annoyed those who feared and loathed revolutions. All the major governments of Europe officially declined the invitations distributed by the French Ministry of Foreign Affairs. These abrupt refusals were partially a result of the lonely and awkward diplomatic position of France in the 1880's, but it seemed to the diplomats of the monarchies that to accept the invitations would be to celebrate the destruction of a political institution for which they naturally had tender feelings.

The French planners were able to take heart from the willingness of foreign firms to participate and to ignore the official censures. However, a stricter official boycott allowed the Germans (who had not exhibited in 1878) to show just some art objects, and these only if they were excluded from the judging. In any case, demands of major governments for area were much less than expected. Space permitted costly displays by poor nations, particularly the republics of the new world, who were eager to make a great show in Paris.

Monarchical disrespect was only part of the political background of this exposition. Its final preparations and opening were intertwined with the most serious political crisis of the eighties in France, the Boulanger episode. Construction on the grounds was well advanced when crowds at military reviews demonstrated in favour of the handsome, *revanchard* general, Boulanger, who threatened to topple the Republic which the exposition celebrated. Two-thirds of the Eiffel Tower already loomed over Paris in January 1889 when the Boulangists tested the appeal of their candidate and won a smashing electoral victory in a traditionally republican and working class district in Paris. The posting of Boulanger's enormous majority led to frightening demonstrations by slogan-chanting mobs who urged a coup d'état to end the inaction, corruption, and economic stagnation of the Third Republic. Ordinarily disputatious republican politicians rallied, and the man on horseback wavered, weakened, and then fled to Belgium. Boulangism seemed to dissipate with the revelation of its hero's cowardice. However, the incident revealed deep fissures in republican society and planted durable fears of similar threats to political stability.

In the face of foreign disrespect and the threats to the Third Republic by its passionate internal dissidents, most Frenchmen were surprisingly unified in defence of the coming fête. They hoped that it, like the Exposition of 1878, could cool political passions. There were few disputes over the new exposition's purpose in the intellectuals' reviews or in the newspapers. What debates there were centred mostly on a critical matter of taste.

Gustave Eiffel, an engineer and not an architect, had a scheme to raise on the Champ de Mars the tallest structure yet erected by man. This was to be a tower 300 metres high, entirely of steel and iron. Moreover, it was to be the central point, the capstone, the theme structure (soon to be called *clou* or main spike—a word that later became hackneyed in exposition jargon) of the whole exposition.

Because of techniques already used in railroad bridge construction, a few experts knew some time before 1886, when construction on the tower began, that Eiffel's project was technically possible.[31] The administrators of the exposition favoured the scheme because of the attention it would draw to the fair it straddled. They encouraged Eiffel by offering him a subsidy of 1.5 million francs and a guarantee of the admission fees to the tower for twenty years after it was finished. After that time the ownership and income from the tower would revert to the city of Paris.[32]

Few people, then or later, have defended the Eiffel Tower for its beauty or its utility. Its enduring éclat is best attributed to its abstract purpose, the scaling of the atmosphere with man-made steel. Artistic notables who felt that such a monstrosity would be a national scandal gave a well publicized collective cry of pain. Well-known artists who signed a protest to block construction of the tower were Charles Gounod, Charles Garnier, Alexandre Dumas, Victorien Sardou, Guy de Maupassant, Charles Leconte de Lisle, Sully Prudhomme, François Coppée (who wrote a poem against it) and the popular painters Jean Louis Meissonier, and Adolphe William Bouguereau.

Here are some parts of their long public letter to the Minister of Commerce:

We are entitled to proclaim aloud that Paris is a city without a rival in the world. Above her streets, from her broadened boulevards, beside her impressive quays, from the midst of her magnificent promenades rise the most noble monuments that human genius has conceived. Italy, Germany, and Belgium so justly proud of their artistic heritage, possess nothing that compares with ours; Paris arouses interest and admiration in all corners of the earth. Are we now going to allow all that to be profaned? Is this city going to continue to be associated with the glories of the baroque, or with the commercial fancies of a builder of machines, making herself hideous beyond repair, dishonouring herself? For without a doubt the Eiffel tower . . . is a disgrace to Paris. Indeed, when visitors from abroad come to see our Exposition, they will shout in astonishment, "What's this? Is this the horror that the French have created in order to impress us with their vaunted taste?" And they will be right in mocking us, since the Paris of the sublimely Gothic . . . will have become the Paris of M. Eiffel.

Moreover, let us consider the prospect of this dizzily ridiculous tower dominating Paris like a gigantic black factory chimney, overpowering, with its barbaric mass, Notre-Dame, the Sainte-Chapelle, the Tour Saint-Jacques, the dome of the Invalides, and the Arc-de-Triomphe; all our monuments humiliated, all our architecture shrunken and disappearing in this horrifying dream. And for twenty years to come we shall see, stretching over the entire city—still quivering with the genius of so many centuries—we will see, like an inkblot the hateful shadow of that odious column of riveted sheet metal.[33]

With lively irony the Minister of Commerce replied that, though Notre Dame and the Arc-de-Triomphe were not really threatened, he *had* been able to save and even beautify the then notoriously grim site of the Tower,

. . . that incomparable square of sand called the Champ de Mars, so worthy of inspiring poets and of charming landscape painters.[34]

Construction, of course, proceeded without a hitch, since, while an exposition was in preparation, its administrators were purposely isolated from legislative supervision in order to ensure continuity and independence from the fickle public. In any case, the protests came from a small group. It seems likely that Frenchmen admired the rising tower, especially since its progress was being followed with wonder all over the world.

A second architectural attraction was the colossal Galerie des Machines. This graceful hall was the ultimate development in the tradition of lean steel and glass in exposition architecture which was started by Paxton. But the impact of the huge hall was due not only to its size and grace, but to what it showed the public from the raised galleries. The Galerie des Machines was filled with examples of the most modern machinery in actual operation. Since it was so striking, and housed goods of central importance to the exposition's purpose, some observers referred to the Galerie des Machines as the "sanctuary of industry."[35]

The sight of two architectural wonders on the Champ de Mars helped only a little to dispel pessimism concerning the exposition's likely success. Plans seemed too big. Foreign opposition was discouraging. Shortly before the opening, the market price of the *bons*, exchangeable for admissions, fell sharply. Though by opening day it was clear that there would be substantial participation on the part of monarchical industrialists, the monarchies adamantly withheld congratulations.

Though slightly larger in area than its predecessors, the Exposition of 1889 showed few advances in intellectual or technical grasp. The Eiffel Tower and the Galerie des Machines excepted, there was little new in decoration. Monumental architecture, for the most part, continued to be eclectic, allegorical, and strenuously decorative as in all the previous nineteenth-century exhibitions, French and otherwise.

One innovation was that Europeans saw pre-Columbian American art in quantity for the first time. And in the section devoted to French decorative art, one might have noticed the exquisite, small, glass, cameo vases of the nancien Emile Gallé. These had floral or sensuous abstract designs that presaged the Art Nouveau movement.[36] But Gallé was still experimenting, and the forms he chose to work in were small and apart from the dominant grand tradition of European painting, sculpture, and architecture.

This was the first exposition that saw the use of electricity as a possible practical servant rather than as a curiosity and plaything of physicists. There were exhibits of small dynamos, transformers, and some large electric motors, all harbingers of an industrial transformation. Small parts of the amusements sections of the exposition were electrically lit at night. One of the sensations of the exposition was a group of electrically illuminated fountains. Some petty speculators rented ten-centime chairs overlooking the spectacle shortly before dark and then re-rented them to affluent visitors for two francs.[37]

A popular amusement at the exposition was an area called the "Rue de Caire." With some accuracy it evoked the indolent, incense-laden atmosphere of the teeming Egyptian city. It had bazaars selling souvenirs (made in Batignolles, many claimed), imported burnouse-clad Arabs, passive and unselfconscious before bubbling hookahs, and noisy, smelly donkeys. Most notorious on the Rue de Caire were the Egyptian dancers (possibly also from Batignolles) who did a suggestive *danse du ventre* that was whispered about everywhere. Appeals for censorship inevitably made the dances more widely notorious, and these tough, provocative ladies usually played to full houses of provincials. The Rue de Caire was always crowded. It seemed, with its fakery, its sweat and dust, and the crowds of ignorant sensation seekers, to be an affront to the predominantly serious purpose of a universal exposition.

In 1889 the increasing world-wide proliferation of knowledge and scholarship assured that there were more international congresses than in 1878. Among them were three international socialist congresses, including one for the followers of the American, Henry George. But the decline in official international participation (except for the recklessly extravagant exhibits by some South American republics) made this largely a French exhibition. Even some apparent internationalism was French in that it was offered by the oddly decorated pavilions of the French colonies and by specially imported colonial Asiatics and Africans. ("Voilà, nos esclaves!" boasted the great critic Eugène Melchior de Vogüé.)

The number of convening interest groups ensured that the exposition would be the occasion for hundreds of banquets, parties, and festive meetings. So did the symbolic and ceremonial use of banquets at the time. The biggest banquet, and in some ways the most charming event of the summer, was the banquet of mayors in which 13,456 guests, 11,250 of them mayors of French towns, sat down to one meal at the exposition.[38] Newspapers for days afterward revelled at a distance in statistical details of pounds of meat eaten, bottles of wine uncorked, and white napkins belched into. But the appeal of the banquet in a deeper sense was its symbolic affirmation of a striking domestic victory for the Republic and republicanism.

Shortly before the inauguration of the Exposition of 1889, someone had conceived the novel idea of starting and closing each day of the exposition with a cannon shot from the top of the 300-metre tower. The shot came from the highest point of the tower, above the apartments of M. Eiffel himself, on a tiny platform to which only eight persons had access. Now, late in November, the boom of the cannon rolled across Paris for the last time. Eyes were misty, chests tightened. The spectacle had enchanted France for half a year and was receiving a funeral worthy of a sovereign. "L'Exposition est morte, vive l'Exposition!"[39]

There were few dissenting voices as the exposition closed. Frenchmen of all classes had loved it. De Vogüé happily assured his readers, "L'Europe est unanime à saluer notre triomphe."[40] The cardinal index of success, attendance, showed that the exposition was indeed a triumph. Almost 40 million people had visited the exposition. Parisians naturally spent more than they ordinarily would, but the out-of-town visitors left behind them about 1,250 million francs. Five million provincials spent an estimated hundred francs each while in Paris, and an estimated 1.5 million foreign visitors, mostly English, left about 500 francs each behind.[41] Every restaurant in the exposition grounds earned its owner a fortune. There were large increases in gold holdings of the Bank of France, in receipts of the *octroi* of Paris, and in passenger miles of the railroads. A happy and unprecedented surprise was that the exposition itself showed a modest profit.[42]

Much of the self-congratulation and gratitude focused on the obelisk, the totem, the maypole that was the chief attraction of the exposition. At the top of the tower, de Vogüé, a constant visitor, was thrilled and tried to rationalize the structure's apparent uselessness. He felt

. . . a tremendous sensation, an expansion of the spirit, at the very least a sense of pleasure and of relief. Each gram of iron which constitutes this massive object has already been paid for by a moment of pleasure for a human being. Is not that a usefulness more valuable than many others?

For him the Eiffel Tower symbolized

. . . one of the most interesting phenomena of the Exposition: the transformation of the techniques of architecture, the substitution of iron for stone and the search made by this metal to find its own form of beauty. Soon we shall study a new form of design which one sees dawning as he inspects the Galerie des Machines; but the tower is a witness to its arrival. It symbolizes as well another dominant characteristic of the Exposition: the search for everything that might make communication easier and accelerate exchanges between and fusion of the races.

De Vogüé imagined a drama where the venerable monuments of Paris address an admonitory prayer to the Eiffel Tower for its rawness, its impiety. Mockingly the new monument replies:

Old abandoned towers, no one listens to you now. Don't you see that the poles have shifted and that the world now turns on my iron axis. I represent universal force disciplined by design. Human thought runs through my limbs. My brow shines with light taken from the source of all light. You are ignorance; I am knowledge. You keep man a slave; I make him free. I know the secrets of those miracles which terrified your faithful. My limitless power will refashion the universe and will establish your childish paradise here on earth. I have no need of your God, invented to explain a creation whose laws I understand. These laws are enough for me. They are enough for those souls I have won from you and which will never return.[43]

The tower's engineer became a national hero; peasant children were named Eiffelin and even Eiffeline.[44] Eiffel himself did very well. Since the ascension fees were high, the popularity of the tower made it an extraordinarily *belle affaire*, for it paid for itself shortly after the exposition closed. Eiffel kept the receipts of the next nineteen years as profit. A technical *tour de force*, uniquely French, admired the world over and, moreover, supremely profitable, the tower overshadowed and embellished all the festivities.

In short, the whole nation "knew a short period of euphoria" as the exposition closed.[45] Some sober analysts noted that it had had exceptional luck. The weather in Paris had been unusually regular and pleasant from the time of the opening of the exposition until it closed. Paris itself had enjoyed good public health. Despite expectations to the contrary, food prices stayed steady all summer.[46] The large numbers of foreign visitors attested to the quiet diplomatic situation in the summer of 1889.

Patriots, however, sought explanations that had nothing to do with the fortuitous. The exposition, they felt, was a creation—and therefore a proof —of French genius. But even the foreigners saw Frenchmen apparently delivered from internal dissension and concerned only with art, industry, and labour—the works of peace and domestic satisfaction. The whole exposition confuted foreign critics who claimed that France lacked energy because of her political crises and moral degeneration.

Not to discount the powerful influences of both luck and French genius, the success of the exposition might better be viewed in its political setting. The triumph was a bright spot in an era of political corruption and humiliation that had been climaxed in the Boulanger episode just before the Exposition of 1889 opened. Some observers were aware of the exposition's salubrious effects at the time. Even before the year ended, one writer noted that "France, diseased with politics, went to the exposition as to a cure."[47] That the nation seemed recovered from Boulangism was shown by the solid affirmation of republicanism in the elections of September 1889.[48]

But relief from politics was brief. Fond memories of the centenary exposition became even warmer as the tawdry papier-mâché decoration that made up most of the architecture and decoration was torn down and removed. Though ostensibly put on to delight the universe (as its name suggested) the Universal Exposition of 1889 was strikingly beneficial to French republican politicians. The political and diplomatic humiliations of the next decade made the exposition year of 1889 seem in retrospect like an oasis of happiness.

Origins and Opposition • The triumph of 1889 was one of few that France produced in the last decades of the nineteenth century. Politically tranquil during the exposition, the Third Republic again fell into parliamentary disorder after the visitors left. Political corruption and uncertainty were accompanied by economic stagnation and, most importantly, by demographic weakness. Some French intellectuals even suspected that France was losing her pre-eminence in art and literature.

Rumours of an impending financial debacle in Panama began to pop up in 1889, the very year of the exposition. Since 1885, until about 1894 when the golden flow stopped, French investors sank 500 million francs in a colossal project to pierce a canal through the Isthmus of Panama. Ultimately the failure was due to the unhealthy climate and unforeseen technical difficulties. But, in a series of moves to gain money and time to overcome these obstacles, officers of the Panama company used its treasure to bribe many politicians and journalists into silence or acquiescence. The slow and ugly airing of the scandal (incomplete to this day) brought with it the realization that many bourgeois fortunes had been wiped out.

The whole mess, involving, as it did, old and young French technological and political heroes, the newspapers, and the French reputation for sagacity in general, smudged and blackened the whole republic. Gustave Eiffel himself and even Georges de Lesseps, the engineer of another French triumph, the Suez Canal, were covered with shame. Georges Clemenceau's enemies used some of his equivocal friendships of those days to hound him from the Chamber of Deputies. Fallen from political power, Clemenceau had to begin the hard struggle back by learning and mastering the trade of journalism. Dozens of other reputations were ruined. No other political scandals in France, not even the Dreyfus Affair, poisoned the political atmosphere as long as this one did.

Widespread indignation arising out of the Panama and other scandals in turn nurtured several opposition movements that further disrupted French political life. Some Jews had been singled out as villains in the scandals; anti-Semitism was stimulated. Widely publicized anarchist outrages not only terrified many Frenchmen, but the brutal and summary repression of the anarchists also weakened the reputation of the Republic for justice. Another more durable political movement, though it was long ineffective, was that of parliamentary socialism. Much of its rise was no doubt the result of widespread disgust of Frenchmen with the inaction, quarrelling, and venality of many of their republican political representatives. In these years, however, the socialists only caused an increase in parliamentary bickering. Of social legislation, proceeding famously in Germany at the same time, the Republic produced almost none. The accomplishments of republican diplomacy (i.e., the expansion of the colonial empire and the Russian alliance) were really the work of high bureaucrats and nearly independent military adventurers. Elected republicans were usually only called on to ratify these victories. Such successes could not add to the prestige of the Republic as such.

The decades of the Boulanger crisis, the Panama and other scandals, and the Dreyfus Affair, were also the years of near economic stagnation. France had begun the century with a stronger economic base than her competitors. Until 1860 she was still the world's wealthiest nation.[1] But in the eighties and nineties Frenchmen tended to invest in land or in the securities of foreign governments rather than in their own industry. The traditional balance between agriculture and industry remained nearly stable. Liquid wealth was concentrated in relatively few hands. Though taxes were high, they were indirect—on consumption rather than on income—and thus were a disproportionate burden on the working classes. Stagnation was accompanied by urban unemployment, strikes, and a steady fall in France's proportion of international trade.

The decline was, it should be said, only relative; France was basically not badly off. An achievement of French national economic policy was the Méline Tariff of 1892. The purpose of the tariff was to preserve both farmers and manufacturers from threats by invading foreign products. It was a successful tariff.[2] The economy remained relatively autonomous, but the reverse of the coin was high agricultural prices and inefficient manufacturing labour, the bases for the decline in exports. Still, however, most Frenchmen were reasonably satisfied with their lot. Social stability, no doubt, rested ultimately on this basic contentment.

Statistics of wealth and literacy climbed slowly but steadily and demonstrated the march of progress, even in France. However, with the increasing collection, perfection, use, and interpretation of statistics throughout Europe in the later nineteenth century, it became apparent to more and more Frenchmen that Progress was having a startlingly better time of it elsewhere.

During these years, France produced relatively few compensatory artistic or architectural triumphs. The control of taste was firmly in the hands of the academies, which were devoted to the study and elaboration of the historical styles. To be sure, painting continued to evolve among a small group of dispersed radicals. But the later Impressionists and other experimenters were perhaps better known outside France than in their own country. Except in the expositions, the lethargic economy offered few opportunities for new or experimental architecture.

Though increasingly attracted by the literature of Russia and Germany, French writers and poets retained their vigour and originality.[3] French literature, art, and music had a great past. In fact, an intelligent Frenchman, while acknowledging his nation's material weaknesses as demonstrated by statistics, might recall the great artistic tradition and point proudly to its durability and importance. Taste and spirit: these were what counted.

But it was certain that France was not pre-eminently the only intellectually creative nation. Some intellectuals, especially the younger ones, were bored with the great traditions of rationalism and verbal clarity. They wanted something new. As with other threats to French autonomy and self-confidence, these energizing intellectual tendencies, the peering into the irrational, the bestial, the mystical aspects of human existence, often had their origins and their most brilliant exponents in foreign lands.

Basic to France's political, economic, and even intellectual problems was her unique demographic situation. Population was expanding all over the world. France's very slow growth was not the result of a rising birth rate but only of greater longevity. Political stability may be traceable to rule by ostensibly irascible, but basically conservative, elders. One writer has called France at this time a "gerontocracy."[4] After 1870 politics became a matter of tactics rather than ideals, for the gap between clever, young seekers of positions and available positions was narrow by the end of the century.[5] An almost stable internal demand was the reason for France's economic growth, or rather for the relative lack of it.[6] But the growing cognizance of France's demographic weakness had important psychological effects as well.

The serious study of French demography can be dated from the appearance, between 1889 and 1892, of Emile Levasseur's scholarly statistical study, *La Population française*.[7] At that time, Levasseur was not gloomy as to the likely consequences of French demographic stability. France, he believed, could remain strong by promoting better education and by urging her people to live more productive lives.[8] The anguish and fear came later.

The crucial difference in the later and ever more frequent writings was that they made comparisons. Nations that were possible military threats were undergoing extraordinary growth.[9] A burgeoning population is a proportionally younger one, with consequently greater supplies of potential soldiers. It was the military implications of the low birth rate that horrified the French observers of their demographic situation.

In the 1890's, then, French intellectuals and statesmen, as never before, were being forced to consider France's power (or lack of it) vis-à-vis the rest of the world. Parliamentary instability caused France to be disrespected; she appeared foolish and ineffectual before the world. This was, of course, embarrassing, but the real evidence of foreign dangers came with comparative statistics of economic performance and population growth. Most disquieting of all was the striking performance by the traditional enemy on the other side of the Vosges.

After about 1891 Germany's birth rate was double that of France. In 1897 a noted statistician wrote, "It is inescapable that within fourteen years [Germany] will have twice as many conscripts [as France] then this nation that detests us will devour us. The Germans say this, print it, and they will do it."[10] He cited German writings demonstrating the implacable hatred.[11]

Typical of a new kind of fear of Germany was an essay, "La conquête allemande," published in 1897 by the twenty-five-year-old Paul Valéry.[12] The article was filled with all the alarm of a threatened patriot. But Valéry felt that the "conquest" was economic and not military. Its basis, he believed, lay in the German talent for organization, a talent the French lacked. "We battle these organized troops like bands of savages," he

"L'Allemagne nouvelle": a design, by Caran d'Ache, for a statue symbolic of the modern Germany.

wrote.[13] Frenchmen waited for customers. The Germans sought out their clients and conquered them with technical virtuosity and meticulous concern for their special tastes. Remarking on the German industrial laboratories, Valéry stated, "The client of the Germans has no idea how many chemists are caring for him."[14] Valéry felt that the aims of Frederick the Great and especially of von Moltke, who deliberately planned not to be indispensable to the State, had been carried over into the method of German science, education, and commerce. In this concentration on method, Valéry believed he saw the seeds of one of the world's future transformations.[15]

More observations on German economics appeared as a series in *Le Figaro* during 1896. Their author was Jules Roche, an economist specializing in the analysis of national budgets, and a politician who had been the Minister of Commerce in 1892.[16] Visiting a local exhibition in Nuremberg, Roche commented on the bad taste, ugliness—and solidity—of German manufactures.[17] He noted that Germany had the second largest foreign trade in the world and, most frightening, that in the previous fifteen years France's trade had fallen as much as Germany's had risen.[18] Like other contemporary observers of Germany's ambition, he dwelt on the extraordinary growth of Hamburg as an international port. Roche was one of the first Frenchmen to remark on Pan-Germanism.[19] Germany's demands for a great fleet and colonies, he believed, were a natural result of her burgeoning population.

However much France saw her strength and glory slipping in other areas, there was one cultural manifestation in which French supremacy was unchallenged—the organization and staging of the universal expositions. For Frenchmen, by this time, thoughts of the expositions produced emotions remarkably similar to those aroused by thoughts of the French colonial empire. In the face of political embarrassment, humiliations in diplomacy, and economic stagnation, expositions and empire compensated somewhat for other defeats. Though hardly the creation of the Republic *per se* (the empire was forwarded by freebooting adventurers, the expositions by autonomous bureaucrats) both showed (or appeared to— the important matter) a dynamic, richly inventive French Republic to the world. Even before the success of 1889, Frenchmen and most Europeans believed the great shows to be almost wholly a creation of French genius. Understandably, Paris was shocked to learn, in June 1892, that a society of German merchants and industrialists was planning to have a great world's fair in Berlin in 1896 or 1897. This was arrogance. Were they hoping to inflict another defeat on France? Newspapers in both nations were soon trading insults, giving the impression that national honour was at stake.

Rather alarmed, *Le Figaro* announced on June 24, 1892 that the German universal exposition was intended to take place not in 1896, but in 1900. The Germans felt that 1896 was too close to a very large American fair planned for 1893. Many rich and powerful Germans, *Le Figaro* went on, thought the later date would be a providential opportunity to demonstrate that the nineteenth was a German century, just as the eighteenth had been a French one. France had not a minute to lose! The previous three expositions had taken place at eleven year intervals. The traditional periodicity of eleven years after 1889, now evoked as sacred, led coincidentally to the year 1900. If France chose that year for its next exposition, the act could not be interpreted as hostile to Germany. It was deft, peaceful, competition and that was all.[20]

Le Figaro urged the government to get the ball rolling, to form commissions, appoint officials, and to begin planning the most magnificent exposition of all time.[21] Traditionally close to the government, *Le Figaro* was more likely reporting hurried preparations than instigating them. On July 2, a deputy had submitted a resolution to the government in the name of the Chamber of Deputies requesting that an exposition take place in Paris in 1900. On July 3 Jules Roche, then minister of commerce and industry, discussed various projects for an exposition and received the entire approbation of the cabinet. The ball was rolling.

The German press was annoyed at the first reports of French initiative.[22] Several newspapers reproached the Chancellor, Georg-Leon Count Caprivi, and other government officials for sloth. They urged that the German government assist in the formation of a society to guarantee the expenses of a grandiose exposition in Berlin. They felt that Germany could not pass up this opportunity to demonstrate the brilliance of her civilization. Industrialists met in Berlin to put pressure on the Imperial Government. The Bürgermeister of Berlin promised a credit of ten million marks if an exposition was launched. Chancellor Caprivi, who apparently believed that his country should concentrate on fairs in other countries, gained time by sending out a circular to provincial German officials and businessmen asking for their advice.

With a mixture of amusement and satisfaction the odd competition was followed by foreigners who wished to see one or both nations embarrassed. The *Times* of London predicted that France would be unable to thwart "this German idea." French determination was supposedly causing consternation not only among supporters of the Berlin project, but "some irritation in Government circles." The *Times* was pleased that the two nations "instead of competing with improved artillery, seem likely to compete in a tournament of arts and industry." This was "a subject for congratulation," but the dispute was "childish" and "difficult to treat as serious." It would probably be wiser to "wait a while before fixing these pacific gatherings, and not . . . make them defeat their own ends by fomenting discords."[23]

In the middle of June 1892, Count Münster, the German ambassador to Paris, had conferred with Alexandre Ribot, then foreign minister, about the probable French reactions to a German exposition. Initially, Ribot was reasonable. Then, toward the end of June, he broke off discussions, declaring that invitations were about to be sent to foreign governments requesting their participation in an exposition that would take place in Paris in 1900.[24] While the German government was apparently assessing the views of her whole political and business community, the French government was audacious. As usual, French businessmen, who would be saddled with great outlays once an exposition was under way, were not consulted at all.

The French government published a decree on July 13, 1892, announcing that a universal exposition would be held in Paris from April 15 to October 15, 1900. Jules Roche, in his preface to the decree, pointed out that the date, marking the close of the century, required that this exposition be especially magnificent.[25] French expositions, it was known, had usually been announced much closer to their opening. France was declaring this one eight years in advance because of the preparations necessary for a celebration that would close the century in which France had led the development of exhibitions. The Exposition of 1900 would be a majestic and solemn ceremony "for a working and expanding nation." It would be a "summit from which we shall be able to appraise all that we have accomplished."[26] Three governmental committees were established to study space and means of transport, construction and organization, and finance.[27]

In the meantime emotions cooled in Germany. On July 16, the *Freisinnige Zeitung*, the organ of Eugen Richter of the German Progressives, published a long editorial in which he doubted that Berlin could attract the number of people Paris could.[28] Another paper admitted that Paris represented more the "soul" of France than Berlin did that of Germany. German iron and steel producers declared that they could draw no particular advantage from a German exposition, but, not retreating entirely, agreed to support the government if it favoured one.[29] A newspaper in Cologne predicted that if the government asked for a credit of 30 million marks from the Reichstag, it would be opposed by the conservatives, the agrarians of the centre, all the clericals of South Germany, and probably the majority of the Progressives.[30] The reports from which Caprivi was to gauge provincial opinion were not due in Berlin until July 26. By that time France had stolen the march. Germany then centred its efforts on the coming world's fair in the United States.

In some ways (e.g. in area), the World's Columbian Exposition of 1893 was grander than the one in Paris four years before.[31] Opening a year late, it celebrated the 400th anniversary of the discovery of America. It demonstrated the first successful effort of an exposition's organizers to impose architectural consistency.[32] The Chicago exposition was also the first really large fair to assert the importance of a new area rather than affirm the vigour of an old one.

Had it not been so very distant, the Exposition of 1893 might have shaken French self-confidence more than it did. Many French writers published their observations of this fair.[33] *L'Illustration*, for example, had frequent articles on the exposition, but chiefly commented on the apparent inability of Americans to enjoy themselves, or on the surpassing beauty of the official French pavilion, a reproduction of the Grand Trianon containing French mementos of the American Revolution and of Lafayette.

A few Frenchmen were astonished at the American material accomplishment. The Marquis de Chasseloup-Laubat, assigned as official observer to the many international congresses in Chicago, asserted that the United States was already the richest nation in the world.[34] Another writer noted that French locomotives were puny alongside their American counterparts.[35]

The French government organized and financed most of the French exhibits at Chicago. The emphasis was on the arts. Partly because of the rigidly protective tariff system of the American government, this exposition saw only small and poorly organized efforts on the part of French heavy and light industry.[36]

Of all the foreign representatives the Germans made the most vigorous attempt to penetrate the almost punitive American tariffs.[37] An envious French reporter explained that they counted on American sympathy because of large numbers of German immigrants in the Midwest. The Germans, he also claimed, were munificent in 1893 because plans for their own exposition in 1900 had come to nothing.[38]

The German official pavilion, which alone cost a million francs, was modelled after the rich bourgeois mansions of the Middle Ages. The whole ground floor of the pavilion held a display of the German publishing industry, and illustrated the richness of German cultural life.[39] Conversely, Krupp's pavilion showed cannon and other war material.

In the meantime, in Paris, a preparatory commission of fifty members, most of whom had had experience at earlier French expositions, was planning the greatest exposition of all time. The committee considered various suburban sites, among them Versailles and Vincennes, since the centre of Paris could not hold an exposition significantly larger than the one in 1889. In March, 1893, the commission definitely decided to keep the exposition in the centre of Paris, but to have an annex in the Bois de Vincennes for many agricultural exhibits, the sporting events, and displays of railroad equipment: the parts of an exposition that required the most room.

On September 9, 1893, the government published two decrees: one outlined the administrative organization of the exposition, the other named Alfred Picard commissioner general. Picard had graduated from the Ecole des Ponts at Chaussées in 1867 and was an engineer concerned with building canals in France in the 1870's and 1880's.[40] He had written the official report for the Exposition of 1889. The first volume of this report contains one of the best histories of international exhibitions ever written. The new commissioner general was thoroughly familiar with the objectives and administrative problems of an exposition; he was also deliberately shielded from the uncertainty and carping of parliamentary politics. He had more time than any of his predecessors in which to stage his project. There can be no doubt that he was able. A tall bachelor with a deeply lined face, Picard impressed everyone with his imperturbability.[41] Apparently he never lost his temper. He had a fine sense of irony and "tempered his gravity with a malicious verve."[42] Surely Picard was joking when he later described his relations with his counterparts from other nations as "perfect."[43]

The new commissioner general had extraordinary powers. His deliberate insulation from the possible nosiness of elected politicians was further enhanced by the state of republican politics at the time. A ministerial decree assigned Picard to his post. He then appointed his own assistants, a small advisory body, and various sub-commissions to administer such aspects of the exposition as publishing catalogues, the congresses, relations with foreign commissioners general, architecture and landscaping, and engineering categories such as hydraulics, mechanics, and electricity. Among the men who assisted Picard there were almost no provincials, no politicians, no businessmen, no free-lance specialists. The men who moulded the exposition were the most secure teachers in the state schools of engineering and art, civil engineers, and a few army officers who were chosen because of their administrative skills. Many of Picard's helpers were experienced at earlier expositions; they were highly trained civil servants and had the *esprit de corps* of that group.[44]

The formal nexus between Picard and the elected representatives of the French people was the commissioner general's theoretical subservience to the Minister of Commerce. The Minister of Commerce was to award funds to the administration, approve the plans as a whole (he could not criticize parts), maintain liaison between the Chamber and Senate, and approve Picard's nominations of assistants and advisors. Because of cabinet instability during the preparatory years, the successive ministers of commerce brought neither administrative pressure nor expositional expertise to their positions. Nor did any minister feel secure enough in his post to impose his ideas on Picard. The great exposition, with its implied involvement of the prestige of the whole nation, was, to a great extent, a "one-man show."

After his appointment, the stolid Picard had three main problems to face. The first was to determine the nature and amount of foreign participation. Secondly he had to plan the general layout and content of the exposition. His third problem was to arrange for financing the whole affair.

The year 1900, unlike the date of the previous exposition, appeared to offend no one. Nineteen-hundred had no political innuendos. Optimistic for international participation in all fields of culture, Picard did not intend the exposition to be specifically French, but hoped it would celebrate the progress of all civilization during the nineteenth century. A government decree of August 4, 1894, stated that all nations were to convene for "this great demonstration of labour."[45] In September 1895, the Foreign Minister ordered the representatives of France abroad to acquaint foreign governments with the purposes of the exposition and to invite these nations to take part in it. This was an anxious period. Who could tell? Perhaps great nations would participate tepidly or not at all, as in 1889. Finances, traffic flow, facilities for accommodating visitors—all would have to be planned accordingly.

Forty-seven nations accepted, including all the great powers.[46] For various reasons eight minor states refused; these were Abyssinia, Andorra, Brazil, Chile, Egypt, Hawaii, the Orange Republic, and Siam. Later acceptances and withdrawals took place among countries of this rank. More than forty countries, including almost every nation that had sovereignty over a significant portion of the globe, eventually participated officially. That all the great powers accepted promptly and requested adequate space in which to set large exhibits, demonstrates not only the great attractiveness of the occasion, but the fact that the Republic as such was much more welcome in the world than it had been eleven years before. It meant also that this exposition, more than any other, would be practically universal in geographical representation as well as in cultural scope.

The most significant inclusion was that of Imperial Germany. Germany's participation in 1878 had been out of the question in view of the propinquity of the war of 1870–71. Neither France nor Germany was especially eager that the imperial government be represented in 1889. This time, however, Emperor William II accepted quickly and immediately demanded area in Paris sufficient to demonstrate Germany's grandeur. The old enemies haggled continually over space, customs regulations, precedence, and other matters connected with the exposition, but during the four years following the acceptance of the invitation their diplomatic relations were unusually tranquil.[47] This hiatus in the traditionally poor relations was no doubt in part caused by France's difficulties with Great Britain, but must have been at least partially attributable to the eagerness of both France and Germany not to compromise the likely success of the coming exposition.

All participating nations had to appoint commissioners general, who would be the sole authorities to deal with the French commissioner general in Paris. Picard hoped thereby to be able to reduce confusion resulting from diffused and uncertain authority among the foreign delegations. Thus the extreme centralization of authority was enforced among the foreign delegations as well. Evidently this simple organization of command produced results. Disputes within the exposition were usually settled between the chief delegates without embroiling domestic politicians.

What was the role of the business man in the exhibitions that we have been discussing? Business men had—and still have—a great deal to gain or lose at exhibitions, whether local, special, international, or universal. Manufacturers and producers with established reputations are apt to be reluctant to interrupt their commerce for temporary exhibits, but a vigorous new company with a fresh product may be eager to compete for international esteem. International exhibitions bring new customers to the entrepreneur and add international renown to local specialties; potential buyers can compare similar products and conclude contracts more advantageously in a competitive atmosphere. Even before 1900, national governments recognized the stimulation given to their foreign trade by organized participation in international exhibitions. Some governments assisted businessmen, usually by subsidies to their trade organizations, for their presentations abroad. Germany, particularly, rendered this type of assistance to businessmen beginning with the Exposition of 1893 in Chicago. In fact, one major reason for the great increase in size and number of international exhibitions in the late 1890's was just such aid from many national treasuries.

All through the later nineteenth century, French governments were concerned only with the huge political expositions in the capital. Businessmen were barred from having any voice in these and were also forced to struggle almost alone to represent French commerce abroad. After about 1880, various groups of private individuals organized French foreign participation, for example, in Moscow in 1891 or Chicago in 1893. To these groups—sometimes in competition with one another—fell the tasks of looking after advertising, transportation, insurance, installation and dismantling, and negotiations with the bureaucrats of the nation that was host.

Gradually one group of businessmen, first formed after a local exhibition in Nice in 1884, became a recognized leader.[48] Shortly before the annual meeting in 1890, their single-minded president, Roger Sandoz, distributed a circular to the members which said in part:

Putting aside all moral or political considerations and considering them solely from a commercial point of view, expositions are much less profitable to the exhibitors of the host nation than they are to those of the other nations that participate. To be sure, the Exposition of 1889 showed the entire world the grandeur of French genius; tourists brought a great deal of money to France, and it demonstrated most impressively the moral resurgence of our country. Yet, despite its great political advantages, it did not produce for our exhibitors the economic benefits that certain foreign nations have derived from it. In fact, the majority of the buyers were apparently Frenchmen for whom our sections seemed to offer less incentive for on-the-spot purchasing than the foreign displays which were only temporary.[49]

Soon this group called itself the Comité français des expositions à l'étranger or C.F.E.E. It steadily gained allegiance until it was able to organize almost all the French participants at a large exhibition in Brussels in 1897. "Les expositions aux exposants" was the simple slogan of the C.F.E.E. Roger Sandoz believed his organization had to counter the narrowly political policies of the government in domestic and foreign exhibitions. The C.F.E.E. continued to lobby for subsidies without success. At their meetings the businessmen regularly passed resolutions in favour of abandoning the committee's functions if the government would take them over.[50] By the late 1890's the C.F.E.E. was the admitted bargaining agent for French commerce at French and foreign exhibitions, yet it was without political influence or official recognition in Paris. In 1900 the organization gave several lavish banquets for foreign and domestic businessmen and politicians, but still had no voice in the themes or administration of the exposition itself.

The ingenious and satisfactory financing of the previous Exposition of 1889 made it almost certain that the Exposition of 1900 would be similar. Picard proposed an outright state subsidy and a subsidy by the city of Paris, with the bulk of the financing to be arranged by private bankers, who, long before the exposition, were to sell books of admission tickets. But before negotiations could begin with the municipal council of Paris and with the bankers, Picard had to produce a workable estimate of the number of paying visitors. By boosting spendable incomes generated by new construction and by attracting tourists, a huge exposition would raise the tax receipts of Paris and thereby justify a larger subsidy. The larger the number of visitors the bankers would accept as a sound projection, the more lavish the financing, and consequently the better the exposition. A high estimate of prospective visitors would also justify high rentals for the terrain available to restaurants and privately financed exhibits and amusements.

Admissions to the Exposition of 1889 were 39 million; no one doubted that admissions in 1900 would surpass that figure. The enthusiastic acceptance of all the great powers could be expected to lead to a significant increase in attendance. A more efficient transportation system would be made yet more attractive by special excursion rates while the exposition was open. Besides, the Exposition of 1900 would be a greater show than that of 1889, there was no question of that. Optimists predicted the splendid round figure of 100 million. Hemmed in by conservative statisticians and bankers, Picard forecast an attendance of 60 million.[51] Few cavilled at this estimate. The banking syndicate used this figure as the basis of the advance ticket sale that would produce the bulk of the exposition's financing, 60 million francs. The project for the exposition that the government prepared during the autumn of 1895 called for a state subsidy of 20 million francs and an equivalent subsidy from the city of Paris.[52] Thus the whole project was assured of about 100 million francs from the beginning.

At the request of the government the five principal banks, the Comptoir national d'escompte, Crédit foncier, Crédit lyonnais, Société générale, and Crédit industriel et commercial, agreed to sell, through their offices, 3,250,000 booklets each containing twenty tickets called *bons*, which, it was noted earlier, were exchangeable for admission tickets to the exposition (figure 13). Each *bon* was valued at one franc. The books of tickets were released to the public in lots of 1,000. Of the expected receipts of 65 million francs, five million would pay the bankers' expenses and commission. In spite of the fact that the financial scheme received almost no advertising, the first issues were quickly oversubscribed.[53] Later issues also sold well, even better than they had before 1889. Great numbers of Frenchmen thus affirmed their confidence in Picard's estimate, in the probable success of the exposition, and possibly in the inevitability of progress as well.

Each exposition, with its own particular splendour and (we must admit) mixed motives, was an expression of the very soul of France at the time. However, it appeared in the late 1890's that preparations for the coming exposition were not going to be just passively observed. Well-placed dissenters could not tolerate the deliberate insulation of Picard and his task from the salient institutions of the Republic. Nor were they uncritical about the proposed role of expositions in the development of Paris and the nation, or, for that matter, in the march of progress itself.

Until the late summer of 1895, groundwork for the great exposition proceeded smoothly. Picard was isolated from the senate and chamber, which as yet had only consented to grant small sums for preliminary studies. When the foreign ministry at the Quai d'Orsay sent invitations to the foreign powers, there was little notice of it in the press. In fact, it rather appeared that the preparations for this vast enterprise were taking place in secret. When the implications of the exposition were finally aired in the chambers and in the nation's press, it became clear that this exposition had vigorous enemies and that it could not expect the almost entire approbation of intellectuals and politicians that had accompanied earlier ones.

The germ of opposition to the Exposition of 1900 appeared first in Nancy. For some time Nancy had had in Léon Goulette, the editor of its principal newspaper, *L'Est républicain,* a crusading decentralist. Goulette detected a sensitive issue in the projected exposition. In June 1895, he convinced the municipal council of Nancy to debate its advisability. Since *L'Est républicain* was watched in Paris and in other parts of France as a harbinger of provincial opinion, Nancy's action was well known. It was surprising, however, that opponents of the exposition found so much sympathy. By August 13, when the municipal council of Nancy passed a resolution against the exposition, the germ of opposition had already proliferated into a nation-wide epidemic of angry editorials, pamphlets, articles in reviews, and lively political debates.

Part of the general criticism in 1895 and 1896 was similar to that faced by the previous four universal expositions. Like the official reports of Prince Napoléon in 1855 and of Frédéric Le Play in 1867, these objections cited the possible damage to commerce of a universal, as opposed to a special, exhibition. In 1895 these views were best and most significantly stated by Jules Méline, the very influential politician and apostle of protectionism, in his newspaper, *La République française.*[54]

Méline favoured expositions in principle. A basic fault of Frenchmen, he believed, was that they did not search out customers. The expositions brought customers to France. Although Paris benefited most from the augmented influx of cash into France, actually, Méline asserted, all of French industry and thus the whole nation profited.

His views were more censorious than condemnatory. This exposition, he said, would be too large and plans included classifications that would make France look second-rate in comparison with the displays of the other competing nations. Worst of all, this exposition was being handled autocratically and without the consultation of the elected representatives of the people. Méline warned that the preparatory commissions should deliver to the Chamber "a clean drawing board (*une table rase*)," not a building already half constructed.[55]

Méline's opposition was possibly the type of complaint to be expected of a man whose whole political life had been devoted to strengthening French republicanism. Since 1871 the expositions, like colonization, had taken place under republican auspices, but were hardly quintessentially republican events. Though the Exposition of 1889 celebrated the Revolution, its theme hid the fact that the centenary triumph was staged by a set of independent civil servants remarkably similar to those who had always arranged the French expositions. The next exposition was to mark only a date on the calendar of no special importance to France and of even less significance to the Republic as such.

Compared to most of the opposition, Méline's wise critique seems quite reserved. Goulette, the editor of *L'Est républicain*, formed a so-called "Lorraine Decentralization League" the same day Nancy passed its resolution against the Exposition of 1900. Later Goulette assembled the more strident polemics on the topic in a pamphlet, *Pas d'Exposition en 1900!*, which he published in October 1895.[56] The pamphlet was then distributed to municipal councils and local officials all over France. The Nanciens were eager for support from the provinces. However, they really intended their pamphlet for the deputies and senators in Paris who could presumably stop the government's project. In the pamphlet's condemnation lurked the decentralist political ideology of Maurice Barrès, who was quoted heavily. The quotations of Barrès came from two articles that he had published on front pages of the widely read and politically weighty *Le Figaro* in August 1895.[57]

This pamphlet marshalled its arguments according to the political, economic, provincial, and moral objections to the exposition. In actual fact, the classifications were badly jumbled. It was essentially provincial pride and hatred of the political and economic power of Paris, both enthusiasms typical of Maurice Barrès, that dominated the arguments.

Goulette's pamphlet granted that the previous republican universal expositions had brought political benefits. The one of 1878 had been necessary to demonstrate France's recovery from her very worst humiliation, the defeat of 1870–71. The year 1889 had celebrated a great anniversary; 1900, however, had no patriotic significance, and its vaunted internationalism would be a curse.[58] With regard to Germany and Italy as prospective guests in Paris in 1900, one writer said he would prefer to tell them, "Stay at home!"[59] Concerning the claim that the exposition would promote international amity, all Frenchmen should realize that the Treaty of Frankfurt, settling the Franco-Prussian War, had made this forever impossible.

The economic results of the expositions, claimed the pamphlet, were evil, but most especially for the provinces. A lack of statistics prevented the proving of the thesis that the provincial economy suffered exceptionally in years of expositions, but the pamphlet cited such things as *octroi* receipts from Nancy to show that they had dropped in 1889 relative to 1888.[60] The Nanciens claimed that expositions were disastrous for France outside of Paris. The continued growth of Paris at the expense of the countryside was sharply accelerated in exposition years by the influx of the required additional construction workers and by peasants who saw the bright lights of the metropolis and refused to return to the land. Peasants saved for years to go to expositions. Many, it was claimed, even pawned their furniture to make the trip. This centripetal movement of talent and capital accentuated both the outrageous wealth of the capital and the poverty of the countryside. It was a mark of Parisian arrogance that in the preparation of any French exposition the provincial chambers of commerce had never been asked for advice.

Businessmen could expect few benefits in 1900. The whole project was designed to gain esteem and not a clientele. Businessmen, understandably, were interested only in the latter. It would not thrill them to know that hordes of foreign tourists would see that "the French are a very nice people and that they inhabit a lovely country."[61] The worst consequence for French industrialists would be the increased sales of foreign manufacturers who used the free market in the centre of the capital to hawk their cheap wares.

These warnings about the dismal commercial consequences of the expositions were really peripheral to the central theme of the pamphlet— that the expositions led to the depravity of a moral people. The whole tone of outrage can be attributed to Maurice Barrès. By tempting Frenchmen with "lemonade and prostitution," the expositions led to the deterioration of their integral virtues. Paris in exposition years disastrously weakened the hold of the countryside upon French youth. The prodigious expense and effort of the proposed exhibition would waste the economic and unique spiritual resources of the whole nation.

Even the peerless riches of the capital were being "denatured" by the expositions. Of all major cities of Europe, Paris already had the highest proportion of foreigners. She was being poisoned by vulgarity, frivolity, and the influence of foreign degenerates. Paris was no longer "the intellectual, elegant capital, the centre of friendly sociability and conversation." It had become "the central point of prostitution." Barrès was especially alarmed by rumours that Picard's plans for 1900 called for a clean sweep of all previous exposition buildings and a destruction of many of Paris's ancient monuments and trees. There was nothing, the patriot from Nancy claimed, "more humiliating than this squandering of past professional artistry, skill, manual labour, and materials." Barrès predicted a spreading wave of provincial indignation. He believed the whole country would watch a march toward the next "hideous fair" with disgust.[62]

This kind of attack on the principle of expositions was quite new. The experience of Picard's predecessors had led him to expect that his plans would be criticized in detail only. Now, with the distribution of the pamphlet, *Pas d'Exposition en 1900!*, there was a sharp increase in the number and ingenuity of pamphlets, articles, editorials, and meetings against plans for the coming exposition.[63] An important article was written by the famous economist, Paul Leroy-Beaulieu, and published in his own journal, *L'Economiste français*. Leroy-Beaulieu believed that expositions no longer increased opportunities for technical education, that the awards system was now a lottery with far too many prizes, and that businessmen participated only because there was no rallying point available for them in order to resist pressure from the government. Since Le Play's great educational experiment in 1867, Leroy-Beaulieu felt that the French expositions had become increasingly degenerate. The organizers of 1900, he claimed, were no longer interested in progress; they wanted "mere disgusting amusement."[64]

Octave Mirbeau, a well known novelist, dramatist, and critic, published a witty, mordant attack on the principle of expositions in the highly esteemed *Revue des Deux Mondes*.[65] This provoked a brilliant reply in the *Revue de Paris* by Henri Chardon, a political journalist who favoured them.[66] *Correspondant*, another of the thick, influential, political and intellectual reviews, adopted opposition to the planned exposition as part of its editorial policy. Newspapers took sides. Such factors as a supposed decline in sexual morality, a rise in the crime rate, and heightened dangers to France from plague and even famine were all brought into the dispute.

Bombarded by polemics, Picard and his committees steadily kept their plans moving forward. In the meantime, the Chamber of Deputies had not been consulted. Legally, it had the ultimate responsibility for approval of the government's plans, but had, until the winter of 1895–96, been able to show its interest only by the voting (or opposing) of 200,000 francs for preliminary studies. The deputies had as yet had no voice in the taste, theme, content, or expense of the exposition. Some had even been rebuffed when they had questioned the bureaucrats who were already working out details.[67]

In the meantime the government's project for a comprehensive law to regulate the Exposition of 1900 had been approved by all the commissioners who worked under Picard. The then Ministers of Commerce and Finance submitted Picard's scheme to the Chambers on November 21, 1895. The plan outlined the spatial design, the themes, attendance, novelties, and a projected financial balance sheet including, of course, the expected grant of the 20-million franc subsidy. At the end of the document the Deputies and Senators were told:

In voting for this draft bill, the Chambers will perform an act of high policy and of patriotism. The Exposition of 1900 will stir initiative, re-activate the movement of business, give a new impetus to our industry and commerce, provide a period of employment for the working classes and give rise to inventions and further progress. It will also constitute a vast study and teaching centre. It will stimulate our exports and affirm the peaceful intentions of the government; it will demonstrate once again the growth of the nation's prosperity and, what is still more important, add to its glory and its import abroad. Paris and all of France will emerge from this solemn meeting yet more splendid. The Republic will close the nineteenth century with suitable dignity and will attest to its desire to remain in the vanguard of civilization.[68]

Jules Méline was president of the eleven-man committee of the Chamber of Deputies formed to examine the proposal. Jules Bouge, *rapporteur* of the committee's report, was one of the seven members known to oppose the government's project.[69] The report was ready for the consideration of the deputies on February 3, 1896. Debate on the project began March 13, 1896.

During the four-day debate in the Chamber of Deputies and also in the day-long debate in the Senate, it was clear that the pamphlet distributed by the Lorraine Decentralization League had reached its mark. Especially during the debate in the Chamber, it was obvious that the rather shrill tone of its writing had touched many of the deputies. In fact, most of the evidence given by deputies who were opponents of the exposition was taken directly from the pamphlet. The long opening speech in the debate in the Chamber, clearly a paraphrase of the pamphlet, closed with the exclamation, "Pas d'Exposition!"[70] This coda was greeted with many cheers of approbation and some shouts of derision. Thereafter the vigour of the opinions and the passions of their supporters led to frequent unruliness. The presiding officials in both houses often had difficulty keeping order.

Both sides of the debate could draw from a lot of material published in the previous months. The economic arguments focused on the already thoroughly aired argument, unresolved for lack of statistics, of whether or not the exposition would hurt the provinces. The moral arguments against the planned exposition were strongly reminiscent of, if not identical to, those of Maurice Barrès. The most forceful defender of the government's project was the unruffled commissioner general himself. Picard corrected deputies who were misinformed on such things as detailed expenses, the alleged probable devastation of the beauties of Paris, or the extent to which imported labour would be used. Picard repeatedly recalled the glories of 1889 and promised that 1900 would surpass them.

Two recurring topics in the Chamber and Senate debates had not been discussed much in the press. Though extremely dissimilar in subject matter, both were used at least as much to torment the government responsible for the exposition as to attack the exposition itself. These were long discussions about the exposition's architectural concepts and about the invitations to foreign powers.

An ambitious and expensive part of the coming exposition was to be the piercing of a new Parisian boulevard that would open a vista from the Champs Elysées across the Seine to the Hôtel des Invalides. Two new permanent palaces of fine arts would flank the boulevard on the right bank. The avenue would continue over the river on a bridge to be named after Tsar Alexander III, and then to the majestic dome of the Invalides itself (figure 1).

These plans called for large-scale demolitions on the right bank in the long wedge formed by the Champs Elysées as it approached the Seine.

The major loss to Paris would be the Palais de l'Industrie, a vast hall built by Napoléon III for the Exposition of 1855 and thereafter used irregularly for salons, ice skating, and horse shows. The Palais de l'Industrie was surrounded with rank shrubbery. Its vicinity was a gathering place for suspect individuals and the walls were smeared with "des inscriptions et des dessins à faire rougir un singe."[71] Long hated by Republicans as an oversized reminder of the Second Empire, and widely deplored for its ugliness and advanced decrepitude, the Palais de l'Industrie suddenly found champions.

Bouge, in his report to the deputies, cited a petition of a society of architects which claimed that the Palais de l'Industrie was worthy of preservation. Its intended demolition would also deface the Champs Elysées for years. Anyway, it was immoral, Bouge claimed, and here he returned to an argument of Barrès, to squander the labour and artistry of past generations of Frenchmen. Though once loathed (concurrently an article in *Le Figaro* recalled the horror of Frenchmen as they watched it go up in 1854) the Palais de l'Industrie was a familiar and therefore beloved part of the Parisian landscape.[72]

Always an impressive, cool figure, Picard defended his project.[73] He quickly destroyed Bouge's claim that architects favoured the preservation of the Palais de l'Industrie. Charles Garnier, architect of the Opéra and president of the Société centrale des architectes français had published a letter saying that no important architect favoured the preservation of the Palais de l'Industrie. Bouge had to confess in the Chamber that in his report he mistook an obscure group for the most influential organization of architects in France.[74]

Picard quoted a report of the municipal councillor of the *arrondissement* near this part of the Champs Elysées who stated that the Palais de l'Industrie was in bad, perhaps irreparable, condition, and should be pulled down. Nevertheless, Picard then promised to keep it up as long as possible so that the annual salons could continue to take place there. He showed that when the old structure was removed Parisians would have a splendid vista of the Hôtel des Invalides (*"le dôme de Mansart"*). Anticipating warnings that an intervening rise in the land had to obscure François Mansart's dome, Picard said that trustworthy figures demonstrated that only the bottom 1.5 to 1.75 metres of the Invalides would be invisible from the Champs Elysées.

This led, as these discussions often did, to matters of principle. A deputy claimed that the reason for architectural horrors at expositions was that there was never time enough to prepare anything really fine. In a fast interruption, Bouge exclaimed, "The architecture of expositions and true architecture are two distinctly different things."[75] Another deputy suggested that if the *clou* in 1889 had been the Eiffel Tower, a *clou* in 1900 might be Paris without the Eiffel Tower. At this another shouted, "We'll decorate whoever demolishes it!"[76]

Many of the deputies were worried about the parks near the site. To warnings of an intended "massacre" of the gardens of central Paris, Picard countered that the exposition would encompass 5,711 trees of which 545 would be removed. But landscapers would add 647 trees that would be permanent: a net gain of 102 trees.[77]

Near the close of his long defense, Picard noted that the United States had recently spent 140 million francs for its exposition. France ought not to compete with America in prodigality, but she had her own high standard to maintain. To uphold his projections of total cost, Picard attacked Bouge's report, which claimed the government's project could not be accomplished for 100 million francs. For one thing, Bouge had counted the cost of the new bridge twice. Picard then appealed to the deputies to unite with him to offer France's magnificence to the world:

You will effectively combat this slander if you rally around the government's project. By doing so you will have given renewed proof of your astuteness and patriotism, assured a triumph for this labouring nation, and guaranteed the Republic a glorious future.[78]

Enthusiastic applause greeted the end of this stirring speech.

Shortly after Picard's defense, it became apparent that though some deputies objected to having any exposition at all, far more were nettled that the government had acted arrogantly and independently (or more correctly, had others do so) on a project that would present the Republic to the whole world. In a speech replying to Picard, Bouge emphasized that thought Picard's plans were far advanced, the Chamber had supported only studies.[79] For nearly two years there had been protests in the Chamber of Deputies against the mysteriousness and evasions of Picard's commissioners. A deputy had also warned the Minister of Commerce that there would be a demand for an accounting of the government's intentions.[80] Bouge noted that invitations for all previous expositions, had been sent out two years in advance. This time they were sent four-and-a-half years before the opening, without the consultation of the

Chamber. Why would the government not even consider modifications of Picard's plans?[81] Then, shocking everyone, Bouge declared he was in favour of an exposition in 1900. Amid astonished murmurings, he finished his speech with moderate criticism of Picard's planned layout.[82]

The debate over the Palais de l'Industrie was really an opportunity for the deputies to declare their offence at bureaucratic presumptuousness. A far more serious problem was posed by the fact that foreign nations, many more than ever before, had accepted invitations and had already advanced their plans for 1900. The government had, in fact, surreptitiously sent out invitations while the deputies were on vacation in September 1895. Could even the most vigorous and highly principled opponent of Picard's plans now urge retreat?

In one oration during the painful debate over this problem, a champion of Picard reminded the deputies that the nation's honour was involved. He allowed that if you invite someone to dinner and later learn that the dinner cannot take place, you write a note and it is settled. Your intended guest may decide that you could not afford it. You may thus slip in his opinion and arouse his pity, but nothing very serious has occurred. "It is exactly the same with the great powers," he observed. If there is no exposition, France will "incur ridicule, but will certainly give rise to no *casus belli*." The deputies laughed. Turning serious, the zealot soberly charged that France had "duties vis-à-vis foreigners and duties vis-à-vis herself." She should "charge ahead, do it grandly, do it splendidly, so as to guarantee a brilliant success." Stinginess and complaining would lead to a most deplorable defeat. France had to surpass her performance of 1889, or the whole world would be disappointed.[83]

In this discussion, the vigorous debater Jules Méline again insisted that he did not oppose expositions on principle. However, too often France had shown merely banalities. What was needed (returning to the advice of Le Play in 1867) was more careful selection.[84] In another vein, he felt there was no need to put the people of the world in closer communication—they were too close now. Méline summarized the arguments previously voiced, but near the end of the long debate rather resignedly admitted that the honour of the nation was engaged because of the accepted invitations. In fact it was impossible now to retreat gracefully.

During the airing of views on plans for the exposition, it became apparent that there was a right and a left position. The tumult in the Chamber was indicative of deeper differences which aspects of the discussion reflected. Conservatives, nationalists, agrarian deputies, and deputies from the wealthier parts of Paris opposed the principle of expositions. The majority of deputies in the centre probably favoured the government's project, though many resented Picard's independence and secrecy. However, they were resigned, though rather bitterly, to the fact that they could do little to alter the government's plans in the face of such determination to keep them intact. A spokesman for the socialists said that they had opposed the Exposition of 1889, seeing in it only a speculation, but that now the socialists favoured expositions because they would provide work for many unemployed.[85]

Socialists dominated the debate that led to the vote. Jules Guesde reminded the deputies, as he frequently did, that no civilized nation was more backward than France. It was the conservatives, he noted, who approved better conditions for labour in Great Britain and Germany. A motion for an eight-hour day for workers on the exposition was defeated 308 to 150. A motion for an obligatory day of rest, though supported by Catholic deputies, met a similar fate.[86] After the raucous confusion of several ballots and repeated counts, the final vote was 419 for accepting the government's project *en bloc*, 67 against.[87]

Debate in the Senate took a similar course. The nine-man senatorial commission that had considered the government's project contained five members who favoured it. Three opposed the government, wishing to preserve the Palais de l'Industrie. The remaining member and chief debater was Albert Le Play, son of the organizer of the Exposition of 1867. Although admitting that he was indeed "a minority of a minority" in the Senate, he cited the well-known figures who shared his views, mostly drawing from the arguments in the pamphlet *Pas d'Exposition en 1900!*[88] Lively response in the Senate, however, showed that he had many sympathizers there.[89]

Henri Boucher, the Minister of Commerce, tried to focus controversy on a single issue, the same one that had settled the quarrel in the Chamber of Deputies. The only real question, he said, was whether or not the invitations to foreign governments were to be revoked. Boucher even tried the fashionable Russian gambit (for the alliance was everywhere popular in France at that time) by declaring that Russia needed the opportunity of a great exposition to demonstrate how she had been transformed.[90] Another zealous senator reminded his colleagues that they were being asked to consent to a great work of peace that cost very much less than the 800 millions they voted each year for military expenses. Charles Freycinet, the former Prime Minister, a great engineer and an advocate of public works, defended the proposed exposition as the next manifestation of a noble French tradition. He told the Senators that it was "by these solemn occasions that a nation demonstrates its power and indelibly imprints its grandeur."[91]

The crenellations of the Palais de l'Electricité, drawn from the roof of the building.

Though there were fewer interruptions and difficulties in keeping order in the Senate than in the Chamber, the one-day debate was quite spirited. But, because of the invitations, as *Le Figaro* predicted, the decision in the Senate as well as in the Chamber was "in the bag."[92] The government's measure was passed by a voice vote.[93] This marked the end of organized internal political resistance to the exposition.

It would be easy to exaggerate the extent and depth of the hostility to the approaching exposition. Though some of its critics were imported people, few Frenchmen were really determined opponents. Even in the provinces, as Picard pointed out, no municipal council or chamber of commerce was as eloquent in its denunciation as were the Nanciens.[94] It was just that those people who aired their objections did so prominently and with considerable spirit. It all meant, however, and this was significant, that the Exposition of 1900 was the first to have a thought-out opposition that was well and widely stated. Many Frenchmen probably had a wait-and-see attitude. Most were no doubt enthusiastic about the coming fête.

A well placed enthusiast was the editor of one special newspaper (of many) published for participants in the exposition. Henri Gautier started his bi-monthly *L'Exposition universelle 1900* shortly after the exposition had been instituted. The journal reprinted documents, debates, reports of banquets, lists of committees, and even gossip likely to be interesting to anyone with a stake in the preparations. Gautier's editorials and anecdotes were close to all events that affected the exposition, and were a first-hand record of the climate of its preparation and fruition.

Gautier was, of course, nettled by the opposition to the exposition. However, when the controversy died down, his worries took a new form. Would this planned 100-million franc, 60-million visitor exposition fulfil the hopes of its promoters and supporters? Moreover, would it be ready in time?

Preparations • As the debate over the exposition flourished, Commissioner General Picard and his lieutenants were already working on the details of the fair—or at least on the planning of them. The centre of Paris was not yet upset with the re-routed traffic, demolitions, and earth-moving that such a project required. However, great numbers of surveyors in Paris and Vincennes peered down vistas, plotted paths and gardens, and tapped down little wooden stakes over areas that would present a very different appearance four years later. To Picard in the summer of 1896, it seemed that the financing and the conservative estimate of attendance augured well. He was a favoured bureaucrat; his isolation from the unruly Parliament of the Republic permitted him to work on the exposition with little fear of interruption. As will be seen later, politics were by far the greatest threat to this exposition, but in the happy years of 1895, 1896, and 1897, it seemed that Picard had the glorious task of directing a triumph greater than that of 1889.

The credits for preliminary studies allowed the administration 50,000 francs to finance an architectural competition for both the general layout and individual French buildings.[1] Aside from the additional large area in Vincennes, available grounds in Paris were about the same as in 1889: the Champ de Mars, the Trocadéro, the Esplanade des Invalides, the Cours la Reine, and the banks of the Seine between the Point de l'Alma and the Place de la Concorde.

Curiously, unlike the Exposition of 1889, there were to be no striking innovations in exposition technique. It appeared that with the marked devotion to education of 1867, and the adding of international congresses in 1878, further evolution would be toward greater size. A planned emphasis in 1900 would be retrospective displays in technology and the arts that would sum up all that the nineteenth century had accomplished.

The competitors were told of this. They were also given general allocations of space; French agriculture and chemistry, for instance (one critic hoped the two wouldn't be confounded), were each assigned 15,000 square metres and told to go ahead.

The competition was no small event; 664 contestants announced that they would submit projects and 108 of these were accepted. The plans, consisting of models and renderings, were viewed by crowds in twenty-three rooms of the old Palais de l'Industrie. The exhibits were on display for almost a year and were frequently viewed by escorted groups of foreigners with an interest in the exposition.

Picard offered the competitors *carte blanche*. Within the assigned limits they could destroy or alter any building except the Trocadéro. This sweeping allowance was supposed to accommodate the unlikely and unexpected appearance of a new Michelangelo. Some projects, such as one for covering the whole area with a single roof of glass, or for multiple towers twice as high as Eiffel's, were visionary schemes. Others were not.[2] There seemed, in fact, to be two kinds of projects:

It is a conflict between the art of the engineer and the art of the government schools. It is like a discourse in which mathematical language blends with the elegant traditional expressions of classical rhetoric.[3]

The outcome of this struggle could have been foreseen. Of the jury of thirty-one members, more than half were professors or officials of the École des Beaux-Arts. The rest were high-ranking bureaucrats or former cabinet ministers like Agénor Bardoux and Léon Bourgeois. The three first prizes of 6,000 francs went to the architects Charles Louis Girault, Eugène Alfred Henard, and Edmond Paulin. There were fourteen additional prizes of 4,000 to 1,000 francs. All of the winners were graduates of the École des Beaux-Arts.[4] A few of the plans that suggested far-reaching alterations in the existing site received honourable mention. But Picard, by the winter of 1894–95, had already been working on his own plans for almost two years. The competition was a spectacle for Paris, and merely a gesture to artists outside the favoured circles of the government art schools. Significantly, the administration kept the right to amalgamate or edit any of the plans as it wished. Considering the composition of the jury and the training of the prize winners, it became clear that the decoration and the architecture of the Exposition of 1900 would be dominated by the eclecticism of the academies and would turn away from those examples of engineering architecture so striking in 1889.

Picard's permission to the competitors to make a clean sweep of previous architecture had included even the Eiffel Tower over which controversy still flourished. Significantly, of the projects accepted by the admitting jury (also dominated by the Ecole des Beaux-Arts) more wanted to preserve the Galerie des Machines than to retain the *clou* of 1889.

"But, what will be the *clou* of the Universal Exposition of 1900?" "Rastignac," the satirical columnist of *L'Illustration,* wrote in July 1897, that this question was debated everywhere in Paris now that the form of the exposition was definite. The papers foretold the great variety and seductiveness of dozens of attractions. Nevertheless, no architectural or other kind of theme seemed to be forthcoming, though there were many candidates: new palaces, gates, views, banquets, even unusual royal visits. Picard hoped that the new vista of the dome of the Invalides would be the most memorable spectacle of 1900. But critics noted that the Invalides dated from the seventeenth century. It was old and therefore not a vital issue at all. Besides, another view of open space excited no one, for Paris already had many splendid vistas opened by Baron Haussmann during the Second Empire.

It was hoped that one of the more ambitious commercial attractions might become a central theme. A successful principal attraction in an exposition in Brussels in 1897 had been "Bruxelles-Kermesse," an interpretive reproduction of Brussels in the middle ages. In 1900, Paris planned to evoke her own past with a "Vieux Paris," which would feature quaint mediaeval buildings and streets with actors in mediaeval costume. Similar candidates were a planned Palais de l'Électricité and a large structure, more fountains than architecture, called the Château d'Eau (figure 22).

Henri Gautier, a sort of cheerleader of the exposition's progress, might have been grasping at straws when he suggested that the expected visit of Menelik, King of Ethiopia, be turned into a kind of pivotal festival. The oddness of the prospect, Gautier believed, would attract great crowds. The suggestion was not to be scorned, he felt, since few monarchs had made irreversible promises to visit Paris personally in 1900. Gautier, recognizing Menelik as authentic, was willing to snatch him up.

"Rastignac" invented his own major themes: Why not a great spiral railway going up the 300-metre tower, each stage of which would sum up the progress of each of the arts all over the world? This could be called "Musée en Hauteur." Alternatively, the authorities might build two statues of pyramid size, one called "War," the other, "Peace." The spectator could walk in front of them saying first, "Good Lord! War is ugly!" and then, "Ah, but Peace is sweet!"[5]

A leading candidate for *clou* and one that illustrates very well the merger of both aims of the exposition—international co-operation and national competition—was the Quai or Rue des Nations (pp. iv, v). This was a row of national pavilions that would cover a sturdy platform raised over the right bank. The principal nations were allowed to build decorative palaces in indigenous styles in the first row to make a stunning ensemble from the Seine. A second row would contain the palaces of lesser nations. This ranking was the occasion for terrific squabbles over diplomatic precedence and assertion of importance, quarrels that contradicted the peaceful purposes of the exposition as a whole. In any case, no nation received the space it had requested.

In nineteenth-century international exhibitions the hosting nation customarily kept half the available area for itself. Within France decisions to allocate her space led to such elegant and rhetorical debates as whether the arts were more important than industry, or colonization than education. Further down the organizational pyramid, less serious decisions concerned how much area should be given to the cheese-makers of Normandy or to the automobiles of the Comte de Dion. The jockeying among Frenchmen was amiable, since space was adequate for all displays that were both French and considered by the admitting juries to be of potential interest to visitors.

Concern for international approbation and the pride of the folks at home made the allocation of space among foreigners quite another matter. Space for 1900 was originally awarded on the basis of participation in 1889, with the significant addition of Germany. Americans were gravely offended upon learning that they had not, indeed, been considered for placement among the first rank on the Quai des Nations. Upon first hearing of the coming exposition, many states, particularly New York and California, planned pavilions of their own in Paris. The French turned down their requests, mentioning that the exposition was international, not interstate.[6] The American commissioner general, Ferdinand Peck, while agreeing that the inclusion of all the states would cause a "hodge-podge," nevertheless believed the space allotted the Americans to be insulting, and the intended second-rank placement of the American official pavilion intolerable. The United States immediately demanded "a maximum amount of area" and "extra space for a national pavilion and certain other buildings which circumstances demanded for the United States." In Paris this request met an "official, definite, and gracious refusal."[7]

The French ambassador in Washington, Jules Cambon, decided that the space for the United States should be increased.[8] Planted articles in the French press listed statistics demonstrating the prodigious growth of the American economy. The French government eventually forced the exposition authorities to increase by 40 per cent the space allocated to the United States.[9] All the powers on the Quai des Nations squeezed their pavilions closer together so that the Yankee pavilion could be inserted between those of Austria and Turkey (figure 00).

An increase for the Americans meant, of course, that the already meagre space of others was further constricted. The Germans, who had more space than any other foreigner, felt that France had broken early promises for adequate area to demonstrate the German industrial transformation. Great Britain at first confounded these matters by imperiously insisting on the allocation of as much space for herself as that promised any other nation. Austria had to sacrifice an intended great retrospective show of her art. In fact, Picard's planned emphasis on retrospective displays was only rarely observed. Many of the planned large educational exhibits were abandoned by nations who preferred to show what would make the greatest impression: new, marketable products. A distant power with little impact on the administrators or deputies in Paris, Japan had her request for more space repeatedly turned down and her allocation diminished. Upon the arrival of the Japanese delegation, "the insufficiency of the space became still more shocking."[10]

This agoraphilia and the ensuing battles of diplomatic courtesy brought with them complications for the individual commissioners general who had to accept or reject their numerous national applicants. Peck of the United States confessed that the weeding out produced

. . . some slight disaffection in the minds of certain applicants whose appreciation of their own merits did not, unfortunately, harmonize with the judgement of those who were compelled to make the selection.[11]

One rejected Englishman who had a large Parisian clientele was desperate to show his scarves in a French display and was told that, alas, Article 33 of the general law regulating the exposition permitted only goods of French origin in the French display.[12] The participation of practically all the civilized nations, which had at first been so gratifying, was causing domestic nightmares and was a source of international friction rather than of harmony.[13]

As in 1888, it again appeared that a whole new city was growing in the centre of Paris. Gas lines were disconnected, traffic diverted, trees uprooted. A high, pale green fence, decorated like a trellis in a lacy jigsaw pattern, hid the frantic activity on the exposition grounds. The aesthetic barrier exemplifies Picard's wish not to arouse the ire of those who feared the desecration, even though temporary, of the capital's beauty. One humourist remarked:

> Alors commença la ballade
> Entre poutres et palissade[14]

As he had promised, Picard had delayed pulling down the old Palais de l'Industrie because it was customarily used for the annual *salons*. Construction of the two new palaces of fine arts began long before the older structure in the same area was demolished. By the summer of 1899, the smaller, called the Petit Palais, was progressing smoothly. It was the work of one architect, Girault, a prize winner in the competition of 1894. On the other hand, discord among three architects was hampering construction of the larger Grand Palais which would house French art since 1800. Furthermore, the committee selecting the works to be displayed in the Grand Palais was reviving all the critical controversies of the century.

In July of 1899 the arch of the Pont Alexander III was complete, though the bridge itself was still covered with scaffolding. All over the exposition grounds cement foundation pillars marked the sites of intended pavilions. Piles of construction materials were everywhere. The Quai des Nations did not yet show the pavilions of the foreign nations, but the territory of each was marked out with little flags.[15] During late summer evenings Parisians strolled to watch the mounting growth of the extraordinary variety of thin lath frameworks that would soon take their light coatings of plaster to masquerade for a while as solidity.

As the buildings rose and Paris approached political tranquility in the late autumn of 1899 (see Chapter 5), there were a great many annoyances for its administrators to deal with. One threat arose with reports of plague in several places in the world, and most alarmingly, in Portugal. *Le Figaro*, seeing possible evil consequences in a recent invention, warned, "Today one comes to Paris in less than thirteen hours and from Bordeaux in less than six. Next year the microbes will travel by automobile."[16] The Chamber voted an additional 300,000 francs for the prevention of plague.[17] Refusing to panic at another rumour, this time of an influenza epidemic, *Le Temps* warned:

The terrors inspired by the flu could have more horrible consequences than flu itself and, naturally exploited by our foreign rivals, they are very likely to compromise the success of the exposition.[18]

A final public dispute in Paris over the exposition focused on a matter of artistic taste. One of the prime candidates for the *clou* was the gigantic main entrance gate of the exposition, officially called "Porte de la Concorde" (see p. i) because of its proximity to the famous *place* in Paris. Its architect, René Binet, had desired to be "modern."[19] The dispute centred on the statue of a confident woman in a tight skirt, elegantly coiffed in the latest mode, bust aggressively thrust forward, who was to perch atop a gold sphere on the cupola of the entrance gate. She was dressed in jewel and peacock colours and smiled, it seemed, like a harlot. Her official title was "The City of Paris," but she quickly became known as "La Parisienne". In a passionate controversy, some deputies tried to prevent this *soi-disant* motif from being erected: it was too gauche, too sensual, too modern, too likely to become a symbol for the exposition itself. Despite their last-minute efforts, the statue, still smiling, was raised to the top of the cupola by a great crane—and the public would judge. *La Vie Parisienne*, during the controversy over this figure, printed a cartoon of France, the mother, advising her daughter, the statue of Paris, "Monsieur Émile [Loubet] is going to inaugurate you, my dear. You must behave prettily."[20]

Preparations for opening ceremonies were well under way when the Americans created a furor over the scheduled opening date, April 15, which was Easter Sunday. A "New York Sabbath Committee" had the matter carried to Congress. Eventually the date for the opening ceremonies was moved to April 14, 1900.[21]

In March 1900, Gautier complained that Paris had a new kind of bore. This fellow leaned against you and asked earnestly, "Do you think it will be ready on time?"[22] The question was being posed all over Paris.[23] It had been a wet and very cold winter. For some of the buildings special paints had to be developed. Parisians had only to walk near the site to see that many big buildings had a long way to go before completion. The grounds, especially around the Trocadéro and Champ de Mars, were quagmires.[24] Some of the exhibitors were pressing for a delay in the opening.

Picard used the strongest language to tell all exhibitors that under no circumstances would the date of the opening be changed.[25] One wag remarked

> Le palais le moins en retard
> Dit le Commissaire Picard
> C'est celui de l'agriculture
> Il ne manque que la toiture.[26]

Le Temps, on April 11, assured its readers that five-sevenths of the total of 35,000 tons of the material intended for emplacement was already on the exposition site. It could not, however, assure the readers that the material was in place (figure 23). The fenced-in area of the exposition grounds was an ant-hill of workmen rushing completion, for it became clear that Picard was adamant about permitting no postponement.

Almost all of the dignitaries who would supervise the foreign pavilions and exhibits had arrived. The pace of banquets, receptions, and official welcomes was accordingly stepped up.[27] The largest banquets took place in one or another of the few exposition buildings that were complete. To celebrate one such event a chef called his dessert *Bombe Palais de Costume*. One wonders how Loubet, Millerand, and Picard could speak at so many banquets and still carry on their administrative duties. Tourists were starting to fill the hotels. The *Berliner Tageblatt* noted that already in the restaurants the waiters were ruder, the prices higher, and the filets smaller.[28]

Rains in early April further bemired the grounds, but the same moisture made the flowers bloom and the trees of the boulevards send out fine greenery. On the morning of April 14 the president left the Élysée Palace in his ceremonial calèche, preceded by a squadron of *cuirassiers*. He was followed by four gilded landaus carrying members of the cabinet and high military officials, all wearing their decorations. Crack regiments marched or rode in breastplates, with pikes, bayonets, and other jangling, flashing hardware; all officers wore parade uniforms, rows of medals, and plumed helmets. Cannon boomed the whole way to the Champ de Mars. Alas, the ooze and water that filled the carriage ruts slowed this section of the journey and the party arrived

> Moitié sautant, moitié nageant
> A la suite du président.[29]

As the orchestra played the *Marseillaise*, Picard and Millerand greeted Loubet at the tribune of the *Salle des Fêtes*, an immense, ornate chamber constructed within the great Galerie des Machines of 1889.[30] After Massenet's *Marche solonnelle*, Millerand reviewed the purposes of the Exposition of 1900. His speech closed with a curious blend of republican pomposity and obeisance to his socialist past:

Oh, Work, sacred, liberating Work it is you that ennobles and that consoles. Before your march ignorance is dispelled and evil flees. Through you, Humanity, emancipated from the night of slavery, climbs, climbs ceaselessly towards that luminous and serene region where one day an ideal and perfect fusion of power, justice, and goodness will be realized.[31]

A few excerpts from President Loubet's speech give an idea of the tone of the dedication:

France has sought to offer a brilliant contribution to the coming understanding among nations. She has consciously worked to benefit the whole world at the end of this noble century whose victory over hate and error is, alas, still incomplete, but which bequeaths to us a continuing and lively faith in progress. . . . Despite the harsh battles which nations still fight in the fields of industry, commerce, and economics, they have never ceased to give the highest importance to studying means of easing suffering, organizing public assistance, expanding education, improving the lot of the worker and to ensuring support for the aged.[32]

Like Millerand, Loubet also felt that the exposition marked the beginning of a new and more beautiful era:

. . . soon, perhaps, we shall have completed an important stage in the slow evolution of work towards happiness and of man towards humanity. It is under the auspices of such a hope that I declare the Exposition of 1900 open.[33]

After the cries of "Vive la République!" had settled, the orchestra played *The Hymn of Victor Hugo* by Saint-Saëns and a *Heroic March* by Théodore Dubois. Picard then led the cortège across a monumental staircase to the galleries of the new Palais d'Électricité, which offered a view of the Champ de Mars.

Pausing there, the procession then marched along the Champs de Mars toward the Pont d'Iéna accompanied by the din of artillery salvos and the great bells of the pavilion of Asiatic Russia, which played French patriotic songs.[34] On the right bank the President of France, the presidents of the Senate and the Chamber, the ministers, and members of the diplomatic corps boarded a ceremonial barge. Two additional barges followed with more uniformed and beribboned dignitaries. They cruised slowly past the Rue des Nations. Most of the official pavilions had orchestras in front of them playing their respective anthems. The jangling mixture of musical and architectural themes must have produced a peculiar dissonant blare—auguring confusion perhaps—but the procession appeared pleased.[35]

There were more speeches at the inauguration of the Pont Alexander III. After this Loubet, who was handsome, but quite short, and Picard, who had a lined, sober face at the top of his long frame, marched toward the Champs Élysées. At an appointed moment, both stopped and turned about, dramatically forcing their cortèges to turn with them. Yes, at the end of the admirable panorama the whole dome of the Invalides was splendidly visible (figure 3). Loubet once more mounted his golden carriage to return to his palace. The crowd of dignitaries dispersed. The exposition had been opened on time. Workers turned at once to their tasks. Soon the greatest international exhibition of all time would be ready for its millions of curious visitors.

At the Fair • Confronted with its complexity, one enthusiast complained of the Exposition of 1900:

No man has been able actually to see, much less is any able to show, this vast, indeed too vast, labyrinth of labyrinths, this enormous multitude of collections, this museum of museums. How can one briefly give an idea of what needs shelves of volumes for its mere catalogue?

Despite the 350 acres, all is too crowded; and twice the space would not have been too much.[1]

In addition, the extraordinary voluptuousness and experimental liberties of the architecture at the Exposition of 1900 produced a medley of colours and styles that was, perhaps, an abrupt contrast to the regularity of Baron Haussmann's Paris outside the gates. But, however dazzled he might be, the sincere observer of 1900 felt he *had* to try to absorb this great exposition, to make the content mean something to him, to draw lessons from what the exposition summarized and predicted. This investigation, undertaken so many years later, will attempt to absorb the exposition too. It will be divided into three main parts: first, a general tour of the grounds in the centre of Paris, next an attempt to draw some lessons from art and architecture in 1900, and then an appraisal of the national competition and its outcome at the exposition. The chapter will end with a chronology of the exposition's season.

The fairgrounds in the centre of Paris resembled a vast, flattened "A" truncated lopsidedly at the top (see map at front). A broad swath of the city stretching from the Champs Elysées to the Hôtel des Invalides formed the left leg of the "A"; the Champ de Mars plus the Trocadéro formed the other, thicker leg. The horizontal bar of the "A" (in this case a gentle bend in the Seine) was formed by both quays of the Seine between the Pont Alexandre III and the Pont d'Iéna.

In Paris itself, the exposition occupied only a little more area than the centennial eleven years earlier. The increases were around the new Grand Palais and the Petit Palais and along the right bank of the Seine.[2] In 1900, the Bois de Vincennes (see map at front) was an annex for exhibits and displays (e.g. stock and horse shows, agricultural exhibits, railroad equipment, some other heavy machinery, and the athletic competitions) that required spaciousness. The atmosphere in Vincennes was probably similar to that of the more bucolic parts of a great Middle Western state fair. Though Vincennes was newly connected to the centre of Paris by the first line of the Métro, almost no one went there. The main attractions were in Paris.

Except for the annex at Vincennes and the landscaped grounds around the two new palaces of fine arts, there were few open areas. Also, for this exposition many pavilions were two or three stories high. Commissioner General Picard had tried, at least, to satisfy the unprecedented demands for exhibit space. As in all the French expositions, though the proportions varied with the classifications, roughly half the space was devoted to French displays, half to the displays of other nations.

Most visitors entered the grounds from the Place de la Concorde through René Binet's new Porte de la Concorde (page i), one of the many so-called *clous*, in 1900. Since the buildings were somewhat squeezed together, one could "do" much of the exposition in a few days with little difficulty. From Binet's gate to the furthest corner of the Galerie des Machines at the northern end of the Champ de Mars, the distance was about 2½ miles by foot. One of the major private speculations, and a novelty in 1900, was a raised electric moving sidewalk, with bands of varying speeds. This gave the cartoonists an abundance of inspiration and subject-matter (figure 39). They depicted peasants wide-eyed in fear or astonishment, or very fat ladies worriedly negotiating the change from one band to the other. The *trottoir roulant* was widely talked about, but not much used: as at any fair, almost everyone walked.

Just to the visitor's right after he passed through the monumental gate was a large structure, the new Petit Palais which contained a retrospective display of older French art. This area was one of the best planned and most heavily visited of the exposition. On the other side of the new

Avenue Alexandre III stood the larger Grand Palais (figure 16) containing the best modern painting and sculpture of all nations. In the Grand Palais the French (justifiably, they believed) had awarded themselves far more than half the space.

The promenade down the Avenue Alexandre III, across the broad new bridge of the same name (figure 4) revealed Paris' new vista of the Invalides, Picard's candidate for *clou* of the exposition. As the commissioner general predicted, from a great distance only the bottom few feet of the Hôtel des Invalides were hidden; the view of Mansart's imposing dome was unencumbered (figure 1).

On either side of the Esplanade des Invalides, were the many lightly built, though lavishly decorated, buildings devoted to the broad classification of decorative art. This included jewelry, costumes, ceramics, furniture, carpets, and all aspects of interior design. Here were the separate pavilions of the great French department stores and the private pavilion of S. Bing, the impresario of the Art Nouveau movement (figure 24). French decorative art, divided according to provincial areas, occupied the west side of the Esplanade des Invalides; foreign decorative art shown by nations was displayed on the east side (figure 28).

As the visitor returned to the right bank and walked along the Seine toward the Trocadéro, he passed through a section of the grounds which, if he chose to enjoy it fully, compelled him to dip into his pocketbook. Here, and also on the Champ de Mars near the Seine, were most of the more ambitious commercial enterprises, as well as the theatres, the ethnic restaurants, and the carnival-type "rides."

Most of the commercial *attractions*, as they were called, represented huge investments.[3] Some attempted to re-create distant geographical regions or historical periods by means of architectural copies, murals, or dioramas.[4] One, more tasteful than the majority of the others, a Swiss village, covered about as much ground as that enclosed by the four supports of the Eiffel Tower. One tour that visitors were able to make without leaving the exposition grounds was Andalusia at the time of the Moors (figure 37). Another, Vieux Paris, with strolling actors in mediaeval costumes, stretched along the quay of the Seine and was a sort of temporary French Williamsburg (figure 5). The most extraordinary shift in geography was the Tour du Monde, a bizarre catch-all, that took bargain seekers all over Africa, South America, and Asia by dioramas and fragmented plaster reproductions."⁹ of such places as the imperial palace at Peking and a terraced tower of Angkor Wat.

Leaving the earth entirely, the *cinéorama* took one on an imaginary voyage in a balloon. Even more ambitiously, *le globe celeste* seated the visitor in an easy chair to enjoy a voyage in outer space, accomplished with the help of a rolling canvas. There was an aquarium at the Palais de l'Optique, where one could watch a drop of Seine water magnified a thousand times ("Horrid sight!" commented Paul Morand) or observe the moon through the biggest telescope yet made. A simulated naval battle on a "sea" 800-metres square showed the French fleet, including its first submarine, the *Narval*, on manoeuvres. It attacked an "enemy" fleet (English, no doubt) and sent it to the bottom.

The wide range of theatre and dance in Paris in 1900 was not neglected. At the exposition a Maison de rire had two halls that provided varieties of Parisian street entertainment. Grand Guignol was at the exposition, as were musical comedies, puppets, and marionettes. Outside the grounds many theatres had been renovated for the influx of easy spenders. Sarah Bernhardt was playing to wealthy, international audiences in *L'Aiglon*.⁵ Called the "Japanese Bernhardt" or "Duse the Lesser," Sadda Yakko is an example of a short-lived exposition triumph. The aesthetes flocked to see her bring long-popular Japanese prints violently to life.⁶ Amid spare oriental sets she was tender, cunning, or wildly furious with a vividness that challenged Westerners' confidence in their theatrical tradition.⁷

Sadda Yakko performed at the special pavilion of the American dancer, Loie Fuller, another critical sensation (figure 14). Loie tossed shawls of ineffable polychrome gauzes before concealed, shifting, mauve and Nile-green spotlights. As "light, flame, flower, star, dragon fly" she was "the queen of the impalpable, the goddess of evocation," a veritable priestess of Art Nouveau in motion.⁸ There were more dancers from Japan, as well as a number from other countries, including Java. To the *dense du ventre* of 1889 the Javanese added the *danse de la gorge*. Miscellaneous Algerian and Egyptian dancers offered the "shake that thing" kind of entertainment that so alarmed those who favoured only an elevated moral tone at the exposition. On the other hand, the Spanish restaurant, in vogue among high society and very dear (as in New York in 1964–65), had sixty-six dancers whom "one never saw turn without their accompanying castanets."⁹ Some renowned Parisian restaurants set up branches within the exposition's gates. Dining tended to be a shockingly expensive undertaking. As suited wealthy parvenus, the German restaurant, a calculated effort to dispel the *Wurst und Bier* image, was among the most luxurious. Friedrich Naumann wisely bought his German beer in the Norwegian restaurant.[10] As at any world's fair, the prudent people brought their picnic hampers or ate outside the exposition grounds, where meals were cheaper.

Some commercial amusements, as at most fairs, thrilled visitors by contracting their stomachs and disturbing their inner ears with motion and noises rather un-natural to humans. (The electric sidewalk with its three speeds was for more passive visitors.) One noteworthy "ride" was the "Grande Roue," or Ferris Wheel.[11] As in 1889, the expensive elevator ride up the 300-metre tower, painted golden yellow by its owner Gustave Eiffel for the occasion, though a trifle *déjà vu*, was again an outstanding favourite of the crowds.

The Trocadéro palace and the hilly park between it and the river were given over to celebrating the diffusion of that culture of which the exposition was itself the supreme expression. This was the colonial section; here were arranged the pavilions of South Africa, Indonesia, and the Portuguese empire (figure 38). But it was here, as in the Fine Arts area, that France arrogated far more than half of the area.

Though many people criticized the aggressive spirit behind the inclusion of the French ministries of the army and navy, few Frenchmen perceived the Janus face ("jalousement patriote mais sincèrement humaine") of the Republic here.[12] At the Trocadéro France's interest in the exposition was most clearly revealed. Blithely, almost contemptuously, disregarding her recent diplomatic humiliations, she proclaimed her worldwide power at the same time as she portrayed an altruistic France, benefactor and educator of the universe.[13]

Indo-China, Cambodia, Senegal, Tunisia, and especially Algeria all had pavilions grander than those of several rich sovereign states elsewhere at the exposition. Long before the opening, France had imported hundreds of native craftsmen to erect and decorate these oddly diverse and gaudy palaces. The colonial architects and workers then stayed through the summer for "atmosphere."[14] Paul Morand later wrote:

I passed my days at that Arab, Polynesian, negro town, which stretched from the Eiffel Tower to Passy, a quiet Paris hillside suddenly bearing on its back all Africa, Asia . . . a Tunisian bazaar where you smoke the *narghileh* and watch the dancers, the stereorama, the Kasbah, the white minarets, surprised to find themselves reflected in the Seine, the stuffed African animals, the pavilion of Indo-China varnished with red gum, its golden dragons and its carving painted by Annamites in black robes.[15]

There was even a model of the recently discovered temple of Angkor Wat. Morand observed the

Tonkinese village nestled with its junks and its women chewing betel. [At] a Dahomey village . . . great negroes, still savages, strode barefoot with proud and rythmic bearing, the subjects of ancient kings, old and recent enemies. Their wives pounded millet and peanuts.

Visitors drank tea at the Ceylonese pavilion and watched "slick native waiters and devil's dancers with huge masks with bulging eyes."

All this hillside exhaled perfumed incense, vanilla, and the smoke of pastilles that burned in seraglios, there you heard the scraping of Chinese violins, the click of castanets, the thin wail of Arab flutes, the mystic shrieks of the Aissaous.[16]

Crossing the Pont d'Iéna to the left bank, the Champ de Mars contained the most serious and most portentous displays at the exposition. Here in iron and glass halls, of which the Galerie des Machines was only the largest, were the exhibits of technology (figure 33). The Champ de Mars was divided into sections devoted to various classes of machinery, textiles, chemistry, publishing, and agriculture. To see the products of any one nation necessitated a long and complicated tour. Here, significantly, the demands of foreign exhibitors had been most insistent. Pressure for terrain in the Champ de Mars had even squeezed out the display of mining technology. This was eventually placed under the Trocadéro in a *monde souterrain* which was an appropriately meandering cavern with installed dioramas and groups of modern equipment illustrating progress in the extractive industries.

This was the first exposition to show large numbers of bicycles and automobiles. Since the French automobile industry was advanced over that of the other industrial nations, autos figured prominently in displays and parades. A Swede showed the first practical steam turbine. Other technical innovations were the first demonstrations of X-rays, of wireless telegraphy, and of sound synchronized with movies.

One doctor was accused of unethical advertising when he showed a movie of himself performing an operation. The weekly magazines printed pictures of Edmond Rostand and his family at the exposition listening to

L'Aiglon, several miles away, over a "theatrephone." There was a German coin-slot restaurant, perhaps the first automat. As at any fair, gawkers crowded around such anomalies as a ship made of chocolate, cows made of cheese or butter, and a champagne bottle as high as a house.

Curiously (and this was remarked upon at the time), aside from radioactivity and wireless communication, in comparison with other expositions, the one of 1900 had few startling technical or scientific discoveries on display. What it did demonstrate, however, was the power for change of earlier inventions. It seemed that the previous Paris exposition had demonstrated the promises of modern, particularly electric, technology (figure 25), while this exposition showed the realities. Electric light, known now for decades in Europe, had not been used before to brighten a whole city in such a way that its oudoor festivities could continue into the night. Railway engines, blast furnaces, cranes, and tractors were larger, faster, cheaper, and incredibly more efficient. In a march of material progress that shocked some observers, new machines rendered outmoded and, as if by magic, transformed into junk those that were the ultimates in efficiency just a few years earlier. Germany displayed immense dynamos, and whole factories for producing synthetic chemicals. As expected, Great Britain presented splendid industrial exhibits. But in 1900 the United States, Italy, Belgium, the Scandinavian countries, and, surprisingly, Japan, also demonstrated their growing industrial might.

In the colonial exhibits and in the industrial displays, exhibitors were instructed to prepare their presentations to educate the millions of visitors. In fact the salient purpose of the exposition as a whole was not only to educate in the popular sense, but to ease communication among the world's scholars. In 1900 Esperanto was, "so to speak, placed on the world market."[17] Scholars from everywhere arranged for correspondence in four languages and established systems of bibliographical exchanges.

The international congresses mostly took place in a pure white palace on the right bank near the Pont de l'Alma. Ignored by the mobs, these hundreds of meetings probably best illustrate the aspirations of the exposition's organizers. Almost every imaginable group with interests transcending national boundaries met in Paris that summer.[18] There were orderly conferences on international postal regulations, copyrights, fisheries, libraries, publishing, ornithology, dentistry, public health, hypnotism, numismatics, photography, philately, and all kinds of public instruction, including education for the handicapped. In addition, though their congresses were held outside the exposition grounds, several varieties of socialists had their international meetings in Paris that summer.

In 1889 there had been sixty-nine international congresses; in 1900 there were 127. The largest assembly was for medicine, with over 6,000 participants; the smallest for fencing, with only seventy-five. The congresses were usually presided over by the most distinguished French academicians and intellectuals. In all, 67,638 individuals had official roles in the meetings.[19]

One manifestation of internationalism, not a congress, was a motley competition in sports.[20] These competitions are commonly considered to have been the second modern meeting of the revived Olympics, the first having taken place in Athens in 1896.[21] Like the other parts of the exposition, the sporting events were carefully and minutely organized. The whole competition was divided into ten sections: Athletic Sports, Gymnastics, Fencing, Marksmanship, Horsemanship, Cycling, "Automobilism," Nautical Sports, Life-Saving, and Air Sports (ballooning). Internationally known specialists supervised each of these sections. In addition, for each there were separate systems of juries for both admissions and awards.[22] Each section encompassed a great deal of recreational activity. The track and field events, later glorified by the Americans, were but a small part of the first section, Athletic Sports.[23] The section also included several kinds of football and tennis and even pelote, the Basque game, which had its own awards, schedules, presidents, and juries.

Typical of the muddles that marred the exposition were those that surrounded American participation in the track and field events, the only athletic competitions that saw many American entries. Most of the finals were scheduled for July 15—like April 15th, a Sunday. Many Americans refused to compete on the Lord's day, which in Europe was ordinarily set aside for recreation and games. The hosts, understandably, replied that French athletes could not compete on July 14. The days following the weekend were unacceptable to others of the thirteen nations that offered teams. In the end, the track and field events took place as originally scheduled. The Americans won most of the prizes, but almost all were angry at their hosts and furious with one another. The more pious half of the American team cried "Foul!" at those who profaned the Sabbath. The French retaliated by producing almost no spectators. American runners also objected to the shabby track conditions, being unable to grasp the fact that few Europeans at that time cared for this kind of competitive sport. Composed mostly of Ivy League athletes, the American team also startled European observers with their "savage and gruesome" college yells.[24]

The soothing of the irritations arising out of the athletic meets resembled the effacement of disappointments in competitions elsewhere at the exposition. The athletic meetings ended at a great banquet before the departure of the teams. All the athletes ate heavily and all, or almost all, the wounds to pride were smothered by repeated toasts to international amity and by sentimental singing of the multilingual equivalents of *For He's a Jolly Good Fellow*.[25]

The visual aspects of an exposition—its art, decoration and architecture—were what most impressed the visitor and made it live or perish in his memory. In 1900, in terms of colour, richness of allusion, size, and above all, novelty for its own sake, rivalry was ubiquitous and forced. Yet surprisingly, little of enduring merit was actually accomplished in this great tournament of taste.

As a mixture of the very old and the very new, the taste of that exposition needs some resurrection. This discussion will occupy itself a great deal with the final large effort of nineteenth-century style, a style that even then was believed to be exhausted by almost everyone but the very secure French academicians who taught it. Perhaps corruption itself is worthwhile discussing. In any case, the critical and the public reactions to the dominant taste in the year 1900 may have had a lot to do with the appraisals of the exposition, the future of the exposition movement, and even the shifting in the canons of Western taste after the nineteenth century closed.

The international movement of Art Nouveau (called by various names in various languages) was the "new" in that year. Though largely ignored at the time, it was, through its ideology and its practitioners (if not in its iconography), really the school of the twentieth century.

As we have seen in Chapter 3, all the architects whose projects were executed for the exposition had diplomas from the official Ecole des Beaux-Arts. The director of the Beaux-Arts, Henri Roujon, was also director of Beaux-Arts at the exposition. Even the admitting juries for painting were almost entirely composed of officials of the government school. Thus the canvases of the courageous, rebellious French painters of the era, reproductions of which are now so well known and cherished by us, were barred or placed in such a way that the colours (so important to the Impressionists) were dimmed.[26] One of the glories of France, Auguste Rodin, had to exhibit in his private pavilion in the Esplanade des Invalides, far from the colossal new palaces of fine arts.[27]

Art in the nineteenth century was supposed to be historical, didactic, and ennobling.[28] These precepts did not necessarily have to result in works that were flaccid or boring. In 1900, the contrary was true, for by then the calming influences of the purist, Eugène Viollet-le-Duc, who had been an influential restraining figure in earlier expositions, was obliterated. Throughout the nineteenth century, in the architectural and decorative products of eclecticism there had been a tension between devotion to classical restraint and characteristic (for the time) yearnings for novel effect. It was clear that in 1900 the balance was sharply tilted in favour of a kind of visual grandiloquence and hyperbole—still, however, within didactic and classical moulds. As a result, the visual impressions were chaotic, not radical; sensational, not intellectual (figure 6); and real experimentation was held in check by the directors of the exposition, who had their own ideas as to what role artists should play in amusement, competition, and politics.

The artists of 1900 were craftsmen-creators who, in order to win official patronage or teaching positions, had to master the historical styles. The purposes of art were not those of the artists, but were those of all citizens who were to be inspired by confrontation with past examples of man's nobility. Painting implanted patriotic lessons, moralized and amused. In any case, in the hierarchy of the arts painting no longer occupied the exalted position it had in the first half of the century. Nor was it yet viewed as the most congenial form for the most intense and individual artists of the next decades. The prize-winning paintings (and favourites of the crowds) were of slain patriots of earlier times, well-fed cardinals with parakeets and florid and busty Flemish peasants at dimly lit drinking bouts.

In 1900 architecture was really queen of the arts. Decoration also evoked great epochs, sometimes several at once, of the past. The apparently tireless motifs of Greece and Rome were combined with those of mediaeval Europe and with the voluptuous iconography of the baroque period; they were then produced on a large scale and in multiples, stamping Europe with the florid, sometimes foolish mixtures that characterize late nineteenth century eclecticism (figure 20).

The Pont Alexander III and the Grand and Petit Palais were permanent additions to Paris and can still be seen as examples of the intentions of the exposition's directors.[29] All three have special qualities. The Grand Palais has a fine roof (obscured to pedestrians) of leaded glass (figure 15). The lively and free wrought-iron of its grand, ceremonial staircase shows a vigorous fantasy. The wrought-iron ornament on the Petit Palais, particularly the monumental grill before the main entrance, is as fine as, and freer and more graceful than, anything comparable done in the eighteenth century. The Pont Alexander III is a success in every way. The massive garlands on its arches by the river suit the immensity of the construction. The sculptured large, airy, bronze groups (figure 4) are today perhaps too obscurely allegorical, but the long rows of globed bronze lamps, and especially the stone bas-reliefs which spring organically from the pillars, show that the architect was able to draw something from the Art Nouveau innovators. Every detail of these structures was conceived of and finished with practised skill and devoted craft. They all stand splendidly as noble expressions at the end of a rich period in Western art. Never again could Europe undertake such large projects with so much seriousness, so much exuberance.

As examples of exposition architecture these buildings, though they may appear bombastic now, were somewhat restrained since they were to be permanent. The decorators of the temporary buildings were not inhibited in this way. Continuing a trend in exposition architecture that began in 1851, most pavilions used much prefabricated iron and glass in their construction. Though engineering architecture made a few advances in 1900, the schools of Beaux-Arts mounted a vigorous counter-offensive. As the new structures were erected, hordes of craftsmen

. . . were turned loose to cover all available surfaces with statues and academic trophies, to embellish the cornices with urns or jars and to cap the domes with every sort of ornament. On every hand there were frescoes and polychrome terra cotta friezes and allegorical statues.[30]

Perhaps it was too much to expect beauty of buildings to which "so many artists brought a stone."[31]

Even before the buildings were finished a critic attacked

. . . this exaggerated and banal ornamentation, half Ecole des Beaux-Arts, half Kursaal, with its flying figures, friezed pediments, and pinnacles, all of it out-of-date and ridiculous although accepted by the deferential crowds, and bearing no relation, either to the spirit of the times or to the use of new techniques of construction.[32]

Another compared the buildings to the creations of a confectioner:
"Some resemble soft-boiled eggs—some nougats, sponge cakes, or decorated chocolate creams."[33]

The impression was chaotic:

. . . All the styles are confounded in a frightful merging of inimical periods; disparate materials, piles of artificial stone, artificial marble, imitation gold and iron, and simulated porcelain. . . . Assyrian rubs elbows with rococo, the propylaea of the Acropolis act as vestibules for Swiss chalets; one leaves a painted-paper Alcazar to enter a pink-sugar Trianon.

This was Europe's last great exhibition of allegory and the personification of virtues. Everywhere one looked there were colossal sculptural groups and painted friezes of straining, thrusting, muscular women, taut wrestlers of all the races, rampant stallions, snarling lions and lionesses, obese cherubs, and groups of Hercules with attendants. These groups had titles like "Immortality Conquering Time," "Harmony Destroying Discord," "Nature Disrobing before Science," "Science Advancing in Spite of Ignorance," or "Inspiration Guided by Wisdom". The spandrel of the Petit Palais showed a luscious City of Paris experiencing ecstasy at seeing herself surrounded by the Muses. There were endless numbers of such groups and titles, and their descriptions filled the official literature.

The plethora of conservative architecture, of laboured decoration and sculpture of allegory, which appeared strident and over-ripe when placed in the stream of nineteenth-century eclecticism of which it was a part, can best be understood by relating it to a paramount motive of the exposition's organizers. This aim was to surpass, even overwhelm, all the exposition's predecessors. Perhaps the directors of taste confounded art with luxury and wealth. Certainly the strenuous decoration might be viewed as another attempt (like the colonial exhibits) to compensate for the otherwise weak French international impact at the time. The iridescent colours, the groping, clawing curves, the encrustations of outsize jewels were just the culmination, or better, the furthest statement of a style seen in milder forms in new railway stations or ministries.[35] Had the direction of the exposition's taste fallen into the hands of a committee of engineers, the visitors might have seen technical marvels. As it was, those desiring to excel eschewed technology, and committed follies of Beaux-Arts zeal.

Many of the buildings were generally considered ugly even at that time. This was especially true of "advertising gimmicks" such as a restaurant, the Pavillon Bleu, a tall octagonal restaurant that was overloaded and super-charged with tacked-on "gingerbread" decoration. Another was the opaque glass Pavillon Lumineux which looked as though it had been assembled of tree stumps and stalactites and which offered an eerie night-time spectacle of slowly shifting coloured lights exuding from its interior. Yet another was Loie Fuller's pavilion, a rectangle that was entirely surrounded by a false theatre curtain in plaster.

The most serious effort at novelty was René Binet's entrance gate, the Porte de la Concorde, called by some of its many critics "the salamander." The gate excelled at its function of admitting up to 75,000 ticket bearers per hour. The working apparatus was covered by an immense three-legged cupola of steel. Tall minarets of punctured lattice-work and applied cabochons stood nearby. This structure which, more than any other, was intended to be the main attraction of the exposition, being used on most advertising and souvenir plates, was no technical advance over the Eiffel Tower.[36] It was much smaller. The architect, "a man of florid and luxurious imagination," intended that the Porte de la Concorde should make its impact by the decoration, which would be "ultra-modern."[37]

The method Binet used to be chic was to push eclecticism to its extreme limit. It is true that in his modernity Binet de-emphasized the tired motifs of the Renaissance and the French eighteenth century, but, paradoxically, he turned to far older ones from pre-Columbian Mexico, the ancient Near East, India, and especially the recently rediscovered Angkor Wat in Indo-China. A critic wrote that Binet "demonstrated his knowledge of the architecture of the whole world without excepting the lands of dreams."[38]

The three-legged dome and its minarets were speckled and interlaced with coloured lights, so that the impact of the confection was not lost on evening visitors. With this large structure, eclecticism had drawn its sources from all the world and all the ages. It could go no further. Even then the forced combinations of obscure, irrelevant epochs and the resulting clumsiness produced despair for historicism. Hope for the future, however, might be aroused by some kinds of new art in 1900.

Art Nouveau, seen in a few places at the exposition, was at least alive and dynamic.[39] Art Nouveau had a characteristic ideology which was, briefly, to be modern by using decorative motifs that were anti-historical. The whiplash lines, vegetable curves, female hair, peacocks, sea weeds, lily pads, and swans of Art Nouveau's iconography were supposed to be timeless. By using them, the artists of the movement felt they could break away from the tiring artistic follies of their century.[40] It is widely believed that Art Nouveau reached its culmination in the Exposition of 1900. However, it appears that, with some noteworthy exceptions (few of them French), the Art Nouveau movement was already in its period of lost optimism and decay.[41]

Before 1900 the impresario of the Art Nouveau movement was the wealthy patron and former dealer in Japanese antiques, S. Bing. The passion among radical artists of the West for oriental objects brought Bing wide international acquaintance and, eventually, influence in these circles. In the early 1890's Bing began a series of design inspection tours which took him all over the continent, to England, and even to America. He especially sought out radical designers. Already known as an oracle of taste Bing thought he perceived marketable strains in the artistic ferment of his time. In 1895 he abruptly redecorated his large shop at 22, rue de Provence in Paris and boldly called it "L'Art Nouveau," a name which thereafter assembled disparate currents of reform in art and design.

Bing patronized the best radical designers, regardless of nationality. His first display included works of (among many others) Aubrey Beardsley, Auguste Rodin, Camille Pissaro, Henri de Toulouse-Lautrec, Anders Zorn, Emile Gallé, Louis Comfort Tiffany, Walter Crane, Henry Van de Velde, Mary Cassatt, Charles Rennie Mackintosh, and Réné Lalique.[42] In fact, Bing's sponsorship included almost all the artists and designers now known as the innovators and proto-theorists of twentieth-century design. Bing attracted eager curiosity from abroad and made the venture a brief financial success, though he incurred the wrath of conservative French critics. Indeed, the critical fury was so intense that he slowly retreated from his espousal of the very new. Since conservatives controlled the artistic and decorative themes in 1900, Bing, like Auguste Rodin, was able to show unorthodox art only in his private pavilion. This was in the form of a fully furnished and decorated seven-room house on the Esplanade des Invalides. Bing's artists in 1900 were Eugène Gaillard, Georges de Feure, and Eugène Colonna, who had no reputation outside Paris. In this house, where an enthusiast might have anticipated a vigorous display of radical international art, quasi-floral, quasi-abstract, curvilinear motifs were used modestly to please. The chairs of Gaillard were

gilded and appropriate for an eighteenth-century salon. An English observer described de Feure's dressing room of gilt, muted prints, and soft, bas-
relief female forms as "deliciously feminine."[43] A German critic called the
ensembles "coquettish" and felt they suited the French exactly.[44]

Emile Gallé of Nancy was, as in 1889, one of the heroes of the exposition. In the intervening period he had proliferated his techniques in
glass and marquetry and had become a leading spokesman for the Art
Nouveau movement.[45] Called a "magician," "l'enraciné," or the "Barrès of
art," his work was admired even by the enemies of the new style.[46]
Gallé's best work was snapped up by museums, but still his *œuvre*
illustrates the tendency of radical French artists to work in small forms.
Similarly, the exquisitely inventive personal jeweler of Sarah Bernhardt,
René Lalique, was popular in 1900.[47] Lalique's stylized insects and
reptiles of baroque pearls, cloissoné, aquamarines, and rubies "totally
transformed our concept of jewelry."[48] The *fin de siècle* aesthetes perceived an enchanting contradiction in these dazzling dragonflies and
lizards. But Lalique's works were miniatures, shockingly expensive, and
really only fabulous eccentricities.

Hector Guimard was not only one of the most adroit of the French
artists who worked in the new style, he was one of the very few who
worked in architecture. Guimard designed the archetypically Art Nouveau
Paris Métro signs and many Métro stations which were later demolished.
But at the exposition, Guimard, like Bing and Rodin, had a "stand" at the
Esplanade des Invalides where he showed sample interiors and *objets*
from his ambitious tour de force, the "Castel Beranger," a new apartment
house in Paris which he designed from foundations to door knobs.

To observe the evolving of Art Nouveau in 1900, one really had to look
for examples from outside France. The American, Louis Comfort Tiffany,
displayed large, lushly coloured, and apparently three-dimensional stained
glass windows of graceful, sexless figures and timeless nature scenes.
Tiffany also showed his recent invention, "favrile" glass vases whose
shimmering colours were like oil stains on wet pavement, and objects of
brass whose malleability permitted the full use of Art Nouveau's asym-
metrically curving motifs. Rookwood Potteries of Cincinnati and Grueby
of Boston exhibited vases of muted colours and characteristic vegetable
ornament. Rosenburg of The Hague also showed ceramics with brittle
abstract designs.

The most vigorous displays of Art Nouveau were in the German,

Austrian, and Hungarian exhibits.[49] There, whole rooms in the new style were parts of the government pavilions. Some of these were created by artists whom Bing had first patronized but who had left Paris for an artistic climate more congenial to innovation.

For example, Henry Van de Velde, surely the most versatile, prolific, and quotable of Bing's artists, was represented by his designs for two German industrial pavilions. Just as French Art Nouveau was dying out, Germany was experiencing a wave of optimism in the decorative arts.[50] There the new style was called, significantly, "Jugendstil." East of the Rhine, radical English, Belgian, American, and French designers found livelier markets and princely patronage. A French critic observed that

Germany, in her predilection for radical decorative art, has often achieved unusually felicitous results. In the display cases installed in her various exhibits, [she reminds] one that she is the classic homeland of the fire gnomes, miniature blacksmiths with silvery beards and bowed legs and wearing pointed caps, setting out eagerly to apply their knowledge to the twisting and fashioning of metal and producing ironwork equal to the best. Further on they turn to wood, bending it in simple curves, discretely moulding it, embellishing it with bronze or guilded copper to achieve rich effects. And artistic centres of intense activity are revealed in products of undeniable interest: Berlin, Munich, Cologne, Hamburg, Dresden, Carlsruhe, Darmstadt, where all crafts are favoured—cabinet making, glass work, ceramics, pewter, leather work, tapestry —and where, under the aegis of enlightened princes or of societies of wealthy patrons, regular schools are thriving.[51]

These new schools were to produce most of the great figures of the Bauhaus and were profound influences in the evolving of twentieth-century international style in decoration and architecture.

A large work of great originality, and possibly the architectural jewel of the Exposition of 1900, was the official pavilion of Finland (page 78). This was one of the first designs of Eliel Saarinen, later to become very famous as an innovator and as the father of the famous architect, Eero Saarinen.[52] The pavilion was constructed of native woods: Scandinavian bears, birds, and wild flowers, all taken from nature and therefore not historical, not of the academies, were the motifs. Yet the decoration was understated, and the building well proportioned. In a quiet way, Saarinen's pavilion was a self-conscious declaration of Finnish nationality in the face of a concurrent campaign by their Russian masters to eliminate the Finnish language and culture.[53] The contrast of this romantic, elegant building with the chaotic architecture elsewhere in 1900 was striking.[54]

Its whole effect was lyrical, yet alluded to hidden strength, like the music of Sibelius.

The Finnish pavilion was in a section of the grounds that was the focal area for the most serious competition within the Exposition of 1900. This area was the Quai or Rue des Nations along the Left Bank (see pp. iv, v). Here the official pavilions of the more extravagant nations were

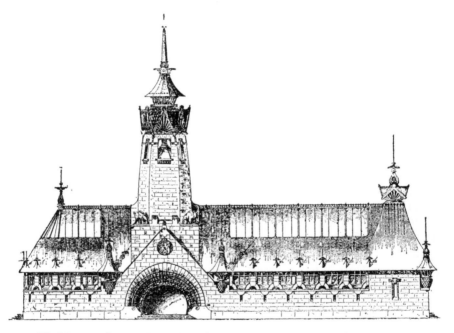

Eliel Saarinen's Finnish pavilion: the architectural "jewel" of the Exposition.

grouped together in order to provide a spectacular view from the Seine and to produce another possible *clou* for the exposition. Optimists about international harmony believed that the ensemble would encourage peace. They were wrong. The Rue des Nations was an obvious starting-point for a tour to establish the ranking of nations according to their performance in 1900. Because of the heightened popular nationalism of the time, the pressure to excel was cumulative and focused more upon nations than upon individuals.[55]

Since so much of the exposition was an architectural creation of the nation that was host, France had no official pavilion. However, in grateful recognition of the Russian alliance, a keystone of French diplomacy since 1893, the Republic gave some prominence to the Russian exhibits. Very likely because of its extraordinary size, the Russian pavilion was not along the Rue des Nations, but at the Trocadéro. Like some other pavilions in 1900, it was a pot-pourri of styles: a spreading, gilded pile, combining a tabernacle, a Turkish kiosk, and a colossal icon.

The Russian exhibits appeared to have the narrow aim of impressing the potential French investor. Russia had last exhibited in Paris in 1867. The new displays were designed to show how she had changed since then. Russian industrialists exhibited a few boilers, some textile machinery, and a few examples of electrical equipment. One Russian exhibit was a grotesque pagoda made only of domestically produced metal tubing. However, most avidly watched were samples of raw materials—furs, ores, coal, precious stones, gold, wheat, oil—and statistical tables showing Russia's large and growing population.

The carillon of the Imperial pavilion often played Russian and French hymns or the two countries' national anthems alternately. A popular curiosity at the exposition was a map of France made by the jewelers of Tsarskoye Selo. It showed France all in precious minerals and rare metals, set in a heavy, ornate frame draped with maroon velvet; each *département* was of a different gem stone. Naturally there were several varieties of malachite and lapis lazuli, both Russian specialties. Railway lines were indicated by fine wires of platinum. Paris was a large ruby, Le Havre an emerald, Rouen a sapphire, and so on. The name of each city was written in gold.

Part of the Russian national exhibit was a joint venture with the travel company Wagon-Lits Cook. This was the pavilion of Asiatic Russia. Visitors sat as passengers on the Trans-Siberian Railroad. The carriages left "Moscow station" and rolled east as scenes of the Caucasus, the steppes, and of the wilds (and the riches, to inspire confidence) of Siberia rolled by the windows on a long canvas. There were also posed vignettes of Siberian and Chinese natives. The "trip" ended when a Chinese boy went through the cars serving jasmine tea, shouting, "Peking! All change here!"[56]

In contrast to the boasting and freshness of many Russian exhibits, it appeared that the confident British were participating in the competition more or less as an obligation. Great Britain's exhibits were costly, disparate, and usually well planned. The British officials deliberately avoided the flamboyance of other rich nations.[57] Since it was constructed of real stone, their pavilion, which reproduced a large, venerable, country house, was the most expensive on the Rue des Nations. Eschewing the look of newness everywhere else in the exposition, the British pavilion aped stability with its drapery of ivy. The stately rooms were decorated to show several great eras of English design. The walls held old and modern British paintings.[58] As in all the previous expositions, British industrial goods were widely displayed, but, since their excellence was known and the wealth that backed them nearly a tacit assumption in the political ranking of the later nineteenth century, the British industrial exhibits received scant attention from visitors who came to the exposition in order to rate the national contestants. The strained diplomatic relations between France and Britain also caused the British displays to be ignored.

Twenty-two of the twenty-three nations that had official pavilions constructed and decorated theirs in an identifiably "native" style. The exception was the United States. A European visitor might have hoped for a Chicago skyscraper or perhaps the mansion or country house of a Philadelphia or New York millionaire. *L'Illustration* commented, "No, the art of Richardson, Burnham, or Root could not appear sufficiently consecrated, official, pompous, triumphant, or imperial."[59] The American national pavilion was a bleached interpretation of a Roman pantheon, demonstrating the impact of the sterile ceremonialism of the "Great White City" of Chicago in 1893 upon American taste (figure 34). An archway over the entrance facing the Seine held a large allegorical group of naked, jubilant, male and female mesomorphs restraining a group of four wild horses pulling a chariot of Progress carrying the beaming goddess of Liberty. The American pavilion was really a social centre for American businessmen. In this "section of American home comfort transferred, as it were, to a foreign land, there was nothing for sale, no peddlars, no fakers, no nuisances."[60] One also had at one's disposal public stenographers, typewriters, newspapers, and daily stock quotations. During the evenings the American pavilion was more exciting. Inside, on floors covered with hygienic linoleum, there were nightly receptions where the "diamonds of the American women, the beauty of their shoulders, and the splendour of their complexions made one pardon the banality and empty pomp of the décor."[61]

This was by far the most costly effort that the American businessmen and their government had made at a foreign exposition.[62] The United States was the most magnanimous foreign exhibitor, spending more money even than Germany, though a disproportionate part of the total cost naturally was for the transportation of American displays.[63]

Though high steamship fares discouraged swarms of touring Americans, their exhibits testified to American wealth, vitality, and aggressiveness. The official pavilion, like its neighbours, was principally an architectural exercise. Elsewhere in the exposition, there were large special pavilions of American agriculture, forestry, publishing, and printing. A large building in Vincennes was devoted entirely to American heavy industry. The McCormick Harvester Company had its own pavilion. So did American bicycle manufacturers. Commissioner General Ferdinand Peck assigned an assistant to see that decoration "provided in a general way for the display of exhibits at the exposition."[64] These "façades, colonnades, pillars, columns, artistic walls, and patriotic features announced in unmistakable individuality the presence of an exhibit from the United States."[65]

Like the exotic Asiatics and Africans in attendance at the colonial exhibits, the Americans were watched with curiosity. Those Americans who chewed tobacco and spat were especially fascinating for the Europeans. A Maize Propaganda Association constructed an American corn kitchen, where foods in all varieties and degrees of delicacy were prepared of corn and daintily served free of charge. But to Europeans maize was only "hog food" and would always remain such, so they stayed away. The corn kitchen became just "an eventual rendezvous for Americans visiting the exposition."[66]

A climax of the American participation was reached on the fourth of July, which became almost a day of fête in Paris. There were colourful parades; American flags were displayed—and hawked—everywhere. President Loubet and a large portion of the Parisian diplomatic corps attended the American presentation of a monument to Lafayette for the court of the Louvre. John Philip Sousa's band, imported for the occasion, gave three rousing concerts that day: one in the morning at the unveiling of the monument, a second in the afternoon at the exposition, and the last in the evening at the Place de l'Opéra.[67]

The American performance at the exposition might have shaken the confidence of Europeans more than it did. But the United States was still immensely distant; it was difficult for observers of the national competitions to translate the statistical indices of American growth into measures or fears of military, commercial, or intellectual power. This was not, however, the case with the German performance at the exposition.

In their exhibits of architecture, the fine arts, the decorative arts, and most especially in the heavy and light industries, the Germans were shockingly good. It was clear to everyone that the German Empire, like the French Third Republic, had chosen the exposition as a favoured area for international competition.[68] In 1892, as was noted earlier, Germany had been thwarted in her tentative efforts to host a great exposition in Berlin in 1900. She then moved on to gain valuable experience through her prodigal participation in the Chicago Exposition of 1893. Their newspapers assured the Germans that their exhibits in 1900 surpassed those of every other nation. Germans came in millions to confirm this superiority and to enjoy it.[69]

The German official pavilion, designed and constructed in the decorated style of a Rathaus of the sixteenth century, had the highest spire on the Quai des Nations. It recalled the days of the Hansa trading towns and evoked Hamburg and Bremen, then booming with exports, the products of German resources and technical and mercantile knowledge (figure 30).

The German technical exhibits on the Champ de Mars revealed "a veritable explosion of method . . . the greatest instance of commercial encirclement the world has ever seen."[70] One exhibit was an industrial crane that lifted twenty-five tons. It made the cranes of other nations look like toys. The Helios firm of Cologne exhibited a quietly hissing dynamo that generated 5,000 horsepower and took just two men to operate it. It was the world's largest, but salesmen from Berlin and Magdeburg promised yet larger ones. As part of the festive atmosphere in Paris that summer, electric spot lights swayed beams through the sky at night. The most powerful of these duplicated a light at the mouth of the Weser River and was part of a large exhibit of the German merchant marine.[71] North German Lloyd and Hamburg-America Lines showed models of crack liners. Among them was the new *Deutschland* which had just crossed the Atlantic in five days and eight hours. One German chemist gave a demonstration of liquid air. This reportedly led to the remark: "Have you seen the Germans? They are amazing! They put air in bottles! They manufacture cold!"[72]

General and pervasive aspects of the German exhibits were organization and method. It was clear that the Germans had decided not to compete as individual firms, but to glorify the Reich. "No German," wrote one French reporter, "seems to aspire to eclipse his neighbor. The sole triumph sought after seems to be that of collectivity."[73]

Only in two major areas were the German efforts negligible. Germany had no colonial exhibits, and out of discretion or perhaps in sly understatement, the German military exhibits were modest. In the international pavilion devoted to "Armes de terre et de mer" were mounted large, menacing exhibits from Austria, Great Britain, Russia, the United States, and Italy. Germany showed only maps, some electric projectors, a model of a military hospital, and a retrospective display of military uniforms. France was less subtle; nearby, on a prominent curve of the Seine near the Eiffel Tower, was the gruesome display of Schneider et Cie., "a huge blood-red dome, the stupendous exhibit of the cannon foundry of Creusot."[74]

Perhaps the most eloquent part of the German participation was their catalogue itself, published in French, English, and German editions.[75] Unlike the multi-volumed compendiums of other nations, this was a single, compact work. It consisted of a series of essays surveying German industry, society, and culture. Lists of exhibits that illustrated the essays followed the chapters. The catalogue gave a picture of an assured, well-ordered state with the best educational and social-welfare systems in the world. It noted that 44.7 per cent of the German population was under twenty years of age, 60 per cent under thirty years of age. Each German marriage was producing about 4.7 children. A careful observer, alluding to the military implications of the above figures, remarked that the German buildings at the exposition, though impressive, were temporary, "but the German official catalogue will remain afterwards and the world will long draw lessons from it."[76]

This catalogue, itself an event in the history of book design, was planned and decorated by Bernard Pankok, one of the cleverest innovators of the Jugendstil movement.[77] Rather than in buckram, the catalogue was bound in soft muslin printed with the swaying vegetable ornament characteristic of early Jugendstil. Illustrations, statistical tables, and even advertisements at the back were framed in graceful and distinctive floral and abstract designs. A special Jugendstil font had been designed for the printing. Perhaps never before had such a radical, though tasteful and consistently excellent, book been an official publication.

It is impossible in a short chapter like this (just as it was impossible at the exposition itself) to give each nation its due. Belgium, Switzerland, and Austria-Hungary, which had large, expensive exhibits, must be passed over. Japan, whose art was a sensation at the expositions of 1867 and 1878, now showed in addition tubular boilers, armour plate, and guns.[78] Eugène Melchior de Vogüé observed, "Il commence bien le siècle, ce jeune triomphateur."[79]

The official pavilions, all declarations of patriotism on foreign soil, were enchanting structures. Italy's was a riotous plaster amalgam of the cathedral in Siena and Saint Mark's in Venice. Sweden's, perhaps the most radical of all, was made of wood and looked like a large version of one of the scaly, mediaeval Norse churches.[80] Turkey's pavilion resembled a mosque; that of Spain was a miniature Escorial. Nations as poor as Mexico, and even Monaco, whose pavilions made a second line on the Rue des Nations, strained their treasuries for palaces to rival those of the great powers. Peru's was meant for reconstruction as a municipal library in Quito. Greece's was planned to be a fine arts gallery in Athens; Serbia's would be one in Belgrade.

The surge of the crowds and the entertainments at this exposition, as at any other, were not at one constant level during its whole seven-month season. On opening day the exposition was perhaps just half ready to receive the visitors. At that time the newspapers denied that the grounds were "a mess," but tales of bad conditions passed by word of mouth. Potential visitors waited. Even when actually finished in May, the exposition was lively and crowded only between the hours of two and six in the afternoon. Despite the electric lighting, the grounds were disappointingly empty in the evening. Everyone asked, "Where is all the fun?"

Henri Gautier noted that the Romans cried for bread and circuses. Thanks to the great number of restaurants in 1900, bread was not lacking at the exposition—but circuses were. In an editorial appeal to the exposition authorities, Gautier asked that they launch a campaign to show visitors that "the old Gallic spirit is not dead. There is still time," he claimed, "to repair the omission; otherwise we run the risk of seeing the Grand Prize for Gaiety pass into other hands."[81]

Accordingly, in early July a "Commission des fêtes de l'Exposition," composed of artists, newspaper editors, architects, the director of the Opéra, and other specialists in amusement, announced that an innovation at this exposition would be a series of fêtes. The first, on September 10,

*The management evolved many ingenious arrangements to make a success of the
Banquet of the Mayors.*

L'ILLUSTRATION

Prix du Numéro : 75 centimes — SAMEDI 29 SEPTEMBRE 1900. 58e Année — N. 94.

was a flower festival with some *batailles des fleurs* in which the public was invited to take part. Another was a wine festival featuring several parades of symbolic groups showing the various operations (a token to the exposition's educational purposes) involved in wine-making, as well as allegorical floats from the great French wine regions. Among the other festivals was one, the harbinger of a new age, for chuffing automobiles that paraded along slowly, heavily festooned with flowers.

The most remarkable fête of the exposition was the Banquet des Maires, which took place on September 22. The competitive spirit of the Exposition of 1900 required that this banquet surpass the banquet of mayors of 1889. It did. Of the 36,172 mayors invited, 20,777 appeared. Many were old and bearded; many were in regional costume. They all paraded, led by President Loubet, before they sat down to dinner in two immense tents in the Jardin des Tuileries. This was the menu[82]:

Hors d'Œuvres
Darnes de saumon glacées Parisienne

Filet de bœuf en Belleville
Pains de caneton de Rouen
Poulardes de Bresse rôties
Ballotines de faisans Saint-Hubert
Salade Potel

Glaces Succès—Condés
Dessert

Preignac en carafes—Saint Julien en carafes
Haut-Sauternes
Beaune-Margaux J. Calvet 1887
Champagne Montebello

[20] TOP *Architectural exuberance: the Palais de l'Enseignement*

[21] BOTTOM *A nineteenth-century baroque allegory adorning the Salle des Fêtes*

[22] TOP *The Château d'Eau with the Palais de l'Electricité behind it*

[23] CENTRE *Some colossal decorative heads waiting to be placed
on one of the pavilions*

[24] BOTTOM *The pavilion of S. Bing on the Esplanade des Invalides*

[25] TOP   *A view of the interior of the Palais de l'Electricité*

[26] CIRCLE   *The Hall of Mirrors, à la 1900*

[27] BOTTOM LEFT   *The architecture of fantasy: this was a pavilion erected
by a French company of slate manufacturers*

[28] TOP   *Hungarian Art Nouveau for a display of textiles and clothing*
[29] LOWER LEFT   *The entrance to a display of German light industry*
[30] LOWER RIGHT   *The official pavilion of Imperial Germany on the Quai des Nations*

[31] TOP   *The Korean pavilion on the Champs de Mars*

[32] LOWER LEFT   *Ecuador made a strenuous architectural effort for her pavilion*

[33] LOWER RIGHT   *Fantasy in steel tubing: an example of French metallurgic art*

[34] TOP   *The official pavilion of the United States of America*
[35] LOWER LEFT   *The eclectic Tour du Monde*
[36] LOWER RIGHT   *The Siamese pavilion on the Champs de Mars*

[37] TOP   *Another evocation of the past: Andalousia in the time of
the Moorish occupation*

[38] BOTTOM   *The pavilion of the Dutch East Indies*

There were eleven kitchens. The chief chef and his staff, more than abreast of the times, capably supervised the setting of the 606 tables by automobile and telephone (page 85).[83] Like the exposition itself, this party was immensely complex and difficult to arrange. Yet it all functioned smoothly. The toasts, the cheers of guests, the harmonious yet variegated spectacle of the assembly of these respected provincial figures, the cordiality of everyone, attested to the persuasiveness of French cuisine, the skill of French administrative ability, and the appeal of the exposition itself. The Banquet des Maires was then and long afterwards interpreted as a striking demonstration of the vigour and solidarity of the republic.[84]

Some time before the Banquet, however, it was clear that the attendance at the whole exposition would be less than expected. Gautier, the editor-watchdog of the exposition, predicted on September 10 that the total would only reach 40 millions, just two-thirds of the official estimate.[85] Some zealous bureaucrats tried to save the estimate by planning a re-opening in 1901. President Loubet himself, one of the most assiduous trudgers of the grounds, sighed, "It doesn't seem possible that all these marvels are to disappear."[86] But these somewhat naïve hopes were dashed with the knowledge that the structures of heavy cardboard and plaster would not survive a winter. By any standards the Exposition of 1900 was immense; but falling short of the planned triumph, it appeared to be foundering.

Then, because of cooler autumn weather and the well-publicized parades and festivals, average attendance climbed to around 300,000 a day, reaching as much as 600,000 on a day of fête. Pressure for a prolongation, at least, was irresistible, especially since there was a precedent in the delayed ending of the Exposition of 1889. *Le Figaro*, incidentally, suggested that attendance figures might be increased by as much as 5 million by a slow, progressive closing of the exposition, leaving the Quai des Nations till the last.[86]

In order to avoid speculation in the negotiable *bons* which had by September fallen in price to the point that the entry to the exposition was nearly free for those who purchased them, the administration put off announcing that the exposition would be extended twenty-seven more days until November 11. Stories were permitted to circulate that the real reason for the stretching of the season was the impending visit of President Kruger of South Africa. An official explanation was, of course, out of the question, because it would further infuriate the British. Despite the reduced numbers of shivering *indigènes* (Gautier called them *les pauvres transplantés*) who remained in the Trocadéro, and the grim vistas of sagging buildings streaked by autumn rains, Kruger's visit drew mobs of patriotic Frenchmen who thus demonstrated sympathy with the underdogs in the Boer War and, while doing so, showed their hatred of Great Britain.

During the last weeks, international juries awarded thousands of certificates of merit and plaques, ribbons, decorations, and medals (figs. 8–11). Publishing houses in Paris worked extra shifts to print the multi-volumed lists of winners. In the international hotels and at the exposition, the pace of banquets quickened. Each ceremonial dinner ended in gushing tributes to the good intentions of the hosts. In the competitions for awards there had to be winners and, alas, losers. Toastmasters stretched their eloquence to heal the wounds made earlier by insults, injustice, and damage to professional and national pride.

Despite fogs and generally melancholy weather, 589,446 people came to the exposition the last Sunday. Large exhibits were already mostly dismantled. The natives had been sent home from the colonial exhibits because of fear for their health. A feeling of finality, of the ending of something unique and great made the crowds reverently quiet. Looking at the dimly perceived sun, an electrician commented in the jargon of the coming century, "The November sun definitely lacks potential."[87]

The great exposition was kept open for one further day for a last Fête de nuit, to be a demonstration of electricity. It rained in the afternoon, but the night was lucid, crisp. All the pavilions were flooded with light; the entrance gate, the arcades, the illuminated fountains drew on all the power they could tap and the speed of changing lights was increased. At ten o'clock a cannon cracked from the Eiffel Tower and coloured filters were changed all over the exposition. At eleven o'clock six cannon shots boomed from the top of the tower, the filters again changed, and the tempo of shifting lights at the fountains speeded up. At eleven-twenty the Château d'Eau extinguished its lights, to be followed by the Trocadéro. Blocks of lights all over the exposition gradually went out. Drums beat a retreat as the crowds, chilled, already nostalgic, went home slowly in darkness. "It was over. The Exposition of 1900 had lived!"[88]

The Affair and the Fair: Politics and the Exposition • In September 1899, *L'Illustration* noted that a harsh English word was entering the French language. *Interdit* or *quarantine* would serve as well, but one read or heard instead *boycottage*:

Boycott here, boycott there, boycott everywhere!
This repetition of the same word, somewhat obsessive, a catchword, is the perfectly natural consequence of the importance which a very topical question has assumed in the press. Certain foreign journalists, unhappy with the outcome of the Dreyfus Affair, which they have made their concern, with a zeal as intemperate as it is indiscreet, have begun a campaign to have their fellow countrymen unite to punish France. If they were listened to, the Exposition of 1900 would be deprived of the co-operation of foreign industry and of the presence of several million visitors.[1]

In Chapter 1 it was noted that the four previous French universal expositions had political origins and political results. Those of 1855 and 1867 had been almost vignettes of Napoléon III's domestic and foreign policy. Eighteen seventy-eight had pacified tempers after the *seize mai* crisis of 1877 and affirmed the vigour of republican France. The triumph of 1889 masked the embarrassing clearing away of the Boulanger episode. Nineteen-hundred, too, had political roots and political fruits. The general political atmosphere during the exposition's preparation and the intertwining fates of the Dreyfus Affair and the fair will be the subjects of this chapter. Chapter 6 will go on to discuss the economic and intellectual results of the Exposition of 1900.

During the late 1890's France suffered several serious diplomatic disappointments. She had been forced to accept a staggering humiliation when she backed down before Great Britain in the Fashoda crisis of July 1898. At Fashoda, on the headwaters of the Nile, a French expeditionary force withdrew before the threats of a superior and stubborn British force. French prestige as well as a large piece of Africa had been at stake and the resulting humiliation was a factor in the several years of serious strain with Great Britain, made even more bitter when France clamorously sided with the Afrikaaners in the Boer War. France had also annoyed the Americans by sympathizing with the Spanish in their war; relations with Italy had also deteriorated badly, and, despite its alliance with France, Russia gave her little support, being apparently absorbed in financing her own industrialization. Some tentative feelers on the part of Théophile Delcassé for closer diplomatic co-operation with Germany came to nothing. This disappointment should have been expected, since neither country could permit any modification of its views on Alsace-Lorraine.

A recurring worry for the enthusiasts of the exposition was the possibility of war which, if it came, would of course cause the exposition to be abandoned. Many Frenchmen sympathized with Charles Dupuy who, in an interpellation concerning the withdrawal at Fashoda, defended the government's policy saying, "From now on we must concern ourselves with justifying the hopes that France has fostered in all nations by inviting them, for 1900, to a solemn meeting of the fruits of labour and of peace."[2] War moved the competition of nations to the battlefields. War was the antithesis of the peaceful progress that the expositions celebrated.

In the midst of great political instability caused by the rapid turnover of cabinets, the president, Félix Faure, died mysteriously (rumours—true ones—were circulated of a fatal heart attack in the arms of a lady not his wife), on February 16, 1899. Two days later the chambers chose a virtual unknown, Emile Loubet, as the new president. Paul Morand claims it was said of him, "He is very amiable, very clean, and he does not spit on the flag when it is presented to him."[3] Dull, honest, suspected of sympathizing with Alfred Dreyfus, Loubet immediately became the object of a campaign of vituperation by the nationalists.

With the formation of the Waldeck-Rousseau ministry on June 22, 1899, France finally attained political stability. However, though a rest from politics was imminent, this was far from apparent at the time. Two appointments to the ministry in particular were alarming. The Minister of War was the Marquis de Galliffet, an outspoken aristocrat and the commander of the forces that crushed the commune in 1871. Galliffet was loathed by the many Frenchmen who venerated the *communard* martyrs.

Alexandre Millerand, the first socialist to enter any European cabinet, was the Minister of Commerce (the tenth since the exposition had been announced in June 1892) and therefore supervisor of the exposition. He immediately caused a stir when he ordered the prefects to arrange for reduced fares for visits of workers' delegations to the exposition "in the interests of public instruction." It smelled of socialism, but Millerand noted correctly that this special arrangement had been provided for in a regulation of August 4, 1894.[4] Millerand's appointment plunged the promoters of the exposition into deep gloom.

During these troubled years France was diligently preparing for the greatest world's fair of all time. Henri Gautier, chronicler of the exposition's progress, felt that France's competitors within the exposition would surely profit from her internal miseries. He noted that the German government had arranged for goods destined for the exposition to receive a reduction of 50 per cent on all transportation rates. Preparations for the German displays, he said, were being directed personally by William II, "while we ourselves at the same time are hypnotized by the Dreyfus Affair."[5] He pleaded with the politicians: "Ah, Messieurs! Finissez-en avec l'Affaire. Songez un peu aux affaires, et beaucoup à la France."[6] Gautier warned French manufacturers that "a defeat would be disastrous from all points of view." Foreign newspapers were filled with columns anticipating the marvels and amusements of the Exposition of 1900. "Ours," he lamented in January 1898, "are full of the Dreyfus Affair."[7]

Captain Alfred Dreyfus had been arrested for treason in October 1894. A short time before, rumours had reached the newspapers that secret documents had been passed to a foreign power. The General Staff was pressed to find the guilty one. Some circumstantial evidence suggested Dreyfus, a Jew and an unpopular officer. Basing their prosecution partially on forgeries, a military court found him guilty. In a hideous ceremony in the court of the Ecole militaire Dreyfus was publicly degraded and sent to life imprisonment on Devil's Island.

The Dreyfus Affair did not become a political and an intellectual *cause célèbre* until some time after the victim's deportation. Independently, the Dreyfus family and a conscientious army officer, Colonel Georges Picquart, searched for evidence to force a new trial. Little by little the family and Picquart gathered proof and, eventually, sympathetic and well-placed supporters. On the other hand, they aroused a counter-movement which was concerned for the army's honour and which was terrified of another scandal analogous to that over the Panama Canal. By the middle of 1897, a growing group of intellectuals, politicians, and publicists were determined to have the decision on Dreyfus revised. Georges Clemenceau took revisionism as a major task behind which his newspaper, *L'Aurore*, should throw its support in October 1897. A counter-movement of equally determined "anti-Dreyfusards" also gathered strength.[8]

On January 13, 1898, Emile Zola published his famous open letter, "J'accuse," in *L'Aurore*, charging many French politicians and officers with obstructing justice. For nearly two years afterward the Dreyfus Affair was a vital crisis in French political and intellectual life and, besides, made world as well as domestic news. During the same period preparations for the fair were in their last and most expensive stages. The Affair, many said, betrayed France and, revealing her as decayed, unjust, unstable, shamed her before the world. The preparations for the fair were planned and arranged in great measure to prove France strongly devoted to the work of art, industry, pleasure, and peace—in short, to display her as she wished to appear before the world.

Concern for the deleterious effects of the foreign interest in Dreyfus were early, specific, and well known. In a long article on February 23, 1898, the influential *Le Figaro* pointed out that foreign newspapers were warning (irresponsibly) that France was near civil war and that their readers should plan to stay away from the exposition. Parisian department stores, the deluxe hotels, and jewelers, all dependent upon wealthy foreigners for their trade, reported a slump which was blamed on the Dreyfus Affair, or more correctly, on foreign bitterness at French handling of the Affair.[9] Later in the year the reactions abroad were summed up by a journalist, André Chéradame, in a series of articles in *L'Eclair*.[10] His observations were the product of an eight-month trip through continental Europe. Chéradame's general and repeated conclusion was that Europe was Dreyfusard. This was, he noted, perhaps to be expected of such near-enemies as Germany and Britain, but the championing of the man on Devil's Island was also deep and passionate everywhere in Europe, even in Russia, then France's only important real friend in the world.[11] Chéradame believed that the sentiment against France would certainly damage the Exposition of 1900.[12]

Like many French observers of foreign criticism in France, Chéradame seemed to be dispassionate about both the technicalities and the issues of the Affair itself. He merely wished that if Dreyfus were innocent, the proper judges would quickly and quietly declare him so in order to end foreign disrespect. Like many other French political figures and journalists and the majority of French patriots, Chéradame and Gautier were not *engagé*, not at all concerned about the victim or justice in the abstract. They saw the Dreyfus Affair as a pure nuisance, a disruptive intrusion into French political life, a corrosion of her world-wide reputation, and a threat to the exposition. The small number of militant Dreyfusists (who were more concerned with the reputation of France for justice rather than her crude popularity) were the sources of most of the foreign news about the Affair.

By the summer of 1899 the Dreyfus Affair had overshadowed all other news coming from France. For foreigners, the endlessly fascinating intricacies of the Affair offered a double enjoyment. They could smugly side with the truth (for the world was convinced of Dreyfus' innocence) and incidentally feel *Schadenfreude* at the distress of France. On June 3, 1899, the highest French court of appeal (cour de cassation) set aside the 1894 condemnation of Dreyfus and ordered another court-martial. This trial began on August 7 in provincial Rennes to avoid jeopardizing the precarious political equilibrium in Paris. Almost all the major newspapers of the world (assisted by hordes of reporters at Rennes and by the international wire services such as Reuters) were carrying transcripts of Dreyfus' second trial. The seven judges were professional military officers. On September 9, 1899, two of the judges voted for acquittal; five found Dreyfus guilty of "intelligence with the enemy with attenuating circumstances." They sentenced Dreyfus to ten years of further detention.[13]

The extent and fury of the foreign reaction to the decision shocked even those who expected the worst.[14] French prestige reached its nadir. In the next few days things moved quickly and the ground was laid for the resolution of the Affair that had been a French agony for years. And the principal issue that forced action was the forthcoming Universal Exposition. This issue led to some surprising departures from principles and a tendency toward a common plan of action among Dreyfusards and anti-Dreyfusards alike. The solvent for French differences was the rage of the foreign press.

In Belgium the press greeted the news of the second condemnation "with exceptional violence."[15] In Holland, where the news was heard "with indignation," newspapers suggested to readers that, if they wished their children to learn French, they should send them henceforth to Belgium or Geneva.[16] The German press was filled with "invective and insults."[17] There the decision was seen as an outright insult to Emperor William II, who had sternly and officially declared that Dreyfus had had no dealings with any Germans.[18] In Switzerland there was "fury against anything connected with France" and demonstrations before the consulates.[19] In many towns in Italy there was "general consternation" and police guarded the consulates.[20] In Sweden and Norway, where the walls of many cities had been placarded with reports of the trial, the news from Rennes caused "a great sensation."[21]

The denunciation of France was most violent in the Anglo-Saxon countries.[22] Paul Cambon, the French ambassador, characterized the mood of London as "a furious madness" and worked with high British officials and the London police to control a protest meeting in Hyde Park of between 30,000 and 50,000 (estimates varied widely) people.[23] In Newcastle emotions reached a pitch of "epilepsy, defamation, and outrage."[24] There were huge public meetings in the large American cities. In Chicago one crowd burned the tri-colour.[25]

Nor was the hostility against France confined to the great cities and large nations. The summer residents of Northeast Harbor, Maine, sent one of the thousands of public letters to Madame Dreyfus. As a demonstration of its sympathy for Dreyfus, Wichita, Kansas, elected Miss Sadie Joseph, a Jewess, as its Carnival Queen.[26] There were protests and outrages against France from small towns in New Zealand and Nova Scotia. Journalists in Oporto, Portugal, were "injurious" to France. The meagre press of Cairo, heavily dependent upon the great wire services, particularly Reuters (which was hostile to France), believed the second decision to be "an insult to the conscience of humanity."[27]

All France was blamed in what was perhaps the first international *cause célèbre* that was not a war or the ending of one. The world seemed eager to punish France. Almost at once, in many parts of the world, journalists, particularly, threatened the exposition.[28] The bitter contrast between the idealism and gaiety of a world's fair and the cruelty of the Rennes decision was grasped almost immediately in Chicago, New York, Newcastle, London, and Rome on September 10 and the movement for boycott spread all over the world within two days. Americans circulated petitions, held public meetings, and pressured their congressmen to urge an official withdrawal from the exposition.[29] In a fit of anger, the

St. Louis Merchant Exchange voted unanimously to boycott the exposition; the San Francisco Chamber of Commerce also passed a resolution for boycott.[30]

Motions for a boycott sprang up almost simultaneously in several places in Great Britain. Meetings in London attacked the exposition, while in Liverpool merchants and manufacturers threatened to remove their exhibits. A large ship owner from Newcastle who was also a commissioner for the British displays declared that he had no desire to go to Paris, and encouraged others to "refuse to tread the soil of France." This he reasoned, would make the exhibition a "fiasco" and "almost ruin Paris which expected to make a great harvest out of people from other countries."[31]

This kind of attack on France was expressed all over the Empire. The Anglican Bishop of Calcutta had proposed from the pulpit that, since France had ceased to be a member of the community of civilized nations, India should withdraw from the exposition.[32] A cartoon in the *Melbourne Punch* showed stereotyped Americans, Englishmen, Russians, and Indians looking tearfully and disapprovingly over a glass case in which "Justice," a lovely lady, lay dead on a black block stabbed by a sword, "the Army's honour." The whole was entitled, "The French Exhibit."[33] There was also pressure for abstention from Canada.[34]

The British journalists were annoyed that other nations, particularly Germany, apparently were not as censorious as they might be. They accused the Germans of measuring their indignation "with an eel wand."[35] But in fact, the German journalists, especially those from Hamburg, were loudly threatening boycott. It was just that German officials and businessmen seemed to be assuming a stuffily proper "wait and see" attitude.

Almost every area of the world seemed to vent its indignation against France and threaten punishment by attempting to ruin the exposition. In their vituperation the journalists of Hungary and Italy rivalled the English; there were strong movements for boycott in Denmark, Portugal, Argentina, and even Turkey. And almost all of this international invective had burst forth within three or four days after the decisions at Rennes.

The same world-wide telegraphic news network that speeded communication among the international Dreyfusards permitted the French to follow closely the rage of the foreign press.[36] That Dreyfus was believed innocent, that France was considered an international pariah, that the exposition was in danger—all this was well known in France. The expected reactions (wails from the Dreyfusards; cheers from the anti-Dreyfusards) had occurred in France at the news from Rennes. However, as a result party differences became blurred and were almost effaced when it appeared that the exposition was threatened.[37] *Le Figaro* and *Le Temps*, close to the government and longtime boosters of the exposition, reported the movement for boycott in great detail and editorialized on the need to forestall it.[38] Georges Clemenceau's *L'Aurore* and *Le Siècle*, which published the views of such Dreyfusists as Joseph Reinach and Georges Picquart, were grief-stricken at the news from Rennes and appalled at the plummeting of France's reputation. Even anti-Dreyfusard papers, such as *Le Petit Journal* were horrified at the foreign insults to France and the threats to the exposition. Only the gutter-nationalist, Edouard Drumont, of *La Libre Parole*, crowed that now, thank God, the exposition would be exclusively French.

Embarrassment and fear led to some desperate, and a few peculiar, attempts to remove France from the obloquy she appeared to be under. Well-publicized letters of sympathy were sent by prominent Frenchmen to Madame Dreyfus. *Le Siècle* began a subscription for an "expiatory monument" before the Palais de Justice at Rennes to protest the second condemnation and laud the two judges who voted Dreyfus innocent. The newspaper urged haste in order that this "might figure in the Universal Exposition of 1900."[39] It appeared to many Frenchmen, and especially to many important ones, that haste and expediency would be required to save the exposition and restore the reputation of France.

Efforts to settle the uproar over the Rennes decision were complicated by the fact that important politicians, most notably President Loubet, had firmly promised to observe the decision at Rennes.[40] However, before making these promises, they had themselves felt sure that Dreyfus would go free.[41] The disappointment of those who carried out a desperate and fruitless search for a legal means to declare Dreyfus innocent added to the confusion. In the meantime, the unresolved Affair was demoralizing the nation and casting all France in the role of an international criminal.[42]

As early as September 11, 1899, *Le Temps*, avidly watched abroad as a weathervane of French official opinion, noted portentously that (*a*) the decision at Rennes was not unanimous, (*b*) the seven judges had voted four to three not to impose the punishment, and (*c*) "attenuating circumstances" could be interpreted as uncertainty.[43] *Le Temps* also remarked that the president's right to pardon was subject to no restriction and a day later suggested this as a solution to the problem. On September 15, *Le Temps* reprinted an article from *La Dépêche* quoting General Mercier, considered a villain by the Dreyfusists, and Commandant Carrière, one of the judges who voted for attenuating circumstances. Both believed that a pardon would settle the matter.

By this time, of course, the motions for bringing about the pardon of Dreyfus were well under way. As early as September 10, the day after the Rennes decision, Waldeck-Rousseau had suggested that Loubet pardon Dreyfus. After a vain search for a means of declaring Dreyfus innocent, the Council of Ministers and the most important Dreyfusists agreed that a pardon could calm the general agitation and restore the reputation of France abroad.[44] Important as it was, the exposition's fate was not the only matter that pressed upon the cabinet ministers. For them these were frantic days oppressed by fears for Dreyfus' health and threats of internal political disruption as well as horror at foreign chagrin. It was clear that something had to be done for Dreyfus.[45]

However, the key man in the negotiations, Loubet, stubbornly resisted signing a decree of pardon. Loubet wished to find a general means of pacifying France and hoped a longer wait would both ease tempers and give time to find a solution.[46] While urging a pardon, Waldeck-Rousseau himself had first suggested that it be signed after a "cooling-off" period of a few weeks.[47] But the pressure for haste could not be withstood. Finally, after Millerand and then Waldeck-Rousseau and Galliffet all threatened resignation, Loubet relented, but only after obtaining promises of help in a programme for a general amnesty.[48] He signed the decree of pardon on the morning of September 19.[49]

That afternoon at 2 P.M. the president toured the tumultuous exposition grounds and spoke there of the peaceful purposes of the impending great fête. He declared, "Fleeting quarrels have not altered the tender and generous soul of France which is absorbed in its mission of progress and peace."[50] *L'Eclair* observed:

He had calculated that a close correlation would be seen between the two events. The pardon of Dreyfus was to be a pardon for the exposition, which was threatened with death by the friends in other countries of the victim condemned at Rennes, who replied to the verdict by shouting, "Let's boycott the exposition!"[51]

On September 22 the commissioners general of Germany, the United States, Great Britain, Russia, Hungary, Austria, Denmark, Spain, Italy,

Norway, the Netherlands, Rumania, and Switzerland met with French officials at the Palais de Transport on the exposition grounds. More a show than a ceremony, this meeting marked the official possession of the terrains their exhibits would occupy. The occasion was a stately one and well publicized.[52] The exposition was saved. One could almost interpret this rite as a symbolic welcoming of France back into the community of great nations.

The pardon began a new stage, the "phasing-out" period of the Dreyfus Affair, the beginning of the whitewash (*passer l'éponge*) or armistice (*trêve*). Unlike the previous stages, this one was characterized by soft motions, euphemisms, and silence.

The seeds of this new development were planted just after Rennes. Realizing immediately that the stability of the nation was threatened by the passions arising out of the Dreyfus Case, Maurice Barrès suggested a resolution:

Let us all journalists and nationalists alike, seal up the Affair on a marble tomb. May it lie in a traitor's grave and never again appear in our discussions. Let us organize a campaign of silence against this unceasing foreign plot.[53]

On September 12 Ernest Judet, editor of the anti-Dreyfusard *Le Petit Journal*, by far the most widely circulated newspaper in France, wrote a front-page editorial, "Si nous n'en parlions plus." Judet believed that silence would not only obliterate the Affair but would save the exposition and restore the prestige of France abroad.[54] Thereafter, to ignore the Affair became part of his editorial policy.[55]

If the movement was begun by the anti-Dreyfusards, it was embraced by their enemies. Ernest Lavisse wrote a widely read and heeded article, "La réconciliation nationale," in *La Revue de Paris* that deliberately de-emphasized the Affair and ignored the victim. Barely using the word "Dreyfus" the article closed with, "Patriots, offer to our country the sacrifice of your hatreds!"[56]

This article was the occasion for the opening on October 19, 1899 of a series in *Le Figaro* with the same title. An inquiry was phrased: "I: What are some practical and rapid means for obtaining appeasement? II: How can we prevent the return of this current misery?" Well-known intellectuals and political figures were polled for solutions.[57]

The tone of the responses was set early by Marcellin Berthelot who suggested an amnesty, and secondly:

To pledge all journalists and publicity agents to cease stunning and bothering the public with private matters and to turn all minds towards general problems the discussion of which has always been the glory of France.[58]

The crucial answer to the inquiry was the one given by Alfred Mezières, a deputy, president of the press corps at the Exposition of 1900 and of the "Syndicat des journalistes parisiens." He wrote:

To achieve the appeasement that you desire, that we all desire, I know only one method: silence. Let us say no more about this Affair whose interest, moreover, is exhausted. The most useful example in this regard can be given by the press. What a splendid occasion, as well, for our diplomacy to carry off one of those peaceful and glorious victories which, while satisfying national pride cures the country of a passing indisposition![59]

In general, the same tone continued throughout the rest of the inquiry.[60] Raymond Poincaré also wrote that the means to obtain reconciliation was "not to speak so much."[61] Actually, several of the correspondents expressed gratitude at being asked their views on such a vital matter, but agreed so heartily with the consensus that they refused even to discuss the issue obliquely in public. On this note the inquiry rather burned itself out.

Le Temps, like *Le Figaro* a salient force in the earlier campaign to have Dreyfus rehabilitated, dropped the matter once the victim was pardoned and was spirited off to recover with his family in Carpentras.[62] The soothing ripples urging reserve spread outwards. Very quickly other newspapers and politicians got the message. If many Frenchmen were uncompromising on the issues of the Dreyfus Affair, they could be as one over the issue of patriotism. Soon even some of the most militant Dreyfusists, Reinach being the outstanding example, were convinced by promises that the silence would be only for the sake of the exposition. To many erstwhile campaigners for justice, however, "silence" was too crude a confession of cowardice. They preferred "armistice." A phrase that occurs repeatedly in journalistic and public pronouncements in the year after Rennes is *la trêve de l'Exposition*. *Trêve* could be interpreted according to one's hopes for the eventual resolution of the Dreyfus case and this became the usual euphemism for referring obliquely to the dying Affair.[63]

Reinach grudgingly agreed to silence for the success of the exposition.[64] Clemenceau, more cynical about the politicians he knew so well, never did. He regretted the brief moment of weakness when he had consented to the pardon. He had done so only because of the explosion of foreign bitterness against France and because he hoped for rapid justice. He was appalled at the armistice, which he quickly perceived would be a smoke screen as thousands of crimes were erased by Loubet's insistence on an amnesty. The Tiger spewed fury at the truce and at the steady progress toward amnesty which Waldeck-Rousseau made his salient task while the exposition was on.[65] Clemenceau, like Zola, Picquart, and Dreyfus himself, did not oppose the exposition, but believed it a gross hypocrisy to present it to the world just as France was callously and expeditiously cleansing the criminals of the Dreyfus Affair of their sins. At the other extreme, Henri de Rochefort of *L'Intransigeant* and Drumont wanted Dreyfus to be degraded a second time and attacked the pardon, the silence, the armistice, and the exposition.[66]

But Clemenceau and Drumont were on the outer fringes of the opinion moulders of France. In any case, they were not regarded abroad as responsible mouthpieces of French sentiment. The fact that legally Dreyfus was still guilty and might never be declared innocent, Clemenceau's grief, was too subtle for foreigners, as it was for all but a few Frenchmen.[67] With the pardon and the *trêve*, the world looked forward to the exposition and it was this that occupied most of the news from and about Paris.[68]

One could overstate the real strength of the movement to wreck the exposition. The world press seemed to be in a state of shock and hysteria at the verdict of September 9. Significantly, however, rapid moves from Chambers of Commerce or legislators came only from a few places in Great Britain and the United States. Many foreign officials, as soon as they heard that a pardon was in the air, assured Millerand, French diplomatic officers, and the commissioner general of the exposition that they intended to participate in 1900. The natural prudence of administrators and politicians had much to do with this. Another significant factor, however, was the still unsatisfied demand for space at the exposition. Individuals and even nations felt that if they acted rashly, there would be less idealistic competitors to seize their staked-out terrain in Paris. This might explain the eagerness with which each *enragé* watched the others to see if, indeed, they would pull out.[69]

In any case France became remarkably peaceful after the pardon. Originally the basis of the truce appeared to be fragile, being a reaction to the brief, though thorough, foreign disgust with French justice and the resultant threat to the exposition. However, to all but a tiny group of militants, the benefits of the armistice were too good to risk losing.

An optimistic view of what would happen to foreign plans to boycott the Exposition.
"Le 'Cinquième Acte'" refers to an article by Zola on the pardon of Dreyfus.

LE « BOYCOTTAGE » DE L'EXPOSITION
par Albert GUILLAUME

DE LONDRES :
« Boycottez l'Exposition! Boycottez la France! Boycottez les produits français! »

DE BERLIN :
« L'agitation contre l'Exposition de 1900 grandit. Dès à présent, plusieurs notables
COMMERÇANTS DE L'INDUSTRIE DU CUIR ont retiré leur promesse d'y participer. »

TROIS MOIS APRÈS
CHŒUR : « Si nous faisions une « boycotte » mâ''taillée ?... »

LE « CINQUIÈME ACTE »
« ... et ils viendront gadailler chez nous ! » (Emile ZOLA, chap. 103, verset 69.)

The opening of the Chambers after the long winter vacation was calm. *Le Figaro* observed:

One cannot quite picture the professional interpellators of the Chamber demanding that the Government set the judicial machinery in motion while the exposition is on, and the whole Chamber going along with this manoeuvre.

Le Figaro added hopefully. "Who knows? Perhaps after the exposition no one will want to hear of these quarrels concerning matters so useless and out of date."[70]

In a speech eight days before the exposition opened, the arch-*syndicaliste*, Joseph Reinach, reiterated a vow he made earlier:

Even we have offered to observe an armistice for the whole duration of this great festival of work and peace the universal exposition. Having once given our word for patriotic reasons, we will keep it. We shall not allow any of our claims to lapse, but be assured that we shall not disrupt this festival that France offers the world.[71]

Reinach was always carefully watched. Curiously, a mis-reporting of this pledge of peace led to what was perhaps the unique brouhaha over the Dreyfus Affair that summer. Reinach, by merely mentioning the Affair, was viewed as a traitor who was trying to re-open it. After a disputatious session (mostly over the wording of the resolution) in the Chamber, the deputy Chapuis's motion "To invite the Government vigorously to oppose the re-opening of the Affair, from whatever quarter such motions may come" was passed and greeted with wild cheering on all *bancs*, right, left, and centre.[72]

Reinach (who did so delicately) and the other militant Dreyfusists (who were more indignant) struggled against the government's massive efforts to heal all the wounds of the Affair by progressively more encompassing amnesties.[73] Before the year 1900 ended, this process was complete: all trials were dismissed, all prisoners released, and all crimes legally wiped out that related to the Affair. Zola, for example, blamed the exposition; said it "strangled truth and justice."[74] But his objections meant little. Because of the news blackout, most of the protests of the Dreyfusists were heard in private.[75] Almost no one would publish them.

Exhausted by emotionalism, one anticipated pleasure and profit. This period of "exposition politics," as it was called, was not very dignified, but these kinds of reactions are the natural aftermath of great public fevers and they are part of the hygiene necessary for restoring health.[76]

The members of some religious orders and many prominent Catholics had erred, perhaps morally and certainly politically, by siding vociferously with what was to be the losing side in the Dreyfus Affair. During 1900 Waldeck-Rousseau worked quietly with the pope to curb the powers of the worst offenders, the Assumptionists. But secretly, plans were made for a more thorough campaign after the exposition closed. After the amnesty of December 19, 1900, Waldeck-Rousseau, believing that the country was pacified, announced that France was "at the eve of a decisive battle to snatch the favourite weapon of the reaction."[77] The allusion was, of course, to clericalism and the least co-operative members of the Catholic church.

There was no election in 1900 (as there was in 1889, for example) to suggest that the exposition had increased the allegiance to the Republic. There were municipal elections in the spring. The nationalists made gains in Paris and the republicans gained strength in the provinces. But these results were very likely only part of a long trend.[78] In general:

The year 1900 was going to be one of a return to calm. Like that of 1878 after the crisis of May 16, like that of 1889 after the Boulanger episode, the universal exposition would contribute greatly to the easing of tempers.[79]

The threats to the exposition frightened almost all parties in the Affair. The *trêve de l'Exposition* produced sufficiently striking benefits of political tranquillity that the politicians were reluctant to jeopardize this peace. Clemenceau observed sardonically:

The Republic is enjoying itself. Never have the ministries been so gay. One goes to parties; to the theatre. It is all a façade. The revolutionaries have discovered reasons for joy in the social order and they have guilelessly communicated them to the conservatives. There are Chinese lanterns, dances, and brass bands everywhere. The Republic amuses itself as it dies.[80]

The Exposition of 1900 *had* served well politically, first as a patriotic rallying point for all but a few of the passionate disputants of the summer of 1899 and then as a diversion and a tranquillizer in the following year. By the time of the final amnesty of December 19, 1900, there was no longer an Affair. There was just a judicial error to correct. Since there was little need for haste, the courts could proceed carefully and quietly to give justice to Dreyfus. He was declared entirely innocent on July 12, 1906.

Was It a Success? • Viewed through the winter that began the new century, the ruins of the exposition looked melancholy and already terribly old. Cold and dampness warped the sham solidity and streaked the colours of buildings slow to be demolished. Oversize figures, allegories of Victory, Progress, Knowledge, Peace, and Science, were stern or jubilant before small squads of relentless wreckers. Many of the *attractions* were hacked at or smashed by vandals. Some of them remained as hulks long afterwards, since their owners were bankrupt and could not afford to remove them. During the long clearing-away of the debris the most bizarre sights were the frosty, snarling foo dogs, the ice-covered temple guards, the sooty arcades, and icicled pagodas of pavilions that had housed the colonial exhibits.

Many of the large national pavilions were dismantled shortly after the closing. Some were being returned to their home countries to become public buildings. Smaller foreign pavilions and many French buildings were sold at auction. Bidding on the modish and controversial statue of "Paris" over Binet's entrance gate was listless. The Hungarian magnate who ended the bidding announced that he was taking "Paris" to the garden of his villa in Budapest.

During the winter as statisticians, editors, and printers of all nations prepared the official reports for publication, politicians, economists, and intellectuals asked each other the same question, the crucial one posed after every exposition: "Was it a success?" We have already seen that the Exposition of 1900 was politically salubrious. But, of course, it was more than a political event; the question had to be posed for other aspects of the exposition as well.

The exhibition had encountered some bad luck. Strikes in 1898 and the bitter winter of 1899–1900 had slowed construction. A month after the official opening, harried workmen still ran about touching up architectural decorations, removing scaffolding or tidying formal gardens. Haste in the installation of mechanical equipment caused failures that cursed the exposition until it closed. Paris was tropically hot in July and August, unusually chilly in November. Outbreaks of plague in Portugal and Scotland convinced many wavering potential visitors to stay home.

France was often the object of international resentments that were due to a generally strained diplomatic situation. Wars were being waged in distant parts of the world. Popular newspapers used the European diplomatic repercussions of these wars to fan the aggressive patriotism of their readers. Much of France's unpopularity probably resulted from an emotional residue of the international espousing of the cause of Alfred Dreyfus. Also, in 1900, the competitive atmosphere of the exposition seemed to aggravate the already strained relations between nations.

Traditionally the British had accounted for the largest numbers of foreign visitors to the Paris expositions. In 1900 a British guidebook had called the *vespasiennes* "offensively conspicuous." A French journalist expressed surprise that the English did not know that such constructions were necessary for the most elegant physiognomies.[1] At the South African pavilion, often the scene of French demonstrations where "one inclined his head as at an altar," there was another incident. An Englishman reportedly spat on Kruger's bust while his wife swatted at some of the venerators with an umbrella. The couple barely escaped, apparently, to the pavilion of British India.[2]

Naturally most Frenchmen wanted British visitors, especially wealthy ones. But in 1900 the English newspapers convinced many readers that they would be badly received in Paris. The Germans thus replaced the British as the largest group of tourists at the exposition. In Paris one heard German everywhere, but the Germans, then as now, were not easy spenders and the mark was no substitute for the more attractive guinea.

In an age when such things mattered, the absence of many crowned heads was "an undeniable repulse and a scathing affront."[3] But to the European monarchs (who had lost one of their number, the king of Italy, by assassination in July 1900), Paris was the hatching centre for anarchist outrages. The King of Sweden and the Shah of Persia, the only ones to appear, would not stay at the special house on the exposition grounds that the administration had confidently provided for them and their royal cousins. While in Paris the Shah of Persia was annoyed by attempted regicide. He also offended the city by leaving a ceremony in the Salle des Fêtes when he perceived, in the decoration, nude figures, the representation of which his religion did not permit. In response to his invitation, the Tsar of Russia deigned to send kindly regrets, but in the reply—and this hurt—he neglected to use the word "Republic."

Henri Gautier sadly summarized the bad luck:

If the Americans and the Spaniards had not spent their millions killing each other, if the English, instead of sending 150,000 troops to the Transvaal had kept them at home, if the king of Italy, instead of falling under Bresci's bullet, had come to visit the Exposition, as he had intended, and had led a procession of sovereigns to Paris. If the Chinese, . . . if the plague . . . etc., etc., [sic].[4]

The bleakest appraisal of the exposition was made by the private businessmen who had hoped to get rich on it. In 1889 the most profitable restaurant had earned its owner 2 million francs; the least profitable earned 40,000 francs. Naturally this good fortune led to vigorous bidding for space in 1900. The essentially idealistic administration, eager for money to finance the more educational, free displays, met the demand. In 1889, 37 spaces for restaurants were awarded; in 1900, 207. The owner of one restaurant—not the largest—paid 180,000 francs for space, 220,000 francs for construction. His fixed expenses were 1,600 francs per day.[5] At an average price of 3.50 to 4 francs per meal, he later reckoned that his break-even point was his millionth meal, which, unfortunately was never served.[6] Nine of the 58 commercial attractions cost between 2 and 4 million francs each to build. Almost all the attractions were expensive to attend; few had artistic or educational merit. It would have cost about 600 francs to see all of them.[7]

In all, the owners of restaurants or attractions charging admission had invested about 80 millions in the exposition. This amount was to be amortized in 200 days (actually somewhat less because of the delayed completion). Assuming an average attendance of 250,000 per day, it would have required the expenditure of 3 to 4 francs per person, 12 to 20 francs per family per day, for the businessmen as a group to break even. Not many families could be so extravagant.[8] It must have nettled the businessmen to see provincials established at the public benches opening their wicker lunch baskets, or a Parisian workman with his family gnawing on a loaf carried from a suburban *boulangerie*.

The anger of the concessionaires reached a pitch on September 14 just before the banquet of the mayors, from which the government expected so much. On that day sixty owners met at the Swedish restaurant and threatened a strike if they did not obtain some kind of financial redress from the administration. They blamed the administration for arbitrarily modified agreements, late completion, and less than promised attendance. The prospective closing of the restaurants was evaded by Millerand just before the most dramatic republican event of the year. The businessmen later were to obtain a partial refund of the fees they had paid for space.

The bitterness of the businessmen apart, the exposition itself was an unusual financial success. There were two methods of making an accountant's report of the exposition. Subtracting receipts of 74 million francs from the expenses of 116 millions at first gave the appearance of a French government loss of 42 million francs. But when one considered the gifts to Paris of the Pont Alexander III, the Grand Palais, the Petit Palais, and other permanent improvements valued by the famous economist Charles Gide at 35 million francs, the loss could be set much lower: perhaps at 7 million francs.

The usual method in France, however, was to consider even new permanent structures as current expenses, and to count the subsidies as normal receipts. Paris and the state had each contributed 20 million francs. By this calculation the loss of 42 millions is cut to 2 million francs.[9] This was less than 2 per cent of the total cost of the exposition.

French expositions were not expected to pay their way. In any case, from a businessman's point of view, any exposition was a detestable enterprise. For the state, however, the Exposition of 1900, like that of 1889, did rather well financially.

There were some indications that the exposition was a national economic stimulant. In 1900 railroad revenues increased by 87 million francs over those of 1899. But this amount was only 9 million francs more than the increase of 1889 over the revenues of 1888—a smaller gain than anticipated. This slight disappointment was probably the result of reduced fares for excursion trips to the exposition, since passenger traffic showed a proportionally larger increase. Because of the increased flow of foreign currency into France (largely caused by tourist expenditures) the holdings of gold of the Bank of France increased steadily during the exposition, rising 400 million francs to a total of 2,300 million. Charles Gide believed that the excess attributable to the exposition in the *octroi* of Paris was 30 million francs. Thus Paris, besides receiving her new permanent monuments, had more than recovered the subsidy of 20 million francs.[10]

The Exposition of 1900 was an expensive affair. In these days of Keynesian dynamic analysis, we know that the injection of new expenditures by public works is an indirect, but effective means of raising employment and production in many sectors of the economy. World's fairs can be compared with public works like road construction or new post offices as stimulants and, indeed, in the past few decades this has been the principal justification for their expected deficits. Spending for the exposition very likely was a significant energizer for the sluggish French economy and certainly was a boon to Paris. However, the statistics that could permit us to be exact about just what kinds of economic stimulation the exposition caused are imprecise or lacking. At the time, the arguments for or against the exposition as an economic benefit were rather primitive, and were often presented in polemics that made them suspect. One writer noted that there were slightly fewer business failures in 1900 than in 1899, though the value of businesses that failed was 30 per cent greater.[11] A French economist, in a long argument against big international exhibitions, "proved" that the Exposition of 1900 caused a depression in the provinces and a sharp increase in the demands made upon the Parisian police force. The exposition, he claimed, also permanently increased the burden upon public charity to support provincials who, having seen the bright lights and sins of the metropolis, refused to return to their farms and villages.[12] The Prefect of Police in Paris declared:

The exposition has unfortunately left us with huge numbers of individuals from every corner of France and Europe. Now they have no livelihood. Some of these pariahs are merely unlucky people, pitiable vagabonds; but there are others! And the others, most often, are bandits, burglars, and thieves or—what is even worse—those who live off them![13]

Another enemy of expositions gravely noted that there were many more strikes in 1900 and in 1889 than there had been in the years that preceded the expositions.[14]

The debate over whether the exposition decreased or increased exports had nationalistic overtones. The protectionist-patriots saw the industrial displays merely as an opportunity for the methodical foreigner to steal the fruits of superior French intelligence.[15] More confident patriots believed the exhibits proved the merit of French products and raised the foreign demand for them.[16]

It should be evident that most of the so-called economic arguments were really moral ones. Many of them referred to the notorious pamphlet of 1895, *Pas d'Exposition en 1900!*, the first organized attack on the national policy of regular universal expositions. In any case, economic analysis was nearly intuitive and statistical evidence was lacking for conclusive judgements. The economic debate was only a mask for a new and pessimistic discussion about French patriotism and about the action to be taken by France in the light of what she had learned about herself at the exposition.

The great exposition was a critical disappointment in one respect: attendance reached only 50,860,801.[17] All plans for the exposition, it will be remembered, had been based upon an attendance cautiously projected at 60 million. Many counted on 100 million. Attendance in 1889 had been 39 million. Each exposition, everyone believed, naturally surpassed its predecessor and this one was to cost more, be more international, and be finer in every way than that of 1889. No one could specify how it was to be finer, but everyone expected this, and other kinds of progress. In the preparatory years, 1893–1899, 60 million became a fundamental figure for planning finances, traffic flow, accommodations, food supplies, and the sale of tickets.

It was ironic that this exposition, so disappointing in its attendance, was the most popular of all time. As in 1889, there was a shabby, informal market outside the gates where one bought the *bons*, at a face value of one franc. The *bons* were usually hawked by tramps or thin old ladies who eked out some profit this way. They weakly shouted at the crowds, "Tickets, tickets à vendre ici!" and until the opening the little negotiables sold well. Later their price dropped, until in October and November Parisian workers and their families could buy them for 15 or 20 centimes, sometimes even for less.[18] On the other hand, the millions of bourgeois who had paid the Association of Guarantee face value for books of twenty tickets felt somewhat defrauded. Purchasers of *bons* in 1889 had had the dim assurance that their tickets were valid for future lotteries. The tickets of 1900 carried no such provision.

The final attendance figure is actually staggering; it is still the largest attendance for any world's fair and was much greater than the population of France at the time. Vast as this figure seems, however, it was a setback, a closely observed and critically placed disappointment, which cast a pall over all appraisals of the exposition and what it attempted to accomplish.

In Chapter 5 it was noted that the Exposition of 1900 was more beneficial to the statesmen than to the state. Except from the point of view of the concessionaires, it was a business and perhaps an economic success as well. Yet after it closed, this exposition, unlike any of its predecessors, had only isolated defenders. Moreover, the few advocates of the maintenance and strengthening of the tradition seemed to be using an optimistic frame of reference that was already stale in 1900. Its critics, who were many and clever, used the language of the new century and immersed themselves in its moods. To them it seemed that the exposition revealed truths to Europe—and most especially to France—that were perhaps better left hidden.

As he listened to the crowds at the exposition, Friedrich Naumann heard Frenchmen say, "We'll have no more expositions. This is the last."[19] Many visitors noticed a feeling of lassitude, of finality; there was perhaps a nagging suspicion that their civilization would never again be capable of such an effort. Though this world's fair was a qualified political and financial success, the prediction overheard by Naumann came true. France turned away from what had become one of her proudest traditions, from the sort of cultural imperialism which, despite the strain on her national wealth, time, and talent, she offered graciously to the world. After 1900, in France as elsewhere in Europe, it seemed that the time for such optimistic demonstrations had passed. The ending of this great series of expositions may be partially attributable to the faults of this exposition, but seems more likely to be part of a new mood or change in the spiritual atmosphere of Europe at the time.

"Nearly all students of the last years of the nineteenth century have sensed in some form or other a profound psychological change."[20] The Exposition of 1900 was a crucially placed and widely observed event of importance to many of the world's intellectuals, and if H. Stuart Hughes' statement is correct, we might expect that the Exposition of 1900, especially when compared with its predecessor of 1889, would support his thesis that the *Zeitgeist* of Europe had changed greatly. And so it does. The atmosphere of the appraisals of 1900 is so different from its predecessors that, when recalling the Exposition of 1889, the historian has the feeling that he has left one intellectual world for another. In France an anti-rational, anti-positivistic reaction was compounded with embarrassment over France's relatively poor showing. Yet the sombre reaction to the century's final exposition, like *fin de siècle* intellectualism generally, was not confined to Frenchmen.

One of the most careful and analytical appraisals of the fair was made by the Scottish biologist, sociologist, and pioneer in city planning, Patrick Geddes. Geddes might have been expected to possess sufficient erudition to be further educated by the exposition. This Victorian cosmopolitan, who spent six months in Paris, was most enthusiastic about the international congresses. He also believed that, however one disputed with them, the juries still stood for "the general desire to advance that widest utilization of the best in which progress lies." Geddes deplored the presence of the fashionable world, which really saw nothing, and of those who came to be impressed by the emphasis on bigness (e.g., "the great diamond and golden image, the high champagne bottle, etc., etc."). As examples of those who profited from the show he cited

. . . the milliners' girls discussing fashions and the shoemakers their lasts, the younger painters, the engineers and electricians among Siemens' or Lord Kelvin's patents, the ironmasters crowding to buy the colossal gas engine which utilizes the hitherto wasted energies of the blast furnace and literally wins the power of a thousand horses from what has been hitherto a useless pollution of the air . . . the show of automobiles, the latest telephotographic lenses, the rival typesetting machines, the best trained apple trees, the newest antiseptics and filters, or the contest in brightness and economy in illuminants—so that gas and even petroleum are again competing with acetylene, and all with electricity. . . .[21]

Geddes even suggested new tasks for later expositions.[22] Yet he was disturbed by the obviously inadequate planning and the chaos of architecture and decoration. He complained of crowding, of the exasperating fatigue of walking so many miles with so many people, so many objects demanding, and deserving, his full attention. Geddes acknowledged the existence of a widespread distrust of exhibitions in Great Britain and blamed the distrust on the observation of failure in the modern era. This "reaction against the rainbow optimism of the Great 1851 Exhibition" had, Geddes believed, now settled on Europe. The only place for an ambitious exposition after 1900 was the United States, where there were broadly similar economic conditions and a kindred spirit to those that led to the Crystal Palace Exhibition of 1851.[23]

A liberal who might have drawn optimistic conclusions from the exposition was the German political theorist and journalist, Friedrich

Naumann.[24] Naumann admired France and publicly pleaded for closer diplomatic and cultural relations between the old enemies. He felt that a cheerful result of the overwhelming of Paris by German tourists might be a closer understanding between the two peoples.[25] He favoured world's fairs and felt that his own country had been delinquent in not staging a large and magnanimous international exhibition.

Unlike his countrymen, Naumann was almost apologetic about the conspicuous superiority of the German technical exhibits to the French ones. He observed that the French electrical machinery was smaller and required more men to operate it than the German or American models. He remarked that it was a mistake, in 1900, for the French to keep half of the exhibit space since France did not have enough good things to show, especially in the industrial displays.

Many of Friedrich Naumann's comments on the Exposition of 1900 were comparisons with the one of 1889, which he had also studied closely. He believed that the lean steel height of the Eiffel Tower made it still the overpowering structure of the fair in 1900. Naumann deplored the new architecture (often supported by incongruous but unobservable steel frameworks) of strained, convoluted plaster and stucco. He acknowledged that the fantasy of the French architects was sometimes charming, but believed that this was an inappropriate way to open the new century. Besides, the over-ripe, swollen style quickly became boring. About the commercial entertainment, Naumann wrote, "There must be foam on the greatest waves, but here there is really too much of it."[26] Nevertheless, like every other serious observer, Naumann was bewildered by the amassing of so much of significance. He was angered by the overwhelming quantity of meaningful exhibits that he could not possibly absorb and raged at his own apathy as he moved amid inconceivable intellectual riches.

For Naumann, as for others, the exposition in 1889 was happy, rational, and French; in 1900 it was inconclusive, confusing, and, where strikingly excellent, not French. In 1889, praise from the intellectuals was general; in 1900 praise of the idealistic principles upon which the exposition was based had become largely passé. The principles for which Le Play had designed the Exposition of 1867, still in effect in 1889, had by 1900 lost their appeal. Illustrations of this changed mood can best be demonstrated by comparing articles written eleven years apart by the critic and literary scholar Eugène Melchior de Vogüé in the *Revue des Deux Mondes.*

In 1889 de Vogüé's articles were a witty, intelligent chronicle of an unmixed French victory. In the final paragraph of the last of a long series of articles, he wrote,

The beautiful fairyland will disappear. All that will be left is the admirable show of strength that France put on for herself and for the world. Europe unanimously salutes our triumph. We must thank the many devoted workers who achieved this, from those who provided the spirit down to the humblest stout arm. . . . From foreigners who were our guests for the first time in twenty years, has come that restored sense of life and of pride that Lazarus must have experienced on rising from the grave.[27]

De Vogüé was delighted with the remarkable progress shown in science and most especially in architecture in 1889. In his praise, in his optimism, he was only one of many chroniclers of an absolute French triumph.

In November 1900, de Vogüé was again literate and deft, but he saw little that was ennobling or reassuring. In technology there was not much that was new. The capacity of electrical machinery had increased greatly, but the motive force behind the generator was still coal. The only significant breakthrough on display was in wireless telegraphy.[28] In architecture, there was a distinct regression. As for Art Nouveau, it

. . . exercises its fantasies on fabrics, and jewelry, on furniture, glassware, and ceramics; it is still painfully searching for its identity and its laws.[29]

France, instead of demonstrating her power, was exposing her decline:

[One could say of this last international reunion that it was above all the exposition of the Germans. On the Champ de Mars, on the banks of the Seine, all over Paris, one saw only Germans; heard only their tongue.] It was rumoured that they [the Germans] had offered to be the exclusive suppliers of the [electrical] power and light required by all the various services of the exposition. The contract was allegedly proposed; and, as there are symbolists even in the world of business, these symbolists apparently recoiled at the formidable symbolism of this simple notion: "Paris receiving from German hands her power and her light."[30]

For de Vogüé another cruel surprise was that Japan surpassed France in the excellence of her characteristic displays of art. Japan also showed some very European examples of efficient industrial machinery. Worse yet, in 1895 Europe had received news of Japanese military victories over China just as the exposition was being prepared.[31]

In his final words gauging the accomplishments of the Exposition of 1900, de Vogüé, the former optimist, could see only the victory of vulgar power. The land he loved was scarcely in the competition. Embarrassed and cynical, he wrote:

[A nation that has no other way to demonstrate its excellence to the world risks presenting to] its guests, in its jubilee exposition in the year 2000, a colossal mirror on which these foreigners will see nothing but the decadence of those who are amusing them.[32]

An extreme example of the depressing impact of the exposition's revelations can be seen in the observations of the brooding American historian, Henry Adams. Referring to himself in the third person, he wrote, "Adams haunted it, aching to absorb knowledge and helpless to find it."[33] What troubled Adams about the exposition was that its power and diversity overwhelmed his ability to comprehend and organize its contents. He tried, but could draw no scheme or moral message from what he observed. Worse yet, Adams could find no one else up to this task either, not even his friend, the astronomer and physicist, Samuel Pierpont Langley, with whom he spent much time that summer. Adams recounts how he himself would

. . . sit by the hour over the great dynamos, watching them run noiselessly and smoothly as planets and asking them—with infinite courtesy—where the Hell they are going. They are marvellous. The Gods are not in it. Chiefly the Germans.[34]

Henry Adams compared 1900 with what he had seen in Chicago in 1893. The increasing power that man had created, he believed, was bound to get out of control and end civilization in wreckage.

To Adams the dynamo became a symbol of infinity. As he grew accustomed to the great gallery of machines, he began to feel the forty-foot dynamos as a moral force, much as the early Christians felt the Cross.

And the most terrifying thing about the dynamo was that it had "no interest in history or in man's fate."[35] Speculating on the meaning of what he saw at the exposition, Adams wrote that it

. . . has brought me so near the end that I hardly care to wait for the last scenes. There are things in it which run close to the day of judgement. It is a new century, and what we used to call electricity is its God. I can already see that the fellow who gets to 1930 will wish he hadn't. The curious mustiness of decay is already over our youth. . . .[36]

The last universal exposition of the century therefore appeared to be the object of two different kinds of pessimistic appraisals: it was considered as a specifically French attempt that failed, and as a crucial point in the decline of European optimism. French observers attacked the Exposition of 1900, of course, because of its perhaps inept·administration (though we might note here that it had more time for preparation than any other), but their most penetrating and bitter complaints were that it was a French defeat, permitting, if anything at all, only some lessons to be drawn from it.

To a group of social scientists one French scholar confessed:

We have offered our rivals, the Germans, the English, the Americans, a unique occasion to display their crushing industrial and commercial superiority. In this field we can barely claim a *succès d'estime*.[37]

French factories, it was true, were all busy, but (sad note) certain cannon could not be delivered from the armament works because of orders for the exposition.[38] France's enemies had the double delight of pleasure in the generous spectacle, and knowledge that the exposition debilitated the nation that offered it.

De Vogüé himself felt that France must finish its traverse of the period characterized by "expositional hypnosis," and he now believed that the advocates of expositions sought a kind of *"lâche"* grandeur.[39] Curiously, de Vogüé had been a prime influence in the Western embracing of Russian literature; a polyglot and a critic whose interests and reputation spread far beyond his national borders. The exposition (or was it the epoch?) and what it revealed had made him a defensive, frightened nationalist. He noted with anger and stupefaction that France, richest, biggest, most powerful in 1800, saw herself "in the microcosm that was the last exposition" placed last among the great powers.[40]

But this exposition also offered unsettling prospects to almost all non-French intellectuals. After 1900 it seemed apparent to anyone who thought about it that material progress had far outstripped moral and social progress. A richly impressive human achievement, the exposition left an impression of human frailty. A corrosive irony, and one remarked by intellectuals of all nations, was the disparity between the basic intellectual purpose of a universal exposition, which was to present all of man's accomplishments in a classified display, with the impression that this one left.

Earlier in the century, intellectuals lived in a milieu that encouraged the formation of philosophical systems. To be sure, the quest for scientific order dates from before the Enlightenment, but systems encompassing *all* fields of knowledge were much more common (and had more knowledge to deal with) later. During the nineteenth century philosophers and scientists enlarged the great encyclopaedias and the classifications of animals, vegetables, minerals, and regions of the earth. They also invented library classifications and universal decimal systems. A kind of classificatory conquest took place during preparations for the expositions as well. Many systems were tried. Though admittedly faulty, Le Play's of 1867 was the most durable and the least criticized. For 1900 a commission presided over by Alfred Picard and comprising Jules Méline, Charles Freycinet, Jules Roche, Léon Say, and others, devised a new one.

In 1900 these men tried to carry out a ranking by importance to mankind. There were eighteen classes, of which the first was education; the second art, and so on. Picard explained: "thus education and teaching took precedence in the classification; through education man enters life; education is also the source of all progress."[41] Picard confidently rationalized other classes with similar introductions.

The new classification might be blamed for some disappointments in 1900. One visitor wrote:

After twenty or thirty visits one had learned, without really having understood it, that to see Japan one had to go successively to the Champ de Mars, the Esplanade des Invalides, and to the Trocadéro; that perfumes were to be found with "yarns and textiles," hygiene with materials of war, and optics with pianos; that Greece was separated from Turkey by Sweden, Spain, Great Britain, Germany, and the United States; that the retrospective exhibition of ancient charitable organizations was to be found in the halls of food science; that one had to seek the Sèvres display among the foreign exhibits; that combs, feather-dusters, and brushes were classed as decorative art; that Marat's bathtub was to be found in the welfare section; and that the sabre carried by the First Consul at Marengo was displayed on the third floor of the waterpower and forestry pavilion.[42]

Picard was surely motivated by the same ideals as Le Play, but in 1900 he could not realize them. It was perhaps idle and really too easy to criticize the layout of such disparate richness. It was the totality of the things classified—or really their unclassifiability—that was attacked, not the details.

The nineteenth-century international exhibitions were meant to be temples or milestones on the route of progress. The French universal expositions were also to educate—or at least to create a taste for education. In 1900 no one cared to deny that the pavilions of education or of social welfare were usually nearly empty. It was perhaps one of the weaknesses of the nineteenth century to have unquestioning faith in progress—that all would be more beautiful and bigger than what preceded it.

Even the reputation of a god of the nineteenth century, science, had suffered. The whole world strove to demonstrate scientific discoveries at the Exposition of 1900. By that year, to the amazement of many intellectuals, science had advanced to the investigation of things that man could never perceive. Apparatus for producing X-rays and sending wireless telegrams were first shown in 1900. Discoveries of nearly instantaneous waves, of things at once destructive and invisible, were confounding to human intelligence. Henry Adams feared X-rays, for they were "occult" and "supersensual," all the more terrifying in that they were incapable of expression in horse-power.[43] One scientist wrote: "these discoveries, while enlarging our horizons, also reveal the narrow limits of our sensibilities."[44]

Nothing the exposition might have produced could reach the heights that its enthusiasts had hoped for. But failure of the exposition went deeper. To nineteenth-century intellectuals raised on faith in science, reason, and progress, it seemed that the most complete and expensive demonstration to celebrate science, reason, and progress produced an impression of human uselessness, finiteness, and debility. Eighteenth-century faith combined with nineteenth-century technique had produced a bewildering glut of knowledge and of the things. The intellectuals who greeted the year 1801 had embarked on the next hundred years with a confidence that was dismally attenuated among their spiritual descendants a century later.

Conclusion: The End of an Era • In Paris in 1900 one disillusioned observer remarked, "Die Welt ist ausstellungsmüde."[1] A new, cold attitude toward world's fairs was most evident in France, but was also manifest elsewhere as the twentieth century began. In France the holding of a comparable display became unthinkable for many years to come. If the Exposition of 1900 did not itself change the world, it was the stage on which a realistic, significant drama was performed that permitted its enormous audience to gain lucid and destructive insights into the happy illusions that held the nineteenth-century intellectual consensus together. Appraisals of the results of the exposition cracked and eroded the European consensus long before the destruction of 1914.

International exhibitions, it is true, continued. And often they were fine spectacles. Some of them provided important leadership in the transformation of design and architecture in the next half-century. They even increased in number, if not in size, for exhibitions were and probably always will be unique opportunities to bring together large numbers of buyers and sellers.

Shortly after the Exposition of 1900 had closed, as a reward for his work in 1889 and 1900, Alfred Picard was given the post of President of the Conseil d'état. This body, like the American Supreme Court, was the ultimate legal authority in France. Prince Napoléon, after the Exposition of 1855, and Frédéric Le Play, after the Exposition of 1867, had both become disillusioned about the general utility and the chances for smooth operation of a large, general exposition. Picard's intimate involvement with this very much larger world's fair had chastened him as well and, though he beamed optimism as long as the Exposition of 1900 was open, he was nonetheless ready to help relieve France of her devotion to these debilitating spectacles.

During the depressing assessment of the meagre moral results of the Exposition of 1900, the Comité français des expositions à l'étranger was the only body that had any definite views as to what should be done about French expositions. This group of businessmen, fortified by a rapidly growing membership, increased its pressure on the government to change its policy of rigid control of expositions. The Comité must have been emboldened by the example of the brilliant, disciplined, German industrial exhibits that had been generously assisted by the German treasury.

In early March, 1901, a French administrative commission informed CFEE that the government could assist only associations "reconnues d'utilité publique."[2] Alexandre Millerand, the controversial Socialist Minister of Commerce appointed as part of the cabinet that disposed of the Dreyfus Affair, had been forced to deal with the exposition as a *fait accompli*; until it was over his duties were limited to signing papers and making flowery speeches. After the exposition, however, he was able to pursue his own policies. Millerand told the assembled members of the CFEE at their banquet on March 20, 1901, that they could count on his support in obtaining the recognition of "public usefulness." Three days later the Comité convened an "extraordinary general assembly" at which it empowered two of its members to deal with the government. In the next few weeks, these men and Millerand and Picard worked together to alter the statutes of the CFEE. Finally, on their recommendation President Loubet signed a special decree on June 12, 1901, declaring the CFEE "d'utilité publique."[3]

Membership in the CFEE grew from 400 in 1900 to 1,300 in 1913.[4] The powers of this organization (later called simply the Comité français des expositions, or CFE) grew to encompass all French policy concerning expositions, special or universal, local or international. By 1928 one could say "it enjoys a sort of monopoly and authority which it imposes on all its members."[5] The CFE even had its own architects.

The temporary abandonment of huge world's fairs after 1900 (the United States held its last really large one in St. Louis in 1904) did not mean that international exhibitions as a whole became unimportant or infrequent. They simply became non-political. Special exhibitions for individual groups of purchasers and sellers, or for art or other limited purposes, became quite common occurrences. Certain small countries, such as Belgium after 1885 and Japan after the Second World War, have used well-subsidized special exhibitions as a means of attracting large numbers of prospective industrial buyers. There was even a revival of so-called "world's fairs" in the 1930's, and France herself tried a large international exposition in 1937. Belgium staged a huge and noble general international exposition in Brussels in 1958. The United States, lacking lavish governmental subsidies, has fashioned "world's fairs" that were more or less dominated by the public relations men of her great corporations. Recent ones took place in Seattle in 1962 and, a much larger one, in New York, 1964–65. None of these later exhibitions approached the idealism, intended grasp, or political significance of the last French expositions of the nineteenth century.[6]

Whether the great Exposition of 1900 itself was a factor for change in France (admittedly a major thesis of this book) is certainly debatable. We do know, however, that France (or more vividly and more correctly, France's image of herself) after the exposition was quite different from what it was before.

Viewed simply, France's expositions were great parties staged by her for herself and for the whole world. In 1900 Patrick Geddes wrote this tribute to France and Paris, describing them as

... the nation and city which have so richly spread the feast, so admirably and courteously fulfilled the part of host amid the many cares and tasks and trials inevitable in such a colossal and motley gathering.[7]

But in a subtle, though pervasive and definite way, the nineteenth-century expositions were forceful and serious demonstrations of French pride, as well as being integral parts of France's domestic and foreign policy. The festivals were designed to remind her own citizens of the glory of France and to demonstrate that glory vividly to her visitors from abroad. Alas, in the last analysis, the evidence of the Exposition of 1900 was embarrassing and shocking for the French: France looked weak and shabby, even to herself, and the hoards of German inventions and tourists spoiled her hopes for political or prestigious benefits to be gained from later expositions. France and Frenchmen in general became less grandiose, less generous, less forgiving, and much more frightened.[8] Their frustrations led to overcompensation: the irrational nationalism of a passionate people who no longer possessed either unchallenged intellectual vigour or adequate military might of which they might feel proud. [9]

To be sure, the Exposition of 1900 was a great one but, viewed as an event of importance to Western civilization in general, it was a failure, and the failure was not confined to France and the French people. Earlier, even a few years earlier, it had been easy to regard mankind as cheerfully developing an ever greater knowledge of the world's workings. This pursuit of knowledge, it was reasoned, would not only result in intellectual improvement, but would lead steadily toward the merging of all men's interests and the attainment of permanent, universal peace. The Exposition of 1900, however, showed Europe so much more than she actually wished to see. It put on full view a glut of facts and of material goods, exposing to all the selfish pursuit of wealth and power that motivated society at large and called attention to the taste of the times. The widespread, optimistic, Saint-Simonian faith was dispelled in the *fin de siècle* spirit of lassitude, scepticism, introspection, and irony. It was a French tragedy that Panama followed Suez; in an analogous, but more universal, sense, it was a European tragedy that 1900 followed 1889.

In 1898 the Palais de l'Industrie of 1855 had been pulled down to make space for the construction of two new palaces of fine arts. Seldom, if ever, has art been so deeply adored: yet only the popular guide books could find the decrepit taste of 1900 laudable. Almost all intellectuals deplored both its paucity of originality and the strained attempts so clearly evident in it. To Augustus St. Gaudens, Henry Adams deplored the lack of a moral force behind the kind of art that appeared at the Exposition. Never before (and never since) had an exposition left so little trace on the art of the generation that followed it.

One of the happy results of the Crystal Palace Exhibition of 1851 had been the boost given to international co-operation on so many levels and in so many areas during the rest of the century. All the expositions prompted and witnessed the advance of idealistic, pacifistic cosmopolitanism over irrational, national exclusivism. By 1900 the world was united in scholarly communities and in many other groups whose interests crossed frontiers. Typical examples of this co-operation were the first International Peace Conferences that took place at The Hague at the time of the Exposition. But side by side with the growth of a spirit of co-operation there had also arisen traces of aggressive nationalism. At the Exposition itself one idealist noted:

> The people crowd the military exhibits, the great artillery works; the cannon and the quick-firing guns are the admiration of whole families; they stand spellbound before the plumes and gold lace, the tinsel and uniforms. Poor creatures![10]

In 1900 the principles and probable outcome of cosmopolitanism had become deeply suspect. The nations that entered into the last cultural demonstration of the nineteenth century did so with the intention and desire not to co-operate, but to compete. The recognized winners at the Exposition were the Americans for mechanical ingenuity, the Japanese for taste, and the Germans for almost everything else. In this exhausting competition France, except in the already outmoded categories of altruism, didactic encyclopaedism, and administrative grandeur, was hardly among the contestants at all.

Bibliography • A major purpose of this book is to encourage the investigation of other world's fairs. The abundant sources for studying the exposition movement could also be rich mines for scholars working in other areas of modern history. Printed sources relevant to all the expositions are enormous in extent and coverage and are sometimes easy to obtain as well. The French administrative report of 1900 alone consists of eight beautifully printed tomes of text, maps, tables, and illustrations. The forty-six volumes of published reports of the international juries are a veritable survey of the state of civilization at that time. In 1900 there were additional hundreds of French publications on art, technology, the international congresses, and the awards. The American, British, German, and other governments also published detailed official reports. The *Annuaire de la presse française* for the year 1900 lists twenty-six periodical publications that dealt solely or mostly with the exposition of that year. In addition, the great exposition was the occasion for the appearance of dozens of guide-books, hundreds of critical articles on taste or technique, thousands of pamphlets, and untold amounts of preserved archival material.

All the fairs were rich in content, incident, and significance. Considering the abundance and availability of materials, the fascination of the subject, and the relevance of the topic, it seems odd that so little has been written on them. The search for new ground to cover still has not carried American historians to the fairs of 1876 (Philadelphia), 1893 (Chicago), or 1904 (St. Louis). Each was important in American intellectual development, art history, and national and local history; each has enough scope for several detailed monographs.

The studies of expositions published after 1900 suffer from nearness to that event. Optimists wailed at the impending abandonment of these ecumenical congresses of progress. Cynics, who were more common, wrote polemics claiming that the big international fairs deluded a nation and squandered its human and financial resources. Almost all later secondary works in this century have been anecdotal. Historians have been dazzled by two (of perhaps fifteen) really large expositions: those of 1851 and 1889. More exactly, and more narrowly, exposition historiography has been unbalanced by studies of the Crystal Palace and the Eiffel Tower. Almost all surveys of significant parts of the nineteenth century (exceptions are those by Carleton J. H. Hayes and Jacques Chastenet, see bibliographical citations) have ignored the expositions. No one has opened the subject. Perhaps this is because of the almost overwhelming quantity of the sources, the complexity of the subject, and the difficulty of classifying it.

This bibliography is in two parts. The first is a comprehensive coverage of the Exposition of 1900. The citations of official reports will only suggest the riches that are listed, annotated, and indexed in the Signat bibliography. The other materials on 1900 are, for the most part, things that Mlle Signat missed: mostly they are citations of materials included in other publications and therefore not within her rubric. The second part of the bibliography is what I believe to be the most comprehensive bibliography on world's fairs compiled thus far. Except for items that were not published separately, the bibliographies of the Institut national des techniques de la documention in Paris give complete coverage of French exhibitions before 1937. The other bibliographies cover almost all the international exhibitions of the twentieth century, though not with the system or care of the INTD bibliographies. There is very little bibliographical coverage for non-French exhibitions (other than the Crystal Palace Exhibition of 1851) or for non-separately published materials on any expositions. The sample official reports reflect the period covered in this monograph. The gaps and weaknesses of the list of secondary works on world's fairs should suggest tasks for subsequent scholars.

The bibliography does not re-list all items cited in the notes. Materials dealing with the Dreyfus Affair or those not dealing specifically with the Exposition of 1900 will be easily identified from the notes.

The best place to study the French universal expositions is, of course, Paris. One should start with the INTD bibliographies (which give locations for libraries in Paris). The Bibliothèque de la Chambre de commerce de Paris is especially rich in official documents and has published its catalogue. The subject catalogue of the Bibliothèque nationale in Paris will direct the scholar to many articles and pamphlets not in the INTD bibliographies. The library of the Ministère des affaires étrangères was extremely useful for my discussion of the Dreyfus Affair. French consular officers watched the other nations' preparations for exhibitions very carefully. These observations reveal and illustrate the French concern for their own and for other expositions.

Brussels is the best place to study the movement for the regulation of international exhibitions after 1900. The Belgian national library has large and excellently catalogued collections dealing with world's fairs after about 1885, when the Belgians became very interested in them. The collection of the Bureau international des expositions in Paris is small and poorly catalogued. Until the Second World War, the Comité français des expositions was a natural place to obtain materials on world's fairs. Their library is still rich, but since a move some years ago, the collection has not been organized and is now inaccessible to the public.

Future North American researchers on world's fairs might save themselves time by going directly to the Widener Library, the New York Public Library, and the Library of Congress. The Library of Congress is useful for the exposition movement only after 1900, since it began systematic collecting after that date. The only special collection on international exhibitions in the United States was the one in the John Crerar Library in Chicago. Lack of interest in the subject has already led to the transfer of tons of its precious and unique documents, periodicals, and books to storage in the Center for Research Libraries (formerly the Midwest Interlibrary Center) in Chicago.

Actually, it might not even be necessary for a scholar to go to Europe to investigate the European international exhibitions. Documentation relating to them was published in fairly large editions and had a wide international distribution. Rows of splendid volumes packed with information are lying unused in many great libraries that were building their collections as the expositions were brightening the world. Unfortunately, they are exasperatingly difficult to locate in a large collection. This difficulty is caused by the requirement of English and American librarians that the main entry for publications by a corporate body (such as a state, a city, a ministry, or a group of businessmen—the usual directors of an exposition) be that of the corporate body. A further complication is that an international exhibition must be entered by its *official* title. The official title of the Chicago Exposition of 1893 is "The World's Columbian Exposition," but too few people know this, and few cataloguers have provided adequately for later generations of the curious. But publications about an exposition may show up almost anywhere in a library, with no author's name as a guide to tracing them. In the Library of Congress scheme most publications on world's fairs are included in "T," under "Technology." To learn of the role that an individual played in an exposition is extremely difficult, because there is no personal approach to the rich, published monuments that the expositions left behind.

In the bibliography I have followed the Library of Congress scheme for main entry and have listed a personal author when known. The novice researcher might profit from earnestly explaining his plight to a very wise old librarian, who might then shuffle through some slips and lead him to great banks of heavy, bound volumes filled with wonderful things.

I • Exposition of 1900

A. *Bibliographies*

SIGNAT, COLETTE. "Bibliographie analytique des documents publiés à l'occasion de l'Exposition universelle internationale de 1900 à Paris" (mimeographed), "Mémoire de fin d'études en vue de l'obtention du diplôme de l'Institut national des techniques de la documentation"), Paris: Conservatoire national des arts et métiers, 1959, 545 refs., 159 pp.
This bibliography includes only items published separately. It is remarkably complete and includes a great many items published in foreign languages. Locations are given for the Paris area. Important items have brief annotations. The bibliography includes directories of illustrative material (*iconographie*) and of music, for which there are ten entries. There are detailed subject and geographical indexes.

WENDTÉ, FREDERICA. "Reading List of Magazine Articles on the Paris Exposition, 1900," *Bulletin of Bibliography*, II, No. 3 (1900), p. 42.
Lists about 100 articles in technical and serious magazines.

B. *Newspapers*

L'Aurore (Paris). 1899–1900.
Berliner Tageblatt. 1900.
L'Est républicain (Nancy). 1894–1900.
L'Exposition de Paris (1900): Publié avec la collaboration d'écrivains spéciaux et des meilleurs artistes. 3 vols. Paris: Montgredien, 1899–1900.
One of the many newspapers devoted to the exposition. It was a weekly intended for the intelligent visitor, and contains descriptions of the attractions and special exhibits, a chronological account of special events, and hundreds of photographs taken specially for this periodical.

L'Exposition universelle 1900: Bulletin des lois, décrets et documents officiels relatifs à l'Exposition. "Directeur-Éditeur en Chef, Henri Gautier." Paris: 1896–1900.
Usually this journal appeared bi-monthly. It was intended for French exhibitors and printed, *in extenso*, documents, reports, legal regulations, and statistics of use to an audience that was vitally interested in anything that pertained to the exposition. It also contained gossip that the editor, Henri Gautier, could pick up in Paris. Since

he was close to the exposition as it developed he was, I believe, very dependable. This is one of the most important sources for this book.

Le Figaro (Paris). 1888–1901.

Frankfurter Zeitung. 1900.

La grande revue de l'Exposition: Supplément illustré de la Revue des Revues. Nos. 1–16 (November, 1899–October, 1900), 260 pp.

A chronological survey of the exposition's progress for the intelligent reader.

The New York Times. 1888–1905.

Le Siècle (Paris). 1897–1900.

Le Temps (Paris). 1892–1905.

The Times (London). 1892–1905.

C. Official Reports

BOUGE, AUGUSTE. *Rapport fait au nom de la commission chargée d'examiner le projet de loi relatif à l'Exposition de 1900.* Paris: Motteroy, 1896, 47 pp.

FRANCE. Ministère du commerce, de l'industrie, des postes et des télégraphes. *Exposition universelle de 1900 à Paris. Combinaison financière. Rapport du commissaire général et pièces annexes.* Paris: Imprimerie nationale, 1895, 34 pp.

—— Exposition universelle internationale de 1900 à Paris. Concours internationaux d'exercices physiques et de sports. *Rapports.* Paris: Imprimerie nationale, I (1901), 393 pp.; II (1902), 427 pp.

Summarizes carefully and in great detail the results of this particular competition. Includes photographs, graphs, and surveys the world of sport at that time. Pages 384–404 analyse American superiority in the track and field events and suggest implications for future athletic education in France.

—— Exposition universelle internationale de 1900. Direction générale de l'exploitation. *Règlements et programmes des concours nationaux et internationaux d'exercices physiques et de sports.* Paris: Imprimerie nationale, 1900, 464 pp.

A good illustration of the difficulties with main entry. Gives the rules and schedules of the planned events. This includes the Basque game, pelote, motorcycling, pigeon-shooting (Bois de Boulogne, Tuesday, June 26th), and ballooning (for which the precise compositions of gas and the dimensions of the vehicles are specified).

GERMANY. Reichskommissar für die Weltausstellung in Paris, 1900. *Amtlicher Katalog der Ausstellung des deutschen Reichs.* Berlin: Selbstverlag des Reichskommissariats, 1900, 440 pp.

Appeared also in a French and an English edition.

GREAT BRITAIN. Royal Commission on the Paris Exhibition, 1900. *Report of His Majesty's Commissioners for the Paris International Exhibition, 1900.* 2 vols. London: H.M.S.O., 1901.

JAPAN. Commission impériale à l'Exposition universelle de Paris, 1900. *Catalogue spécial officiel du Japon.* Paris: Lemercier, 1900, 150 pp.

PARIS. Exposition universelle internationale de 1900. *Catalogue général officiel.* 20 vols. Paris: Lemercier, 1900.

—— *Rapport général administratif et technique par Alfred Picard.* 8 vols. Paris: Imprimerie nationale, 1902.

—— *Rapport général sur les congrès de l'Exposition par M. de Chasseloup-Laubat.* Paris: Imprimerie nationale, 1901, 810 pp.

—— *Rapports du jury international.* 46 vols. Paris: Imprimerie nationale, 1902–1905.
These reports follow the classification scheme and are indexed in Signat's bibliography (see above). They are penetrating and honest. The list of jury members might be considered a partial *Who's Who* of the era.

PICARD, ALFRED. *Le bilan d'un siècle (1801–1900).* 6 vols. Paris: Imprimerie nationale, 1906.
A survey of the contents of the exposition by its commissioner general. Emphasizes the retrospective exhibits in art.

UNITED STATES. Commission to the Paris Exposition, 1900. *Report of the Commissioner-General for the United States to the International Universal Exposition, Paris, 1900.* 6 vols. Washington: Government Printing Office, 1901.
These are Senate documents. The personal author is Ferdinand Peck, the American commissioner general.

D. Books, Collected Articles, and Pamphlets

ADAMS, HENRY. *The Education of Henry Adams: An Autobiography.* Boston: Houghton Mifflin, 1918 (Privately printed, 1906), 519 pp.

—— *The Selected Letters of Henry Adams.* Edited by Newton Arvin. New York: Farrar, Straus and Cudahy, 1951, 279 pp.

ALEXANDRE, ARSÈNE. *L'Œuvre de Rodin.* Paris: Société d'édition artistique, 1900, xix, 29 pp.
An illustrated catalogue of Rodin's exhibition.

BABIN, GUSTAVE. *Après faillite: Souvenirs de l'Exposition de 1900.* Paris: Dujarric, 1902, 296 pp.
Babin's collected articles for this period. He loathed the exposition, and this is a bitter, sad polemic. A extreme illustration of the French turning away from this kind of international idealism. These essays are also an extended harangue against the exposition's architecture and decoration.

Les beaux-arts et les arts decoratifs à l'Exposition universelle de 1900. Paris: Gazette des beaux arts, 1900, 526 pp.
A lavishly printed, favourable survey.

BERGERET, GASTON. *Journal d'un nègre à l'Exposition de 1900.* Paris: L. Conquet, 1901, 63 pp.
Simple and humorous observations "traduit par Bergeret." The exquisite illustrations are water-coloured by hand. An example of a fine hand-made book of the time.

BOYD, JAMES P. *The Paris Exposition of 1900.* No place, published by the author, 1900, 583 pp.
A platitudinous survey that contains photos not available elsewhere. Written by an American chiefly for Americans.

BRISSON, ADOLPHE. *Scènes et types de l'Exposition.* Paris: Montgredien, [1901?].
A collection of previously published anecdotal articles about distinguished visitors, taste, etc. Contains much information about the "tone" of the exposition that is unavailable elsewhere.

CHAMPIER, VICTOR (ed.). *Les industries d'art à l'Exposition universelle de 1900.* Paris: Revue des arts décoratifs, 1902, 254 pp.
A non-official and very critical survey of decorative art at the exposition. Fine illustrations. One of the several authors was Émile Gallé.

Comité du souvenir du Président Alfred Picard. *Cérémonie d'inauguration de la plaque commemorative de sa naissance.* Paris: A. Davy, 1924, 32 pp.
Contains biographical information on the exposition's commissioner general.

L'Exposition et Paris au vingtième siècle. Paris: Magasins du Bon Marché, 1900, 382 pp.
A guidebook.

Führer durch die Weltausstellung 1900 in Paris. Leipzig: Woerl's Reisebuchverlag, 1900, 114 pp.
A German guidebook.

GENTSCH, WILHELM. *Die Weltausstellung in Paris 1900 und ihre Ergebnisse in technisch-wirtschaftlicher Beziehung.* Berlin: C. Haymann, 1901, 104 pp.
Mostly concerned with the technical operation of the exposition. Also contains good statistical tables comparing the Exposition of 1900 with its predecessors.

GERS, PAUL. *En 1900.* Corbeil: E. Crété, 1901, 298 pp.
A variety of anecdotal articles about people at and aspects of the exposition, such as ticket sellers, restaurants, the national exhibits, famous visitors, etc.

HALLAYS, ANDRÉ. *A Travers l'Exposition de 1900.* Paris: Perrin et cie, 1901, 303 pp.
A collection of previously published articles by another writer who hated the exposition.

HÉNARD, EUGÈNE. *L'Exposition de 1900 devant le parlement.* Paris: G. Delarue, 1896, 23 pp.

HOLMES, BURTON. *Round About Paris. Paris Exposition (The Burton Holmes Lectures, II),* Battle Creek, Mich.: Little-Preston Co., 1901.

LAHOR, JEAN. *L'Art Nouveau: Son histoire, L'Art Nouveau étranger à*

l'Exposition, L'Art Nouveau au point de vue social. Paris: Lemerre, 1901, 104 pp.
A fine survey of Art Nouveau in 1900 by an admirer of William Morris. The discussion provides an explanation of Art Nouveau's intellectual and social content.

Ligue lorraine de décentralisation. *Pas d'Exposition en 1900!* Nancy: Imprimerie coopérative de l'Est, 1895, 33 pp.
A clever and strong condemnation of the project then under consideration. Used by all later critics of the exposition, most particularly by certain provincial deputies. An important event in the history of French expositions.

MALHERBE, G. DE. *Le pavillon finlandais.* Paris: Imprimerie de Vaugirard, 1900, 52 pp.

MARX, ROGER. *La décoration et les industries d'art à l'Exposition de 1900.* Paris: Ch. Delagrave, 1902, 130 pp.
A survey of decorative art in 1900. Contains many fine plates not reproduced elsewhere.

MEIER-GRAEFE, JULIUS. *Die Weltausstellung in Paris: 1900.* Paris: Verlag von Krüger, 1900, 211 pp.

MELLERIO, ANDRÉ. *L'Exposition de 1900 et l'Impressionisme.* Paris: H. Floury, 1900, 46 pp.
An attack on the admitting juries for discriminating against the independent painters who, the author felt, were the glories of French art.

MORAND, PAUL. *1900 A.D.* Translated by Mrs. Romilly Fedden. New York: William Farquhar Payson, 1931, 206 pp.
A witty survey of Paris in that year. The chapter "The Palace of Illusion or the Great Exhibition" (pp. 59–108) is a brilliant impressionistic survey of the exposition.

NAUMANN, FRIEDRICH. *Ausstellungsbriefe.* Berlin: Buchverlag der "Hilfe," 1909, 224 pp.
A collection of previously published articles on exhibitions by an exceptionally sensitive German. Pages 52–115 discuss the Exposition of 1900.

The Nineteen Hundred: Monthly Illustrated Journal Containing All The Laws, Decrees and Official Documents of The Paris Universal Exposition of 1900. A Pictorial and Literary History. Paris.
A careful, well-illustrated periodical intended for English-speaking exhibitors. Apparently began publication in 1895.

QUANTIN, A. *L'Exposition du siècle.* Paris: Le monde moderne, 1900, 367 pp.
A periodical, later bound, devoted to the content and progress of the exposition. The tone of the articles and illustrations suggest that this was directed at a mildly chauvinistic, lower middle-class audience.

WAILLY, G. DE. *A travers l'Exposition de 1900.* Paris: Fayard frères, 1900.
A monthly, later bound, of sixteen issues. It is a hypothetical "tour" through the exposition grounds by "types" who observe and comment to one another on what they see. Most commentators are bourgeois or skilled workers; they were probably the intended readers.

WITT, OTTO N. *Pariser Weltausstellungsbriefe.* Berlin: R. Mückenberger, 1900, 145 pp.
A epistolatory record of a tour. It is derogatory of France's performance. The first sentence begins, significantly, "Die Welt ist ausstellungsmüde . . . ."

E. Articles

A. R. "La Russie à l'Exposition de 1900," *La Nouvelle Revue*, VI (September 15, 1900), 201–18.
Uncritical, laudatory article.

AFLALO, F. G. "Promise of International Exhibitions," *Fortnightly Review*, LXXIII (May, 1900), 830–9.
A preview of the Exposition of 1900 for Englishmen. Also good for an explanation of the reasons for British coolness to this exposition.

ALEXANDRE, ARSÈNE. "Le concours de l'Exposition de 1900," *Le Figaro*, July 9, 1896, p. 2.
A scornful critique of the winning projects for architecture and decoration at the exposition.

BABIN, GUSTAVE. "L'Exposition de 1900," *La Quinzaine*, IV, No. 125 (January 1, 1900), 96–108.
A somewhat hostile prediction.

—— "Les ruines de l'Exposition," *L'Illustration*, CXVIII, No. 3049 (August 3, 1901), 72–3.

BARRÈS, MAURICE. "Les allemands à l'Exposition, " *Le Journal*, September 25, 1900.

—— "On peut éviter l'Exposition de 1900," *Le Figaro*, August 2, 1895.

—— "Les parisiens et l'Exposition," *Le Figaro*, September 23, 1895.

—— "Sur l'Exposition de 1900: Note en réponse à M. Picard," *Le Figaro*, August 24, 1895.
The last three are well-written polemics opposing the exposition as an offence to public morality and to French national integrity. These are especially interesting since they are illustrations of Barrès' views on patriotism at the time.

BEER, ÉMILE. "Contre 1900!" *Le Figaro*, August 22, 1895.
Attacks Maurice Barrès (see above) and defends the coming exposition as a needed boost to the economy.

CALONNE, ALPHONSE DE. "L'Exposition de 1900 à Paris, Programme et concours," *Revue des Deux Mondes*, LXIV (January 15, 1895), 354–71.
Reviews some of the early disputes about placement of the exposition, the decorative style to be used, etc.

CHARDON, HENRI. "L'Exposition de 1900," *Revue de Paris*, III, Part I (February 1, 1896), 630–57.
A detailed story of the progress of the exposition to that date. The article is part of the public dispute about the usefulness of the coming exposition, and is a refutation of Mirbeau's polemical attack on the plans (see below).

CHAUDARY, COMTE DE. "L'Exposition de 1900," *Le Figaro*, March 13, 1896. Opposes plans for the exposition, claiming they will inhibit French diplomatic flexibility for years.

CORDAY, MICHEL. "Les étrangers à l'Exposition," *La Revue de Paris*, VI, No. 6 (December 1, 1899), 557–80.

——— "La genèse de l'Exposition," *La Revue de Paris*, VI, No. 4 (July 15, 1899), 430–52.

COSTE, M. "Impressions de l'Exposition universelle de 1900," *Revue internationale de sociologie*, December, 1900, 884–97.
A verbatim report to a meeting of scholars. In considering what the exposition did that was new or that was beneficial to France, Coste says it accomplished little.

FOREST, LOUIS. "L'Allemagne nouvelle," *L'Illustration*, CXVI, No. 3012 (November 17, 1900), 310–13; No. 3014 (December 1, 1900), 342–43.
A survey of the transformation of Germany, written in the light of what it exhibited at the exposition.

GEDDES, PATRICK. "The Closing Exhibition—Paris 1900," *The Contemporary Review*, LXXVIII, No. 419 (November, 1900), 653–68.
A brilliant survey, appreciation, and critique.

GIDE, CHARLES. "La liquidation de l'Exposition universelle," *Revue d'économie politique*, XV, No. 6 (June, 1901), 674–7.
A sober analysis of the costs of expositions. Gide favors expositions for their moral, not their economic benefits.

JOUBERT, LOUIS. "Fin de rêve. L'Exposition universelle de 1900," *Correspondant*, CCI, No. 4 (November 24, 1900), 771–84.
An attack on the administration of the exposition by an anti-republican nationalist.

LAIR, M. "Après l'Exposition," *Réforme Sociale*, XLI (February 1, 1901), 233–50.
An intelligent critique. Lair believes the exposition failed mostly because of exterior causes, *e.g.* hot weather and the war in the Far East. He is pessimistic about the future of expositions.

LEROY-BEAULIEU, ANATOLE. "Les grands inconvénients des foires universelles et la nécessité d'y renoncer," *Économiste français*, December 7, 1895, 729–31.
A vigorous and often-quoted attack on the principle of expositions. This article is an early illustration of a *fin de siècle* defensiveness on the part of French nationalists.

MÉLINE, JULES. "Faut-il faire l'Exposition de 1900?" *République française*, August 24, 1895, p. 1.
A criticism of the government's handling of the plans by a powerful politician. This statement, like that of the Ligue lorraine de décentralisation, was often quoted in subsequent debates.

MIRBEAU, OCTAVE. "Pourquoi des expositions?" *Revue des Deux Mondes*, CXXXII (December 15, 1895), 888–908.
A condemnation of the principle of expositions by a noted nationalist and man of letters.

MOUREY, GABRIEL. "Round the Exhibition—I. The House of Art Nouveau Bing," *The Studio*, XX, No. 87 (June, 1900), 164–80.

NORMAND, MAURICE. "L'Allemagne à l'Exposition," *L'Illustration*, CXVI, No. 2994 (July 14, 1900), 24–7.
A careful article combining admiration with a sober appraisal of German economic power.

——— "L'Exposition, est-elle un succès?" *L'Illustration*, CXVI, No. 3000 (August 25, 1900), p. 111.

——— "La Russie à l'Exposition," *L'Illustration*, CXV, No. 2984 (May 5, 1900), 280–8.
Normand, unlike most other French observers, saw propaganda and vulgarity in the Russian exhibits.

OSBORN, MAX. "S. Bing's Art Nouveau auf der Weltausstellung," *Deutsche Kunst und Dekoration*, VI (April, 1900–September, 1900), 555–69.

ROGERS, J. M. "Lessons from International Expositions," *Forum* (New York), XXXII, No. 4 (December, 1901), 500–10.

ROUSIERS, PAUL DE. "La puissance commerciale de l'Allemagne," *La Revue de Paris*, Part One, VII, No. 15 (August 1, 1900), 506–34; Part Two, VII, No. 18 (September 15, 1900) 280–308.

——— "Le port de Hambourg" *ibid.*, VII, No. 20 (October 15, 1900), 735–73.
Warnings that were especially timely in the light of the German exhibits then in Paris.

LA SIZERANNE, ROBERT DE. "L'Art à l'Exposition de 1900," *Revue des Deux Mondes*: I, "L'Esthétique du fer," CLIX (May 1, 1900), 175–206; II, "Le bilan de l'Impressionisme," CLIX (June 1, 1900), 629–51; III, "Les dieux de l'heure," (August 1, 1900), 587–606; IV, "Avons-nous un style moderne?" CLX (October 15, 1900), 866–97.
An intelligent survey.

VOGÜÉ, EUGÈNE-MELCHIOR DE. "Au seuil d'un siècle: Cosmopolitisme et nationalisme," *Revue des Deux Mondes*, Période 5, I (February 1, 1901), 677–92.
A discussion of nationalism in the light of the exposition.

——— "La défunte Exposition," *Revue des Deux Mondes*, (November 15, 1900), pp. 380–99.
A bitter, pessimistic appraisal of the organization and content of the exposition. Beautifully written. This article contrasts dramatically with Vogüé's praise in 1889.

"Weltausstellungen und Revanchekrieg," *Allgemeine Zeitung* (Munich), July 8, 1892, p. 1.
An example of German alarm at French aggressiveness in declaring the Exposition of 1900 early.

ZACHER, "Ausländische Sozialpolitik und die Pariser Weltausstellung 1900," *Soziale Praxis*, VII, No. 25 (March 24, 1898), 646–9.
An editorial urging heavy German participation in the social welfare sections.

II • International Exhibitions

A. *Bibliographies*

PLINVAL SALGUES, RÉGINE DE. "Bibliographie des expositions industrielles et commerciales en France, depuis l'origine, jusqu'à 1867" (mimeographed, "Mémoire de fin d'études en vue de l'obtention du diplôme de l'Institut national des techniques de la documentation" [hereafter, "Mémoire, I.N.T.D."]), Paris: Conservatoire national des arts et métiers, 1960, 1020 refs., 185 pp.
The most thorough of the I.N.T.D. bibliographies. This gives source materials for all the French national exhibitions as well as for the universal expositions of 1855 and 1867. It also includes tables of area covered, attendance, and costs of expositions through 1867.

FAMY, COLETTE, "Bibliographie analytique de l'Exposition universelle tenue à Paris en 1878" (mimeographed, "Mémoire, I.N.T.D."), Paris, 1962, 193 refs., 71 pp.

MARTINIÈRE, VÉRONIQUE DE LA. "Bibliographie des documents ayant paru à l'occasion de l'Exposition universelle de 1889 à Paris" (mimeographed, "Mémoire, I.N.T.D."), Paris, 1959, 663 refs., 207 pp.

SIGNAT, COLETTE. See entry in section IA of this bibliography.

PELLETIER, MONIQUE. "L'Œuvre civilisatrice des puissances européens vue à travers les expositions coloniales et internationales de 1900 à 1931" (mimeographed, "Mémoire, I.N.T.D."), Paris, 1963, 255 refs., 63 pp.
This covers both French and non-French exhibitions. The coverage is less thorough than it is in the other I.N.T.D. bibliographies.

U.S. Library of Congress. Division of Bibliography. "List of References on Expositions in the United States and Foreign Countries, 1918–1928" (type-written), Washington, D.C., 1928, 16 pp.
—— "A Selected List of References on Fairs and Expositions, 1928–1939." (Typewritten, compiled by Florence S. Hellman), Washington, D.C., 1938, 49 pp.

HELTON, H. STEPHEN. "Records of United States Participation in International Conferences, Commissions, and Expositions" (mimeographed) (Preliminary Inventories, No. 76). Washington, D.C.: The National Archives, 1955, 161 pp.
Rough inventories of materials at the National Archives for studying foreign and domestic exhibitions. A great deal of other archival material (not in this work) related to American participation is in other archival repositories, particularly collections of correspondence between the Department of State and U.S. ministers abroad.

LASNIER, ALBERT (comp.). "Références sur les expositions (1937–1964)" (mimeographed). Québec: Albert Lasnier, 1964, 220 pp.

Not annotated. Useful (although far from complete) for the expositions Paris 1937, New York 1939, and Brussels 1958. The bulk of the entries deal with preparations for "Expo '67" (Montreal).

B. Periodicals

Allgemeine Ausstellungszeitung (Berlin), 1878–1914.
A journal, usually appearing twice a month, that had as its purpose to promote the interests of German industrialists who exhibited at the international fairs.
Comité français des expositions. *Bulletin officiel* (Paris), 1909–1921.
Of varying periodicity and contents. For the most part, it listed news items such as lists of members, schedules of coming exhibitions, and relevant government actions.

C. Selected Official Documents

Conférence diplomatique relative aux expositions internationales, Paris, 12–22 November 1928. Paris: Imprimerie nationale, 1928, 558 pp.

Convention signée à Paris le 22 novembre 1928, modifiée le 10 mai 1948, relative aux expositions internales. Paris: Bureau international des expositions, 1960, 90 pp.

FRANCE. Commission. Louisiana Purchase Exposition, St. Louis, 1904. *Rapport officiel*. Paris: Imprimerie nationale, 1905.

FRANCE. Commission. World's Columbian Exhibition, Chicago, 1893. *Rapport officiel*, 2 vols. Paris, Imprimerie nationale, 1894.
The personal author is Camille Krantz.

GERMANY. Reichskommission. Weltausstellung in Chicago, 1893. *Amtlicher Bericht über die Weltausstellung in Chicago 1893*. 2 vols. Berlin: Reichsdrückerei, 1894.

GERMANY. Reichskommission. Weltausstellung in Saint Louis, 1904. *Amtlicher Bericht über die Weltausstellung in Saint Louis, 1904*. Berlin: Reichsdrückerei, 1906.

PARIS. Exposition internationale, 1937. Ministère du Commerce et de l'Industrie. Exposition internationale des arts et techniques dans la vie moderne (1937). *Rapport générale*. 11 vols. Paris: Imprimerie nationale, 1938.
Personal author is Edmond Labbé, commissioner general.

PARIS. Exposition universelle de 1855. *Rapport sur l'Exposition universelle de 1855*. Paris: Imprimerie Impériale, 1857.
The personal author is Prince Napoléon.

PARIS. Exposition universelle de 1867. *Rapport de la commission impériale. Précis des opérations et liste des collaborateurs avec un appendice sur l'avenir des expositions*. Paris: Imprimerie Impériale, 1869.
The personal author is Frédéric Le Play.

PARIS. Exposition universelle, 1878. *Rapport administratif.* 2 vols. Paris: Imprimerie nationale, 1881.
The personal author is Camille Krantz.

────── *Congrès et conférence du Palais du Trocadéro, Comptes rendus publiés sous la direction de Ch. Thirion.* 24 vols. Paris: Imprimerie nationale, 1879–1881.

PARIS. Exposition universelle, 1889. *Rapport général.* 10 vols. Paris: Imprimerie nationale, 1890–1892.
Personal author is Alfred Picard. Vol. I contains the best history of world's fairs written until that time.

D. Secondary Works

BARWICK, G. F. International Exhibitions and their Civilizing Influence," in James Samuelson, *The Civilization of our Day.* London: Sampson Low, Marston and Co., 1896, 301–13.

BERGER, H. GEORGES. *Les expositions universelles internationales: leur passé, leur rôle actuel, leur avenir.* Paris, Arthur Rousseau, 1901, 164 pp.
Berger believed that expositions produce no economic or political benefits and that in the light of the disappointments in 1900, there could be no more great expositions. Berger assembled many tables of economic data to prove his points, but the emotional tone of his polemics makes all his arguments suspect.

BRANDT, O. "Zur Geschichte und Würdigung der Weltausstellungen," *Zeitschrift für Sozialwissenschaften,* VII (1907), 81–99.
A proposal for even greater German participation in foreign exhibitions, urging that Germany be host at a great world's fair. Summarizes German participation in the world's fairs to that date.

BREVAN, E. DE. "Liste sommaire des publications du Comité français des expositions à l'étranger 1895–1916." Bulletin officiel: *Comité français des expositions à l'étranger.* Nos. 1–10 (January–December, 1916), 23–32.

CHASTENET, JACQUES. *Histoire de la troisième république.* Vol. I: *L'Enfance de la troisième, 1870–1879.* Vol. II: *La république des républicains, 1879–1893.* Vol. III: *La république triomphante, 1893–1906.* Paris: Hachette, 1952–1955.
Volumes II and III each have a chapter, "L'Année de l'Exposition," on 1889 and 1900 respectively.

COCKX, A. AND LEMMENS, J. *Les expositions universelles et internationales en Belgique de 1885 à 1958.* Brussels: "Editorial office," 1958, 176 pp.
The Exposition of 1958 is not covered.

COLMONT, ACHILLE DE. *Histoire des expositions des produits de l'industrie française.* Paris: Guillaumin, 1855, 566 pp.
Though drily written, this is the best survey of the early national expositions.

Comité français des expositions à l'étranger. *Conférence diplomatique concernant les expositions internationales, Berlin 1912.* Paris: Comité français des expositions à l'étranger, 1913, 106 pp.

Comité français des expositions et comité nationale des expositions coloniales. *Cinquantenaire, 1885–1935.* Asnières: Les presses de la S.I.M.A.G., 1935, 328 pp.
Though principally a history of the Comité, this is one of the best histories of expositions available.

Comité français des expositions à l'étranger. *Historique, 1890–1910.* Paris: Bourse de commerce, 1910, 70 pp.

CORNELL, ELIAS. *De stora utställningarna: Arkitekturexperiment och kulturhistoria.* Stockholm: Natur och kultur, 1952, 257 pp.
An architectural history of exhibition and display technique. Good coverage of the nineteenth and twentieth centuries. Unusual illustrations of projected as well as completed exhibition buildings—all from contemporary sources.

CURTI, MERLE. "America at the World Fairs, 1851–1893," *American Historical Review*, LV, No. 4 (July, 1950), 833–56.
These "tournaments of industry . . . provided a mirror for the changing attitudes of the rest of the world toward American civilization" (p. 833).

DEMY, ADOLPHE. *Essai historique sur les expositions universelles de Paris.* Paris: Picard, 1907, 1096 pp.
Long and heavily documented, this is probably the best available treatment of the subject. In writing soon after the Exposition of 1900, Demy was defensive, sensitive, and exceptional in that he proposed the continuation of the expositions as national policy.

DONCOURT, A. S. DE. *Les expositions universelles.* Lille: J. Lefort, 1889, 308 pp.
An apparently hastily compiled survey. Actually discusses expositions very little. Some unusual illustrations.

DORFF, ALFRED AND PHOLIEN, JOSEPH. *Les expositions et le droit: Etude des principales questions juridiques.* Brussels: Misch et Thron, 1910, 288 pp.

DUPAYS, PAUL. *Vie prestigieuse des expositions historiques.* Paris: H. Didier, 1939, 285 pp.
A survey by a journalist. Anecdotal, undocumented.

"Esposizione," *Enciclopedia italiana*, XIV, 361–7.

"Exhibition," *Encyclopaedia Britannica* (11th ed.), X, 67–71.
The articles "Exhibitions and Fairs" in recent editions of the *Britannica* have been variously mutilated and amended versions of the fine article in the eleventh edition. The Exposition of 1900 is not mentioned in the 1965 edition.

FORD, GUY STANTON. "Exhibitions, International," *Encyclopedia of the Social Sciences*. New York: Macmillan, 1930–1935, VI, 23–7.
Interpretive article assessing their importance in history.

FOUGÈRE, HENRY. *Les délégations ouvrières aux expositions universelles sous le Second Empire.* Montluçon: A. Herbin. 1905, 218 pp.
Mostly a discussion of Napoleon III's policy toward the workers' movement.

GEDDES, PATRICK. *Industrial Exhibitions and Modern Progress.* Edinburgh: D. Douglas, 1887, 57 pp.

GÉRAULT, GEORGES. *Les expositions universelles envisagées au point de vue de leurs résultats économiques.* Paris: Larose, 1902, 211 pp.
Contains many useful bibliographical citations of newspaper and periodical articles for the years 1895–1896. The economic evidence against expositions is impassioned and untrustworthy. Gérault believes that expositions drain the countryside to favour a few Parisian profiteers and manufacturers of luxuries.

GIBBS-SMITH, C. H. *The Great Exhibition of 1851: A Commemorative Album.* London: H.M.S.O., 1950, 142 pp.
The most charming and analytical survey of the Crystal Palace Exhibition. Well illustrated from contemporary sources.

GIEDION, SIEGFRIED. *Space, Time and Architecture: The Growth of a New Tradition.* 3rd ed. Cambridge: Harvard University Press, 1954, 778 pp.
A section, "The Great Exhibitions," (241–88), discusses exhibition architecture between 1851 and 1900.

GLEIZE, JULES. "L'Exportation française et les expositions," *La Nouvelle Revue,* XXXV (July 15, 1906), 195–202.
In the light of the dramatic increases in German exports, the writer advises France, like Germany, to participate more heavily in expositions abroad.

HAYES, CARLETON J. H. *A Generation of Materialism: 1871–1900.* New York: Harper and Brothers, 1941.
Has a few paragraphs on the universal expositions of the later nineteenth century.

"Historique du Comité français des expositions à l'étranger," *Annuaire 1912–1913: Comité français des expositions,* pp. 27–63.
Part of the *Bulletin* of the Comité français des expositions for the year 1914.

HOBHOUSE, CHRISTOPHER. *1851 and the Crystal Palace.* Revised edition with an Introduction by Osbert Lancaster. London: John Murray, 1950, 181 pp.
One of the few books on this exhibition that discusses things other than architecture or taste. Contains some good quotations of contemporary sources.

ISAAC, MAURICE. *Les expositions en France et dans le régime international.* Paris: Dorbon aîné, 1928, 350 pp.
Deals almost entirely with the period since 1900 and the role of the Comité français des expositions in the campaign to have expositions strictly regulated by national governments and diplomatic conventions. A careful work; well documented and clearly organized. Reprints many documents.

—— *Les expositions internationales.* Paris: Librairie Larousse, 1936, 406 pp.
Concerned mostly with the organization, functioning, purposes, and rules of the Bureau international des expositions. Contains many documents.

ISAY, RAYMOND. *Panorama des expositions universelles*. Paris: Gallimard, 1937, 229 pp.
A lively, witty survey of French expositions. One of the few works on the subject published in recent years. It appears to be accurate, though undocumented.

LACOINTA, FÉLIX. *Les expositions internationales, universelles ou spéciales, au point de vue du droit*. Paris: A. Rousseau, 1896, 278 pp.
Deals mostly with regulations for the safety of property, insurance, etc. The "Introduction historique" (pp. 5–26) is a good survey of expositions before 1900.

LESSING, JULIUS. *Das halbe Jahrhundert der Weltausstellungen*. Berlin: L. Simon, 1900, 30 pp.

LUCKHURST, KENNETH W. *The Story of Exhibitions*. London: Studio Publications, 1951, 221 pp.
A recent survey. The author is really interested in the Crystal Palace Exhibition of 1851; coverage of other exhibitions is cursory.

PAGÈS, ALBERT. *Les expositions publiques et le droit administratif*. Toulouse: Henri Cleder, 1931, 244 pp.
A good bibliography of books on the law and diplomacy of expositions is on pp. 239–41.

PAQUET, DR. ALFONS. *Das Ausstellungsproblem in der Volkswirtschaft*. Jena: Gustave Fischer, 1908, 353 pp.
An extremely careful book that analyses the reasons for the changes in the movement after 1900. Deals with far more than economics. Is especially useful for its good citations of German works relevant to the exposition movement. New York Public Library has this entered under Jena, Universität, Abhandlungen des staatswissenschaftlichen Seminars, Band 5, Heft 2. Several libraries have a pamphlet (44 pp.) with the same author and title.

POIRIER, RENÉ. *Des foires, des peoples, des expositions*. Paris: Plon, 1958, 258 pp.
Covers all types of fairs and contains many undocumented anecdotes about the French universal expositions. The most recent survey.

REEKIE, GORDON. "Expositions, Exhibits, and Today's Museums," *Natural History*, LXXIII, No. 6 (June-July, 1964), 20–29.
An illustrated general article on how present day museum technique evolved out of the expositions of the nineteenth century.

REGNIER, NOËL. *Revue et examen des expositions nationales et internationales en France et à l'étranger depuis 1798 jusqu'à 1878*. Paris: Sault, 1878, 483 pp.
A careful investigation of the industrial aspects of the expositions. Cites many relevant contemporary documents. Probably used by many later secondary works.

TAMIR, M. *Les expositions internationales à travers les âges*. Paris: Galerie Jeanne Boucher, 1939, 203 pp.
A doctoral thesis at the University of Paris. The notes and bibliographies are unreliable. Also it appears to be a partial plagiarization of Demy, *Essai historique*.

Interesting only because it is rather recent and because it gives statistical summaries of smaller international exhibitions, about which there are no secondary treatments.

THORNE, ANTHONY. *So Long at the Fair.* New York: Random House, 1947, 212 pp.
A novel, the plot of which deals with the serious attitude of the French towards the great expositions. The one discussed here is 1889. This book was later made into a movie.

WATERS, H. W. *History of Fairs and Expositions: Their Classification, Functions and Values.* London, Canada: Reid Bros., 1939, 158 pp.
Pages 34–43 discuss "International or World Fairs."

ZETTER, G. *Évolution des foires et marchés à travers les siècles.* Paris: Comité de la foire de Paris, 1923, 190 pp.
Deals only with small, local, commercial markets, especially in Paris.

Note to Preface

1 *1900 A.D.* Translated by Mrs. Romilly Fedden. (New York, 1931), p. 61.

Notes to Chapter One

1 Kenneth Luckhurst, *The Story of Exhibitions* (London, 1851), p. 64.

2 See Charles Simian, *François de Neufchâteau et les expositions* (Paris, 1889).

3 "Les Français ont étonné l'Europe par la rapidité de leurs exploits guerriers; ils doivent s'élancer avec la même ardeur dans la carrière du commerce et des arts de la paix." Reprinted in *L'Exposition universelle 1900: Bulletin des lois, décrets et documents officiels relatifs à l'Exposition*, No. 74 (April 25–26, 1897). P. 3.

4 Guillaume Deeping, *La première exposition des produits de l'industrie française, en l'an VI (1798) (d'après les documents)* (Paris, 1893).

5 See Comité français des Expositions et Comité National des Expositions coloniales, *Cinquantenaire, 1885–1935* (Asnières, 1935) (hereafter, *Cinquantenaire*) for good summaries and reprinted title pages of the reports of early national industrial exhibitions in France. For a splendid bibliography, see Régine de Plinval-Salgues, "Bibliographie analytique des expositions industrielles et commerciales en France depuis l'origine jusqu'à 1867" (Paris, 1960) (mimeographed).

6 *Cinquantenaire*, p. 11.

7 See Plinval-Salgues, "Bibliographie analytique."

8 "Pourquoi les Expositions sont-elles encore restreintes? pourquoi ne sont-elles pas faites sur une échelle vraiment large et libérale? Pourquoi craignons-nous d'ouvrir nos salles d'Exposition aux manufacturiers que nous appellons étrangers: aux Belges, aux Anglais, aux Suisses, aux Allemands? Qu'elle serait belle, qu'elle serait riche une Exposition Européenne! quelle mine d'instruction elle offrirait pour tous!" Boucher de Perthes, président de la Société d'Emulation d'Abbéville, quoted in *Cinquantenaire*, p. 28.

9 *Cinquantenaire*, p. 22. The discussion here blames the French Chambers of Commerce for defeating these proposals.

10 Quoted in C. H. Gibbs-Smith (comp.), *The Great Exhibition of 1851: A Commemorative Album* (London, 1851), pp. 8–10.

11 In 1854 the building was dismantled and re-erected on Sydenham Hill, where it was a tourist attraction until it was destroyed by fire the evening of November 30, 1936. See Christopher Hobhouse, *1851 and the Crystal Palace* (revised edition with an Introduction by Osbert Lancaster; London, 1950), pp. 147–65.

12 Luckhurst, *Story of Exhibitions*, p. 116.

13 *Ibid.*, p. 114.

14 Paris, Exposition universelle, 1855, *Rapport sur l'Exposition universelle de 1855 (installation, lois et décrets, statistiques, résultats financiers) par le Prince Napoléon* (Paris, 1857).

15 See Henry Fougère, *Les délégations ouvrières aux expositions sous le Second Empire* (Montluçon, 1905).

16 Patrick Geddes called his "one of the freshest minds of the century." Geddes, "The Closing Exhibition—Paris 1900," *The Contemporary Review*, LXXVIII, No. 419 (November 1900), p. 655.

17 Peter Selz and Mildred Constantine (eds.), *Art Nouveau: Art and Design at the Turn of the Century* (New York, 1959), p. 65.

18 Paris, Exposition universelle, 1867, *Rapport de la commission impériale: Précis des opérations et liste des collaborateurs avec un appendice sur l'avenir des expositions . . .* , par F. Le Play (Paris, 1869).

19 "Le dernier écolier de la dernière école, le plus incapable, le plus ignorant, le plus mal doué, est un homme après tout, et puisqu'il est un homme, il est fait pour connaître la verité, pour comprendre et vivre par elle." Quoted in *Cinquantenaire*, p. 43.

20 Pierre de la Gorce, *Histoire du second empire* (Paris, 1905–1907), V, p. 161.

21 See Le Play's appendix to his official report for 1867.

22 ". . . the only International Exhibition which has ever been promoted and supported mainly for political purposes." G. F. Barwick, "International Exhibitions and their Civilising Influences," in J. Samuelson, *The Civilisation of our Day* (London, 1896), p. 311.

23 See Paris, Exposition universelle, 1878, *Rapport administratif . . . par J. B. Krantz*, 2 vols. (Paris, 1881).

24 See Paris, Exposition universelle, 1878, *Congrès et conférences du palais du Trocadéro, comptes rendus publiés sous la direction de Ch. Thirion*, 24 vols. (Paris, 1881).

25 ". . . elle fut utile, elle était indispensable pour montrer à l'Europe étonnée la vitalité de la France, son énergie, ses progrès après des défaites que beaucoup avaient cru irréparables pour nous. Peut-être aurait-on dû s'arrêter là." H. Georges Berger, Les Expositions universelles internationales (leur passé, leur rôle actuel, leur avenir).

26 Guy Chapman, *The Third Republic of France: The First Phase, 1871–1894* (London, 1962), p. 189. See also M. de Marcère, "L'Exposition universelle de 1878," Chap. III of *Le seize mai et la fin du septennat* (*Histoire de la république 1876–1879*, II) (Paris, 1910).

27 The London Exhibition of 1862 attracted more people and exhibited more than the one of 1851. But internationalism was acceptable then; it was not a "first" and lost money. One of its organizers wailed, "Oh, for the opposition of 1851! That's a stimulant that's wanting now." (Luckhurst, *Story of Exhibitions*, p. 130.)

28 See M. Tamir, *Les expositions internationales à travers les âges* (Paris, 1939), for a dry, statistical, and chronological summary of the international exhibitions.

29 See Paris, Exposition universelle, 1889, *Rapport général par M. Alfred Picard* (Paris, 1890–1892), I.

30 Raymond Isay, *Panorama des expositions universelles* (Paris, 1937), p. 200.

31 Paris, Exposition universelle, 1889, *Rapport général*, I.

32 Actually, by the end of the twenty-year period, attendance had declined to the point that the city was not eager to possess the tower. A specially organized corporation took over its ownership and management and later realized repeated windfalls with the installation of radio (later television) antennas and the boom in tourism after both World Wars.

33 "Nous avons le droit de proclamer bien haut que Paris est la ville sans rivale dans le monde. Au-dessus de ses rues, de ses boulevards élargis, le long de ses quais admirables, du milieu de ses magnifiques promenades, surgissent les plus nobles monuments que le génie humain ait enfantés. L'Italie, l'Allemagne, les Flandres, si fières à juste titre de leur héritage artistique, ne possèdent rien qui soit comparable au nôtre et de tous les coins de l'univers Paris attire les curiosités et les admirations. Allons-nous donc laisser profaner tout cela? La ville de Paris va-t-elle donc s'associer plus longtemps aux baroques, aux mercantiles imaginations d'un constructeur de machines, pour s'enlaidir irréparablement et se déshonorer? Car la tour Eiffel . . . c'est, n'en doutez pas, le déshonneur de Paris. Enfin, lorsque les étrangers viendront visiter notre Exposition, ils s'écrieront étonnés: "Quoi? C'est cette horreur que les Français ont trouvée pour nous donner une idée de leur goût si fort vanté?" Ils auront raison de se moquer de nous, parce que le Paris des gothiques sublimes . . . sera devenu le Paris de M. Eiffel.

Il suffit d'ailleurs . . . de se figurer un instant un tour vertigineusement ridicule, dominant Paris, ainsi qu'une noire et gigantesque cheminée d'usine, écrasant de sa masse barbare, Notre-Dame, la Saint-Chapelle, le Tour Saint-Jacques, le Louvre, le dôme des Invalides, l'Arc-de-Triomphe, tous nos monuments humiliés, toutes nos architectures rapetissées, qui disparaîtront dans ce rêve stupéfiant. Et pendant vingt ans, nous verrons s'allonger sur ville entière, frémissant encore du génie de tant de siècles, nous verrons s'allonger comme une tache d'encre l'ombre odieuse de l'odieuse colonne de tôle boulonnée." The full text of a public protest signed by these men and others is available in Paris, 1889, *Rapport général*, II, pp. 268–9. The official report omits the names of the signers, which were obtained from Isay, *Panorama*, p. 192.

34 ". . . cet incomparable carré de sable qu'on appelle le Champ de Mars, si digne d'inspirer les poètes et de séduire les paysagistes." Lockroy quoted in Isay, *Panorama*, p. 192.

35 Paul Dupays, *Vie prestigieuse des expositions historiques* (Paris, 1939), p. 82.

36 See France, Third Republic, Ministère du commerce, de l'industrie et des colonies; Exposition universelle internationale de 1889 à Paris: Rapports du jury international, Classe 19—Cristaux, verrerie et vitraux, *Rapport du M. de Luynes, Président du jury* (Paris, 1891), pp. 24–33.

37 A. Morillon, "Les résultats de l'Exposition," *Correspondant*, CLVII, No. 5 (December 10, 1889), p. 801.

38 *Ibid.*, p. 807.

39 "Le dernier coup de cannon de la Tour Eiffel," *L'Illustration*, November 9, 1889, p. 412.

40 "A travers l'Exposition," IX, "Derniers remarques," *Revue des Deux Mondes*, XCVI (November, 1889), p. 195.

41 Morillon, "Les résultats," p. 792.

42 See Alfred Neymark, *Ce que la France a gagné à l'Exposition de 1889* (Paris, 1889), p. 18.

43 ". . . une impression grandiose, un élargissement de l'esprit, à tout le moins une sensation de plaisir et d'allégement. Chaque gramme du fer qui compose cette masse est déjà payé par une bonne minute pour un être humain. N'est-ce pas là une utilité qui en vaut bien d'autres?

. . . un des phénomènes les plus intéressants dans l'Exposition, la transformation des moyens architectoniques, la substitution du fer à la pierre, l'effort de ce métal pour chercher sa forme de beauté. L'étude de l'art nouveau qu'on voit poindre viendra à son heure, quand nous visiterons la galerie des machines; mais la Tour est le témoin de son avènement. Elle symbolise en outre un autre caractère dominant de l'Exposition, la recherche de tout ce qui peut faciliter les communications, accélérer les échanges et la fusion des races. . . .

Vieilles tours abandonnés, on ne vous écoute plus. Ne voyez-vous pas que le monde a changé de pôle et qu'il tourne maintenant sur mon axe de fer? Je représente la force universelle, disciplinée par le calcul. La pensée humaine court le long de mes membres. J'ai le front ceint d'éclairs, dérobés aux sources de la lumière. Vous étiez l'ignorance, je suis la science. Vous teniez l'homme esclave, je le fais libre. Je sais le secret des prodigues qui terrifiaient vos fidèles. Mon pouvoir illimité refera l'univers et trouvera ici-bas votre paradis enfantin. Je n'ai plus besoin de votre Dieu, inventé pour expliquer une création dont je connais les lois. Ces lois me suffisent, elles suffisent aux esprits que j'ai conquis sur vous et qui ne rétrograderont pas." "A travers l'Exposition, I: Aux portes, la Tour," *Revue des Deux Mondes*, XCIV (July 1, 1889), 197–201.

44 Dupays, *Vie prestigieuse*, p. 77.

45 Jacques Chastenet, *La république des républicains, 1879–1893* (*Histoire de la troisième république*, II) (Paris, 1954), p. 241.

46 Morillon, "Les résultats," p. 796.

47 "La France, malade de politique, est allée à l'Exposition comme au remède." *Ibid.*, p. 809.

48 *Ibid.*, p. 806.

Notes to Chapter Two

1 Rondo E. Cameron, "Economic Growth and Stagnation in France, 1815–1914," *Journal of Modern History*, XXX, No. 1 (March 1958), p. 1.

2 Eugene Owen Golob, *The Méline Tariff: French Agriculture and Nationalist Economic Policy* (New York, 1944), p. 9.

3 See Claude Digeon, *La crise allemande de la pensée française (1870–1914)* (Paris, 1959), Chapter IX, "La menace allemande," pp. 451–81.

4 See G. de Bertier de Sauvigny, "Population Movements and Political Changes in Nineteenth-Century France," *Review of Politics*, XIX (January 1957), p. 39.

5 *Ibid.*

6 Cameron, "Economic Growth," p. 4.

7 Subtitle: *Histoire de la population avant 1789 et démographie de la France comparée à celle des autres nations au XIXᵉ siècle, précédé d'une introduction sur la statistique*, 3 vols. (Paris). The lavish bibliographic footnotes for Joseph J. Spengler's *France Faces Depopulation* (Durham, North Carolina, 1938), p. 121ff. demonstrate that Frenchmen were aware of the problem and speculated on it before this time. Spengler believed in 1938 that France was not unique, only advanced; all the other civilized nations would soon experience the same decline and the population problem of the world in the nineteen-sixties would not be overpopulation, but the contrary.

8 Levasseur, *La population*, Vol. III, p. 496. He also wrote that France ". . . twice, by means of her universal expositions of 1878 and 1889, emphatically demonstrated her economic vitality" (III, p. 271).

9 "In the catalogue of *La Librairie Française* the works listed under the heading 'Population,' include four depopulationist works published during the period 1850–1870; 7 in 1873–79; 4 in 1880–89; 14 in 1890–99; 37 in 1901–9; 31 in 1910–14; 12 in 1915–18; 3 in 1920–21. The list is incomplete, for many other works concerned with depopulation are either omitted or included under other headings" (Spengler, Note 5, p. 122).

10 ". . . il est fatal que dans quatorze ans elle aura deux fois plus de conscrits. Alors, ce peuple qui nous haït nous dévorera. Les Allemands le disent, l'impriment et ils le feront." Jacques Bertillon, "Le problème de la dépopulation," *Revue politique et parlementaire*, XIII, No. 36 (June 1897), pp. 538–39. Bertillon established "L'Alliance nationale pour l'accroissement de la population française." Membership was ten francs per year, except for those who had more than three children, who paid only nine francs (*Ibid.*, p. 531).

11 *Ibid.*, p. 540.

12 This article appeared in French in *The New Review*, XVI, No. 92 (January 1897), 99–112.

13 *Ibid.*, p. 100.

14 *Ibid.*, p. 111.

15 Prophetically, Valéry warned that it was Germany that Japan and Italy watched most closely. It was at this time too that many Europeans began to have a new appreciation of Japan's economic and military strength.

16 Later collected and published in 1898 as *Allemagne et France* (Paris, 1898).

17 *Ibid.*, p. 2.

18 *Ibid.*, p. 36.

19 See "Les nouveaux projets [Pan-Germanism]," *Ibid.*, pp. 115–25. Roche was no monomaniac. He believed that internal political mediocrity was making France a laughingstock in the world. He also made some pessimistic (for France) observations on the probable future growth of the United States and Great Britain (*Ibid.*, pp. 281ff.). Another article (anonymous) illustrating the same concerns as Roche's is "La puissance économique de l'Allemagne," *La Revue de Paris*, IV, No. 1 (January 1897), 206–24. Similar observations of Germany's economic strength increased rapidly after 1896. See the bibliographical footnotes in Digeon's chapter cited above.

20 *Le Figaro*, June 26, 1892.

21 The article, which occupied the most important spot on the front page, was signed, "Un Français."

22 See also "Zur Sache der Berliner Weltausstellung," *Allgemeine Zeitung* (Munich), June 16, 1892. The same paper reported that the French were "terrified" that the Germans might want an exposition in 1900.

23 The *Times* (London), July 6, 1892. See also the article "Weltausstellung und Revanchekreig," *Allgemeine Zeitung* (Munich), July 2, 1892. The article said Germany should make the best of the opportunity.

24 However, the political correspondence from Germany to France shows that Ribot had been assured that there was a gulf between the passions of the German journalists and the sobriety of the Chancellor and his officials. See, Ministère des Affaires Étrangères, *Correspondance politique, Allemagne*, Vol. 108. Nos. 10 to 15 (Berlin to Paris, July 2, 1892). The German newspapers appeared to be unaware of the views of their officials. The *Allgemeine Zeitung* of July 9, 1892, saw the French plans as pure chauvinism and a demonstration of hatred for Germany. The *Hamburgischer Correspondent* still felt on July 5, 1892, that France was morally obligated not to interfere with Germany's plans.

25 Maurice Rouvier, then Minister of Commerce, addressed a report to the president of the Republic on November 5, 1884, suggesting that a periodicity of eleven to twelve years be established between expositions. He noted then that 1889, eleven years after 1878, was a date "d'une Hégire chère au patriotisme français." See Alfred Neymark, *Ce que la France a gagné à l'Exposition de 1889* (Paris, 1890). I have found no evidence that a periodicity of eleven years was discussed immediately after 1889. German plans provoked French action in 1892. The periodicity was only a rationalization of French aggressiveness. Plans for 1889 began five years before; earlier expositions had even shorter periods of preparation. Nevertheless, the official report of the Exposition of 1900 claims that as the Exposition of 1889 closed, exhibitors and visitors thought "instinctively" of 1900. See Paris 1900, *Rapport général*, I, p. 7.

26 ". . . de loin en loin comme des sommets d'où nous mesurons le chemin parcouru." Paris, 1900, *Rapport général*, I, pp. 7–10.

27 *Ibid.*, p. 10.

28 The translation was published in *Le Temps*, July 17, 1892.

29 *Le Temps*, July 20, 1892.

30 *Ibid.*, July 22, 1892. Curiously, these approximate closely the French groups that opposed the granting of credits to the French government for the financing of the Exposition of 1900. See the discussions in the Chamber for March 13–17, 1896.

31 Actually, it covered about as much area as Paris under Phillip-Augustus. See Fournier de Flaix, "Mouvement économique et social aux États-Unis: L'Exposition de Chicago," *Économiste français*, April 29, 1893, pp. 519–21.

32 The exposition grounds at Jackson Park were called "The Great White City." Louis Sullivan believed that the overwhelming impact of this romantic revival in America wrecked any chance for the further development of an already nascent American style. The American artistic accomplishment, however, was noted in France. Henri Roujon, Director of Beaux Arts, afterwards, sent S. Bing, noted critic and

art dealer and an initiator (later) of the Art Nouveau movement, on a mission to the United States to report on American art. See S. Bing, *La culture artistique en Amérique* (Paris, 1896).

33 A useful work for this or similar subjects is Frank Monaghan's bibliography, *French Travelers in the United States, 1765–1932* (New York, 1961), originally published in 1931 and supplemented by Samuel J. Marino in the 1961 edition.

34 Aux Etats-Unis, questions économiques et sociales," *Revue de Paris*, II, No. 2 (February 1, 1895), p. 612. See also his "Les congrès de Chicago," *Revue de Paris* II, No. 1 (January 1, 1895), 108–42.

35 Marquis de Chambrun, "Clôture de l'Exposition de Chicago," *Correspondant*, CLXIII, No. 6 (December 10, 1893), p. 875. See also his "Chicago et l'Exposition colombienne," *Correspondant*, CLXIII, No. 3 (August 10, 1893), 429–46. For another eulogy to American material progress, see E. Bruwaert, "Chicago et l'Exposition universelle colombienne," *Tour du Monde*, LXV (April 29–May 13), 257–304.

36 Jules Violle, "L'Exposition de Chicago et la science américaine," *Correspondant*, CXXII, No. 3 (June 1, 1894), p. 580. Violle claims that France was still recovering from the effort of 1889 and was too busy preparing for 1900.

37 See Germany, Reichskommission, Weltausstellung in Chicago, *Amtlicher Bericht über die Weltausstellung in Chicago 1893* (2 vols., Berlin, 1894) and Germany, Reichskommission, Weltausstellung in Chicago, 1893, *Amtlicher Katalog des deutschen Reiches* (Berlin, 1893).

38 Violle, "L'Exposition de Chicago," p. 580.

39 Bruwaert, "Chicago," p. 302.

40 See Comité de souvenir du président Alfred Picard, *Cérémonie d'inauguration de la plaque commémorative de sa naissance* (Paris, 1924).

41 ". . . jamais un homme ait accompli avec plus de sérénité une mission plus rude," Gustave Babin, "L'Exposition de 1900," *La Quinzaine*, VI, No. 125 (January 1, 1900), p. 68.

42 *Ibid.*, p. 20.

43 Paris 1900, *Rapport général*, I, p. 88.

44 The upper level administration of the exposition is explained in detail in Chapter II, "Organisation des services de l'Exposition: Institution de la commission supérieure, Paris, 1900, *Rapport général*, I, 24–46.

45 *Ibid.*, I, p. 247.

46 The first to respond was Serbia. *Ibid.*

47 For a discussion of newspaper opinion in these years, see Chapter VIII, "England or Germany," in E. Malcomb Carrol, *French Public Opinion and Foreign Affairs 1870–1914* (New York, 1931), 162–82.

48 It was first called the "Société amicale des anciens membres du jury de Nice." For detailed histories of the early years of this organization, see "Historique du comité français des expositions à l'étranger," *Annuaire 1912–1913: Comité français des expositions*, 27–63, and Comité français des Expositions et Comité national des expositions colonials, *Cinquantenaire*.

49 "Au point de vue purement commercial et en mettant de côté toute considération morale ou politique, les Expositions sont moins profitables aux exposants de la Puissance qui les organise qu'aux étrangers qui y prennent part. L'Exposition de 1889 a montré au Monde entier la grandeur du génie français, les visiteurs ont apporté en France beaucoup d'argent et elle a été la manifestation la plus grandiose du relèvement moral de notre Pays; mais si elle nous a donné de grands avantages politiques, elle n'a pas procuré à nos exposants les bénéfices qu'en ont retirés certaines Nations étrangères. En effet, la majorité des acheteurs était constituée par l'élément français pour lequel nos Sections présentaient moins d'intérêt au point de vue de l'achat que les Sections étrangères qui devaient disparaître . . ." *Cinquantenaire*, p. 65.

50 "Historique du Comité français, pp. 35–6.

51 For a good account of how this figure was arrived at, and a description of the negotiations leading to the eventual financial agreements in 1895, see Chapter VII, "Combinaison financière pour la réalisation des ressources nécessaires à l'exposition," Paris, 1900, *Rapport général*, I, 164–93. Also France, Ministre du commerce, de l'industrie, des postes et des télégraphes. Exposition universelle de 1900. *Combinaison financière: Rapport du Commissaire général et pièces annexes* (Paris, 1895).

52 Paris would receive any permanent structures built in conjunction with the exposition as a permanent gift once the exposition was finished. In 1878, in a similar arrangement, the city of Paris had received the Palais du Trocadéro.

53 See Paris 1900, *Rapport général*, I, pp. 185–92.

54 "Faut-il faire l'Exposition de 1900?" August 24, 1895.

55 *Ibid.*

56 Ligue lorraine de décentralisation, *Pas d'Exposition en 1900!* (Nancy, 1895), 39 pp.

57 "On peut éviter l'Exposition de 1900," August 2, 1895; "Sur l'Exposition de 1900: Note en réponse à M. Picard," August 24, 1895. However, *Le Figaro* denied any editorial sympathy with the popular writer.

58 Ligue lorraine de décentralisation, p. 7.

59 Louis Brunet in *ibid.*, p. 8.

60 Ligue lorraine de décentralisation, p. 27.

61 Quote from *Bulletin quotidien*, August 28, 1895 in *ibid.*, p. 16.

62 Maurice Barrès, "Sur l'Exposition de 1900: Note en réponse à M. Picard," *Le Figaro*, August 24, 1895.

63 Comité français des expositions et Comité national des expositions coloniales, *Cinquantenaire, 1885–1935* (Asnières, 1935), p. 80.

64 "Les grands inconvénients des foires universelles et la nécessité d'y renoncer," December 7, 1895, 729–31. Leroy-Beaulieu was also, significantly, an early observer of France's demographic weakness vis-à-vis Germany. In 1881 he believed that Germany's increasing economic ascendancy would make the recovery of Alsace-Lorraine impossible. See *L'Économiste français*, May 7, 1881.

65 "Pourquoi des expositions?" CXXXII (December 15, 1895), 888–908.

66 "L'Exposition de 1900," III, Pt. 1 (February 1, 1896), 630–57.

67 See *L'Exposition universelle 1900: Bulletin des Lois, Décrets et Documents officiels relatives à l'Exposition*, February 1896. Also, France, Third Republic, *Journal officiel, Annales de la Chambre des Députés, Débats parlementaires* (Session ordinaire de 1896), March 13, 1896. (Hereafter, *J.O.*, Chamber, and date).

68 "En votant le projet de loi, les Chambres accompliront un acte de haute politique et de patriotisme. L'Exposition de 1900 réveillera les initiatives, ranimera le mouvement des affaires, donnera une impulsion nouvelle à l'industrie et au commerce, assurera une ère de travail aux classes laborieuses, provoquera les inventions et les progrès, constituera un vaste foyer d'études et d'enseignement pour le public, développera notre exportation, affirmera les intentions pacifiques du Gouvernement, attestera une fois de plus le relèvement matériel du pays, et, ce qui vaut mieux encore, ajoutera à sa gloire et à son rayonnement extérieur. Paris et la France entière sortiront grandis de ces assises solonnelles. La République aura clos dignement le XIXᵉ siècle et attesté son désir de rester à l'avant-garde de la civilisation. Paris, 1900, *Rapport général*, I, p. 194.

69 Four favoured the government's plan. These were Henri Lebon, André Lavertujon, Eugène Farjon, and Alphonse Humbert. Méline, Denys Cochin, Georges Berger (not H. Georges Berger, who wrote *Les expositions universelles* [see Bibliography]), and Eugène Chevallier favoured an exposition, but objected to the government's plan, particularly the use of part of the Champs Élysées as exposition grounds. Three, Charles-Philibert de Lasteyrie, Jules Voix, and Bouge, the *rapporteur*, opposed any exposition whatever.

70 *J.O.*, Chamber, March 13, 1896, p. 575. The speaker is Chapuis.

71 *Ibid.*, p. 588. The speaker is Lavertujon.

72 See *L'Exposition universelle 1900*, Nos. 45–46 (February 5–20, 1896), p. 3.

73 The basis of Picard's defence was the report (later published) by Eugène Henard, *L'Exposition de 1900 devant le parlement* (Paris, 1896).

74 *J.O.*, Chamber, March 13, 1896, p. 591.

75 *Ibid.*

76 *Ibid.*, Denys Cochin and Julien Dumas, respectively.

77 *Ibid.*, March 14, 1896, p. 618.

78 "Vous ferez tomber ces médisances en vous groupant autour du Gouvernement. Vous aurez ainsi donné une preuve nouvelle de votre clairvoyance et de votre patriotisme. Vous aurez assuré un triomphe à la France laborieuse et garanti à la République un glorieux avenir." *Ibid.*, p. 623.

79 *Ibid.*, March 16, 1896, p. 628.

80 Letter from Denys Cochin given in full in *ibid.*

81 For corroboration on the determination of the government, see Paris 1900, *Rapport général*, I, pp. 203ff.

82 *J.O.*, Chamber, March 16, 1896, p. 631.

83 *Ibid.*, March 13, 1896, p. 588. The speaker is Lavertujon.

84 A deputy, Charles Rouse, interjected, "Et aussi la sélection des visiteurs!" *Ibid.*, March 16, 1896, p. 640.

85 Jean Jaurès, Alexandre Millerand, René Viviani, Edouard Vaillant, and fifty other socialists, for example, tried to attach an amendment that would require "humane conditions of work." This meant an eight-hour day, union wages where demanded, and inspection of working conditions by workers' delegates. *Ibid.*, March 16, 1896, pp. 645ff.

86 Fabérat closed his defence of the government's project with a "Vive l'Exposition! Vive la République sociale!" Besides applause on the extreme left, he aroused animosity in the Chamber. This excitement led to a confused debate over the wording of the motion to set before the Chamber. *Ibid.*, March 16, 1896.

87 *J.O.*, Chamber, March 17, 1896, p. 677.

88 *J.O.*, Senate, June 12, 1896, p. 41.

89 *Ibid.*

90 *Ibid.*, p. 44.

91 ". . . par des solennités de cette nature qu'un peuple manifeste sa force et imprime la marque ineffaçable de sa grandeur." *Ibid.*, p. 56.

92 March 15, 1896.

93 During the months of May and June 1896, Picard was busy in Paris speaking at banquets and assuring his listeners that the exposition was never in danger. Henri Gautier, editor of *L'Exposition universelle 1900,* also seemed confident that all would go well after the vote of the deputies. See *L'Exposition universelle 1900*, May-June 1896.

94 *J.O.*, Chamber, March 14, 1896.

Notes to Chapter Three

1 Alphonse de Calonne, "L'Exposition de 1900 à Paris: Programme et concours," *Revue des Deux Mondes*, LXIV (January 15, 1895), p. 361.

2 For illustrations of some unsuccessful as well as some successful projects, see *L'Exposition de Paris (1900),* I, pp. 17–18.

3 C'est la lutte de l'art d'école et de l'art d'ingénieur. C'est comme un discours où le langage mathématique serait mêlé aux vieilles formules enguirlandées de la rhétorique classique." Arsène Alexandre, "Le concours pour l'Exposition de 1900," *Le Figaro*, July 9, 1896.

4 Calonne, "L'Exposition de 1900," p. 354.

5 *L'Illustration*, August 14, 1897, p. 122.

6 U.S. Commission to the Paris Exposition, 1900, *Report of the Commissioner-General for the United States to the International Universal Exposition, Paris, 1900* (Washington, 1901), Vol. I, p. 41. Hereafter "U.S. Paris, 1900."

7 *Ibid.*, pp. 30–31.

8 *Ibid.*

9 The United States finally had 337,000 square feet of exhibit space. In 1889 she had had 179,996 square feet. *Ibid.*, p. 35.

10 Japan, Commission impériale à l'Exposition universelle de Paris, 1900, *Catalogue spécial officiel du Japon* (Paris, 1900), p. a.

11 U.S. Paris, 1900, I, p. 37.

12 *Exposition universelle 1900*, May 10, 1898.

13 There was language trouble too. Peck complained later that the railway bills were "rendered in French and after French methods." This caused "infinite trouble and not a little expense." U.S. Paris, I, p. 47.

14 Quoted in Paul Dupays, *Vie prestigieuse des expositions historiques* (Paris, 1939), p. 102.

15 Michel Corday, "La genèse de l'Exposition," *La Revue de Paris*, VI, No. 4 (July 15, 1899), p. 448.

16 Quoted in *L'Exposition universelle 1900*, September 25–October 10, 1899.

17 *Ibid.*

18 "La terreur qu'inspire le fléau causerait peut-être des ravages plus désastreux que le fléau lui-même, et, naturellement exploitée par nos rivaux étrangers, elle risquerait de compromettre le succès de l'Exposition." Quoted in *ibid.*, October 25–November 10, 1899.

19 Gustave Babin, "L'Exposition de 1900," *La Quinzaine*, VI, No. 125 (January 1, 1900), p. 100.

20 Paul Morand, *1900 A.D.*, Translated by Mrs. Romilly Fedden (Paris, 1931), p. 66.

21 U.S. Paris, 1900, pp. 60–62. Though questions about the change in the date arose in the French press, as far as I can tell the reason for the change was never made public in France.

22 *L'Exposition universelle 1900*, February 25–March 10, 1900. See also the issue for January 25–February 10, 1900.

23 See *L'Illustration*, February 10, 1900.

24 *L'Exposition universelle 1900*, January 25–February 10, 1900.

25 See issues of *Le Temps*, March 14 and 29, 1900.

26 Quoted in Dupays, *Vie prestigieuse*, p. 103.

27 Gautier gave these banquets, especially the expensive ones, good coverage. This included the speeches and toasts *verbatim* and reprints of the lavish menus.

28 April 12, 1900.

29 Dupays, *Vie prestigieuse*, p. 103.

30 De Vogüé called it "la salle des harangues et cantates." It of course destroyed the *éclat* of the building which was now divided into three sections: food on one side, agriculture on the other, with the vast Beaux Arts baroque baldachine in the centre.

31 "Ô travail, travail libérateur et sacré, c'est toi qui ennoblis et c'est toi qui consoles. Sous tes pas l'ignorance se dissipe, le mal s'enfuit. Par toi l'Humanité, affranchie des servitudes de la nuit, monte, monte sans cesse vers cette région lumineuse et sereine où doit un jour se réaliser l'idéal et parfait accord de la puissance, de la justice et de la bonté." *Exposition universelle 1900*, April 25, 1900.

32 "La France a voulu apporter une contribution éclatante à l'avènement de la concorde entre les peuples. Elle a conscience de travailler pour le bien du monde, au terme de ce noble siècle dont la victoire sur l'erreur et sur la haine fut, hélas! incomplète, mais qui nous lègue une foi toujours vivace dans le progrès . . . malgré les rudes combats que se livrent les peuples sur le terrain industriel, commercial, économique, ils ne cessent de mettre au premier rang de leurs études les moyens de soulager les souffrances, d'organiser l'assistance, de répandre l'enseignement, de moraliser le travail, d'assurer des ressources à la vieillesse." *Ibid.*

33 ". . . bientôt peut-être nous aurons franchi un stade important dans la lente évolution du travail vers le bonheur, et de l'homme vers l'humanité.

C'est sous les auspices de cette espérance que je déclare ouverte l'Exposition de 1900." *Ibid.*

34 Noted the next day by the *Frankfurter Zeitung*, which also remarked on the naming of the Avenue Nicolas II and the Pont Alexander III, and the prominence of the Russian ambassador in all the ceremonies.

35 For a full description of the opening ceremonies, see *Le Temps* for April 15, 1900.

Notes to Chapter Four

1 Patrick Geddes, "The Closing Exhibition—Paris, 1900," *The Contemporary Review*, LXVIII, No. 419 (November, 1900), p. 655.

2 For maps of the exposition grounds, see Paris, 1900, *Rapport général, Plans généraux*. For a short summary of the areas used in previous expositions see Albert Montheuil, "Les expositions universelles 1855–1900," *L'Illustration*, No. 2753 (February 8, 1896), p. 118. See also the article, "Exhibitions, International" in the 11th edition of the *Encyclopaedia Britannica*.

3 An *attraction* was considered to be somewhat below a *clou* in drawing power.

4 For good discussions of the attractions and restaurants, see *L'Exposition de Paris (1900)* (Paris, 1899–1901, 3 vols.) This was another special periodical devoted to the progress and content of the exposition. However, it was slanted at the prospective tourist and probably got some support from those who had staked money rather than prestige in the exposition.

5 She also exhibited a "Poisson en bronze" in the modern decorative art section.

6 André Gide said her performance "was as fine as Aeschylus." Paul Morand, *1900 A.D.*, translated by Mrs. Romilly Fedden (New York, 1931), p. 95.

7 Adolphe Brisson, "Madame Sadda Yacco," *Scènes et types de l'Exposition* (Paris, 1900).

8 Morand, *1900 A.D.*, p. 89.

9 Paul Dupays, *Vie prestigieuse des expositions historiques* (Paris, 1939), p. 113.

10 Friedrich Naumann, *Ausstellungsbriefe* (Berlin, 1909), p. 80.

11 The Grande Roue stayed in Paris until the First World War, when its huge cars were moved to devastated northern villages to provide emergency housing units. Dupays, *Vie prestigieuse*, p. 116.

12 Raymond Isay, *Panorama des expositions universelles* (Paris, 1937), p. 187. Isay says this is the true image of the Republic in its "young maturity."

13 Naumann, *Ausstellungsbriefe* (p. 99), was struck by France's pushing forward of colonialism in other parts of the exposition as well.

14 See A. Coffignon, "L'Invasion jaune," *L'Exposition de Paris (1900)* (Paris, 1899–1901), II, p. 231.

15 Morand, *1900 A.D.*, pp. 96–97.

16 *Ibid.*, pp. 96–98.

17 Carlton J. H. Hayes, *A Generation of Materialism, 1871–1900* (New York, 1941), p. 335.

18 See Paris, Exposition universelle, 1900, *Rapport général sur les congrès de l'Exposition* par M. de Chasseloup-Laubat (Paris, 1906), 810 pp. Most congresses also published their reports separately.

19 For a summary table with lists of the presidents of the meetings, see Paris, 1900, *Rapport général*, VI 19–22.

20 See *ibid.*, Chapter II, "Concours d'exercices physiques et de sports," 30–67.

21 John Kieran and Arthur Daly, *The Story of the Olympic Games, 776 B.C.–1956 A.D.* (Philadelphia, revised edition, 1957), p. 33. The authors note, however, that even the athletes competing in the track and field events, the core of any Olympic competition, thought they were competing in just part of the exposition. They were informed by inscriptions on their medals that this was the second revival of the Olympics. The next meeting took place in St. Louis at the Exposition of 1904, thus establishing a modern periodicity of four years.

22 See Ministère du commerce, de l'industrie, des postes et des télégraphes, Exposition universelle internationale de 1900, Direction générale de l'exploitation, *Règlements et programmes des concours nationaux et internationaux d'exercices physiques et de sports* (Paris, 1900). See also Concours internationaux d'exercices et de sports, *Rapports*, 2 vols. (Paris, 1901–1902).

23 Competing with teams from ten other nations, Hook and Ladder Company No. 1 of Kansas City won the demonstration of fire-fighting methods. See U.S. Commission to the Paris Exposition, 1900, *Report of the Commissioner General for the United States to the International Universal Exposition, Paris, 1900*, I (Washington, 1901), p. 57.

24 Kieran and Daly, *Olympic Games*, pp. 35–38.

25 One has to read the newspapers or periodicals, official and popular, of the time to gauge the extent to which banquets punctuated political and intellectual intercourse during these years. An American historian of Paris, Roger Shattuck, has given the period an apt name in his *The Banquet Years: The Arts in France 1885–1918* (New York, 1958).

26 "A few old landscapes of Monet, Pisarro and Sisley. Some portraits by Renoir, almost all (except for 'La loge' and the 'Danseuses') half length figures of women. Two paintings, three or four pastels of Dégas, a rare Cézanne or two, something by Berthe Morisot, a Guillemin, a Boudin here and there—and that's all." André Mellerio, *L'Exposition de 1900 et l'Impressionisme* (Paris, 1900), p. 15.

27 The work Rodin showed was grossly contorted, often very roughly finished, and radical even for him. He seemed to be deliberately challenging the slick techniques of the Beaux-Arts masters in 1900. See the catalogue, Arsène Alexandre, *L'Œuvre de Rodin* (Paris, 1900). For Rodin's polemic against the dominant taste in 1900, see the interview "Chez le cabaretier d'Auguste Rodin," Adolphe Brisson, *Scènes et types de l'Exposition* (Paris [ca. 1900]), pp. 131–42.

28 For a penetrating and convincing analysis of the meaning of "art" in nineteenth-century France, see Joseph C. Sloane, *French Painting Between the Past and the Present: Artists, Critics and Traditions, from 1848 to 1870* (Princeton, 1951), pp. 4–6.

29 For a semi-official survey of art in 1900 see *Les beaux arts et les arts decoratifs à l'Exposition universelle de 1900* (Paris, 1900).

30 Morand, *1900 A.D.*, pp. 81–2.

31 *Ibid.*, p. 82.

32 ". . . ces ornamentations banales et ronflantes, mi-Ecole des Beaux-Arts, mi-Kursaal, figures volantes, frontons frisés, pinacles, toutes choses démodées, ridicules, quoique acceptées par le respect de la foule, et qui ne correspondent en rien ni à l'esprit de ce temps, ni à l'emploi des nouvelles ressources de la construction." Arsène Alexandre, "Le concours pour l'Exposition de 1900," *Le Figaro*, July 9, 1896.

33 Les unes ressemblent à des œufs à la coque, d'autres à des nougats, à des madeleines, ou à des crèmes ouvragées au chocolat. Henri Chardon, "L'Exposition de 1900," *Revue de Paris*, III, Pt. 1 (February, 1896), p. 655.

34 ". . . tous les styles se confondent, affreux mélange d'époques ennemies, de matières disparates, amoncellement de fausse pierre, de faux marbre, de faux or, de fer imité et de simili-faïence. . . . L'assyrien y coudoie le rococo, les Propylées de l'Acropole servent de vestibule à des chalets suisses; on sort d'un Alcazar en papier peint pour entrer dans un Trianon de sucre rose." Octave Mirbeau, "Pourquoi des expositions," *Revue des Deux Mondes*, CXXXII (December 15, 1896), pp. 890–1.

35 "Change the inscription and the allegories and you would have a hippodrome or a library." Alexandre, "Le concours pour l'Exposition de 1900," p. 2.

36 See Paris 1900, *Rapport général*, II, 3–13 for descriptive details and more photographs.

37 Gustave Babin, "L'Exposition de 1900," *La Quinzaine*, VI, No. 125 (January 1, 1900), p. 100.

38 Alphonse de Calonne, "L'Exposition de 1900 à Paris, programme et concours," *Revue des Deux Mondes*, January 15, 1895, p. 370.

39 See Jean Lahor, *L'Art nouveau: Son histoire, l'art nouveau étranger à l'Exposition, l'art nouveau du point de vue social* (Paris, 1901).

40 "We should not be dazzled by its present momentary popularity, for this is the product chiefly of our own special ennui, a dissatisfaction with too much that is implacably rational in post-1945 architecture" (John M. Jacobus, book review of Madsen's *Sources of Art Nouveau*, *The Art Bulletin*, XL, No. 4 [December, 1958], p. 373). The secondary literature, most of it recent, is considerable. The best and perhaps definitive survey is Robert Schmutzler's *Art Nouveau* (New York, 1962; first published in German in 1962). Also valuable are Peter Selz and Mildred Constantine

(eds.), *Art Nouveau: Art and Design at the turn of the Century* (New York, 1959) and John Tschudi Madsen, *Sources of Art Nouveau* (New York, 1955). For a long (91 pp.) bibliographical essay and a guess at the reasons for the recent revival of interest in Art Nouveau, see Jost Hermand, *Jugendstil: Ein Forschungsbericht, 1918–1964* (Stuttgart, 1965). Selz and Constantine (eds.), *Art Nouveau*, has useful bibliographies and biographical notes on the artists of the movement. One can also consult James Grady, "A Bibliography of Art Nouveau," *Society of Architectural Historians, Journal*, XIV, No. 2 (May 1955), 18–27.

41 Some historians of the movement might say that mine is too restricted a definition of what might be encompassed by Art Nouveau. John M. Jacobus (review of Madsen, *Sources of Art Nouveau*) would prefer a larger definition and might include Binet's entrance gate as an example of Art Nouveau. In any case it is wrong to attribute the excesses of taste at the exposition to Art Nouveau as have, for example, Morand, Isay, and Dupays. It is incorrect to say that Art Nouveau "dominated" the Exposition of 1900 as has Greta Daniels in her chapter in Selz and Constantine (eds.), *Art Nouveau*.

42 *Salon de l'Art Nouveau, Catalogue premier* (Paris, 1895).

43 Gabriel Mourey, "Round the Exhibition," *The Studio*, XX (1900), p. 170.

44 Max Osborn, "S. Bing's 'Art Nouveau' auf die Welt-Ausstellung," *Deutsche Kunst und Dekoration*, VI (April 1900–Sept. 1900), p. 569.

45 Emile Gallé, "Le pavillon de l'Union centrale des arts décoratifs à l'Exposition universelle" (104–14) and "Le mobilier contemporain" (115–36) in Victor Champier (ed.), *Les industries d'art à l'Exposition universelle de 1900* (Paris, 1902).

46 Isay, *Panorama*, p. 199.

47 See Léonce Bénédite, "René Lalique," in Champier (ed.), *Les industries d'art*, pp. 234–56.

48 Isay, *Panorama*, p. 222.

49 See Lahor, *L'Art nouveau*.

50 For a German critique of taste at the exposition, see Fritz Schumacher, "Die Architektur und die Dekoration auf der Pariser Weltausstellung," in Richard Graul (ed.) *Die Krisis in Kunstgewerbe: Studien über die Wege und Ziele der modernen Richtung* (Leipzig, 1901), 215–37.

51 ". . . l'Allemagne s'est attachée à des recherches décoratives, souvent avec un rare bonheur, dans l'installation des vitrines de ses diverses expositions, ici rappellant qu'elle est la terre classique des gnomes du feu, des petits forgerons à la barbe chenue, aux jambes torses, au capuce pointu, et s'acharnant à tordre et à morteler savamment le métal et produisant des ferronneries dignes des plus beaux jours; plus loin, s'attaquant au bois, l'arquant en courbes simples, le moulurant discrètement, le rehaussant d'applications de bronze ou de cuivre doré d'un riche effet. Et des centres d'art d'un activité intense se révèlent par des productions souvent d'un indiscutable intérêt: Berlin, Munich, Cologne, Hambourg, Dresden, Carlsruhe, Darmstadt, où tous les métiers à la fois sont en faveur, ébénisterie, verrerie, céramique, poterie d'étain, travail de cuir, tapisserie, et où, sous l'égide des princes éclairés ou des sociétés de Mécènes, de véritables écoles s'épanouissent." Gustave Babin, "Vers l'Art Nouveau," in *Après Faillite: Souvenirs de l'Exposition de 1900* (Paris: 1902), pp. 234–5.

52 For a full description of the Finnish pavilion, see G. de Malherbe, *Le pavillon finlandais* (Paris, 1900), 52 pp. See also G. Moynet, "Le pavillon de Finlande," *L'Exposition de Paris (1900)*, II, 235–7.

53 The pavilion was the scene of some demonstrations of sympathy by Frenchmen who admired the Finnish desire for independence. There were far noisier demonstrations for the same reason before the Boer pavilion.

54 See the comments in "La Finlande," by "M.N.," in *L'Illustration*, September 29, 1900, p. 194.

55 "[Ces] grands tournois internationaux . . . un combat courtois, sans mort ni blessure, dans un décor de fête, une lutte de gala, mais où les adversaires mesureront néanmoins leur puissance, leur adresse, leur somptuosité, et s'efforceront même de trouver le défaut de la cuirasse." Michel Corday, "Les étrangers à l'Exposition," *La Revue de Paris*, VI, No. 6 (December 1, 1899), p. 558.

56 Morand, *1900 A.D.*, p. 103.

57 See Great Britain, Paris Exhibition, 1900, Royal Commission, *Report of His Majesty's Commissioners for the Paris International Exhibition 1900*, 2 vols. (London, 1901).

58 See "La Grand Bretagne," *L'Illustration*, October 6, 1900, p. 215.

59 M.N., "Le Pavillon des Etats-Unis," *L'Illustration*, August 4, 1900, p. 69.

60 U.S. Commission to the Paris Exposition, 1900, *Report*, I, p. 60.

61 M.N., "Le Pavillon des Etats-Unis," p. 69.

62 For an original and provocative discussion of the importance of the American exhibits at earlier expositions, see Merle Curti's "America at the World Fairs, 1851–1893," *American Historical Review*, LV, No. 4 (July, 1950), 133–56.

63 For an American guide with photographs not available elsewhere, see James P. Boyd, *The Paris Exposition of 1900* (n.p., 1900), 583 pp.

64 U.S. Commission to the Paris Exposition, 1900, *Report*, I, p. 34.

65 *Ibid.*, p. 52.

66 *Ibid.*, p. 56.

67 *Ibid.*, pp. 65–67.

68 However, the Germans chose to be guests rather than hosts at the expositions. For a statement of the reasons behind heavy German participation see Otto Brandt, "Zur Geschichte und Würdigung der Weltausstellungen," *Zeitschrift für Sozialwissenschaften*, VII (1907), 81–99. For a history of German participation in expositions with valuable citations of relevant German literature, see Alfons Paquet, *Das Ausstellungsproblem in der Volkswirtschaft* (Jena, 1908), 353 pp. See also Wilhelm Gentsch, *Die Weltausstellung in Paris 1900 und ihre Ergebnisse in technisch-wirtschaftlicher Beziehung* (Berlin, 1901), 104 pp.

69 Maurice Normand, "L'Allemagne à L'Exposition," *L'Illustration*, CXVI, No. 2994 (July 14, 1900), p. 24. One German guide book is *Führer durch die Weltausstellung 1900 in Paris* (Leipzig, 1900), 114 pp.

70 Morand, *1900 A.D.*, p. 77.

71 Normand, "L'Allemagne," p. 27.

72 Morand, *1900 A.D.*, p. 78.

73 Normand, "L'Allemagne," p. 24.

74 Geddes, "The Closing Exhibition," p. 664.

75 Germany, Reichskommission für die Weltausstellung in Paris 1900, *Weltausstellung in Paris 1900; Amtlicher Katalog des deutschen Reichs* (Berlin, 1900).

76 Normand, "L'Allemagne," p. 27.

77 See the short biographical note in Peter Selz and Mildred Constantine (eds.), *Art Nouveau*, p. 178. Pankok also designed the smoking room in the German pavilion.

78 Morand, *1900 A.D.*, p. 80, asked, "Against whom are they preparing? Loti said nothing of this."

79 "La défunte Exposition," *La Revue des Deux Mondes*, CLXII (November 15, 1900), p. 395.

80 See Siegfried Giedion, *Space, Time and Architecture: The Growth of a New Tradition* (Cambridge, 3rd ed., 1954), p. 245.

81 ". . . que le vieil esprit gaulois n'est pas mort. . . . Il est encore temps de réparer cet oubli, sinon nous risquons de voir passer en d'autres mains le grand Prix de la Gaieté." *L'Exposition universelle 1900*, June 25, 1900.

82 *Ibid.*, September 25, 1900.

83 For a full description with excellent photographs see *L'Illustration*, September 22, 1900.

84 Gautier wrote that the Banquet des Maires was a "clou historique et patriotique," *L'Exposition universelle 1900*, September 25, 1900.

85 *Ibid.*, September 10, 1900.

86 Quoted in *ibid.*, October 10, 1900.

87 *Ibid.*, November 16, 1900.

88 "C'était fini. L'Exposition de 1900 avait vécu!" *Ibid.*

Notes to Chapter Five

1 "Boycottage par ici, boycottage par là! boycottage partout. Cette répétition du même mot, quelque peu obsédant, à la façon d'une "scie" est la conséquence toute naturelle de l'importance qu'a prise dans la presse une question de haute actualité. Certains publicistes étrangers, mécontents du dénouement de l'Affaire Dreyfus, dont ils ont fait leur affaire à eux, avec un zèle aussi intempérant qu'indiscret, ont entrepris une campagne en règle pour engager leurs compatriotes à mettre la France en pénitence. Si on les écoutait, l'Exposition de 1900 serait privée du concours de l'industrie étrangère et de la présence de plusieurs millions de visiteurs." "Courrier de Paris," *L'Illustration*, No. 2952 (September 23, 1899). I can find no evidence that the word *boycottage* was used in French before September 9, 1899. Robert's *Dictionnaire*

alphabétique et analogique . . . (Paris, 1960) dates the first usage in French by André Gide in 1914. The *Oxford English Dictionary* cites first usage of the English word in 1880.

2 "Nous devons songer, dès maintenant, à justifier les espérances que la France a fait naître chez toutes les nations en les conviant, pour 1900, au solennel rendez-vous de la production du travail et de la paix." Quoted in *L'Exposition universelle 1900*, October 25–November 10, 1898.

3 Paul Morand, *1900 A.D.*, translated by Mrs. Romilly Fedden (New York, 1931), p. 108.

4 See *L'Exposition universelle 1900*, September 25–October 10, 1899.

5 *Ibid.*, August 25–September 25, 1898.

6 *Ibid.*

7 *Ibid.*, January 25, 1898.

8 I shall employ the distinction between "Dreyfusists," and the early militants, and "Dreyfusards," the late-comers, used by Guy Chapman in *The Dreyfus Case: A Reassessment* (London, 1955), p. 10.

9 Edmond Le Roy, "L'Affaire Dreyfus et le commerce parisien."

10 These were later published together in March, 1899 as *L'Affaire Dreyfus à l'étranger* (Paris), and quotations contained in this chapter refer to it.

11 Chéradame (*L'Affaire Dreyfus*, p. 10) said the Dreyfus Affair was producing an effect on literary circles similar to the impact that would result in France were Tolstoy exiled to Siberia.

12 *Ibid.*, p. 15.

13 The best survey of this period is Joseph Reinach's *Rennes* (*Histoire de l'Affaire Dreyfus*, V) (Paris, 1905).

14 The principal sources for the following discussion are seven volumes of dispatches with appropriate newspaper clippings, cartoons, etc., in the Ministry of Foreign Affairs in Paris. All the diplomatic correspondence relating to the Dreyfus Affair, regardless of its origin, is filed under "Germany." The full citation is "Ministère des affaires étrangères, Correspondance politique, Allemagne, Relations avec la France, *Affaire Dreyfus*." Henceforth these volumes will be cited as M.A.E., *Affaire Dreyfus*.

15 M.A.E. *Affaire Dreyfus*, VI, No. 242 (Brussels to Paris, September 12, 1899).

16 *Ibid.*, No. 307 (Hague to Paris, September 15, 1899).

17 *Ibid.*, No. 321 (Württemberg to Paris, September 15, 1899).

18 *Ibid.*, No. 300 (Berlin to Paris, September 15, 1899).

19 *Ibid.*, No. 235 (Berne to Paris, September 12, 1899).

20 *Ibid.*, Nos. 210, 269, 291, 292, 293.

21 *Ibid.*, No. 273 (Stockholm to Paris, September 13, 1899).

22 One can read the supposedly sober *Times* (of London) of these days to learn of the extent to which Englishmen could legitimately use vicious language when discussing France.

23 M.A.E., *Affaire Dreyfus*, VI, No. 283 (London to Paris, September 14, 1899).

24 *Ibid.*, No. 285 (Newcastle to Paris, September 14, 1899).

25 *Ibid.*, No. 217 (Chicago to Paris, September 10, 1899).

26 *New York Times*, September 13, 1899.

27 Various consulates and embassies, M.A.E., *Affaire Dreyfus*, Vols. VI and VII. News was not uniformly so very depressing. More typically, bureaucrats and important political figures urged a "correct" attitude. The Russian press was heavily censored. For the most part, the French diplomatic correspondents in Eastern Europe blamed the public meetings and demonstrations on the Jews.

28 Menaces of a boycott were in the air before September 9, 1899. Rose A. Halperin ("The American Reaction to the Dreyfus Affair" [unpublished M.A. thesis, Columbia, 1941], p. 39) says the first newspaper to suggest a boycott was the *Jewish Messenger* (New York) on February 25, 1898. The point is that all interested foreigners were convinced that Dreyfus was innocent and were stunned when the French judges did not declare him so.

29 *The New York Daily Tribune* of September 11, 1899 felt that a boycott was too severe: "Non-participation would be disastrous to an already weakened country."

30 Halperin, "American Reaction," p. 41.

31 *The Times* (London), September 12, 1899.

32 M.A.E., *Affaire Dreyfus*, VII, No. 68 (Calcutta to Paris, September 27, 1899).

33 September 21, 1899.

34 Significantly, the French-Canadian press was far more understanding of the plight of France at this time. See M.A.E., *Affaire Dreyfus*, VI, No. 274 (Montreal to Paris, September 13, 1899). For a discussion of the Canadian press, both English and French, see also *L'Echo de Paris*, September 14, 1899.

35 *The Times* (London), September 13, 1899. However, Bernhard von Bülow, the German Foreign Minister, wrote on September 12, 1899: "It is delightful to see foreigners promote their campaign against the exposition in Paris." Bülow was cheered that the prestige of France had sunk so low and even gratified that the German journalists were so exercised, since it permitted him to ask for larger military budgets. See Maurice Baumont, *Aux sources de l'Affaire: L'Affaire Dreyfus d'après les archives diplomatiques* (Paris, 1959), p. 266.

36 Patrice Boussel's *L'Affaire Dreyfus et la presse* (Paris, 1960) deals almost entirely with the Affair before September, 1899.

37 For examples of newspaper articles see "Boycottage," *L'Aurore*, September 21, 1899; "Pour l'Exposition," *Les Droits de l'Homme*, September 15, 1899; "L'amnestie, apaisement et progrès," *L'Eclair*, September 16, 1899; "L'Exposition de 1900 et l'Affaire," *Le Figaro*, September 16, 1899 [this painted an especially bleak and alarming picture]; "Boycottage: L'Affaire, les étrangers et l'Exposition," *Le Matin*, September 15, 1899; "Cela leur passera!" *Le Petit Journal*, September 15, 1899; "Boycottage," *Le Siècle*, October 2, 1899; "L'opinion à l'étranger," *Le Temps*, September 14, 1899.

38 See chapter XIII, " 'Le Temps,' journal officieux de la IIIᵉ république," in Raymond Manevy, *La presse de la IIIᵉ république* (Paris, 1955).

39 September 11, 1899.

40 In a speech on August 25, 1899, Loubet said, "Soon the court-martial at Rennes, in perfect independence will give its judgement. The entire nation must adhere to it, for no society can survive without respecting its laws." *Le Temps*, August 26, 1899.

41 There appears to be little doubt of this. See Reinach, *Rennes*, p. 417. During the early part of the trial General de Galliffet had assured the Dreyfusists that all would go well. See also Henri Dutrait-Crozon, *Précis de l'Affaire Dreyfus* (Paris, 1909), p. 377; Ch. Decotay, *Le bilan de l'Affaire* (Paris, 1899), pp. 3–4.

42 See, for example, the letter of Galliffet to Waldeck-Rousseau (Bibliothèque nationale, Département des manuscrits, Nouvelles acquisitions françaises, 24878 [Reinach papers], nos. 203 to 205) of September 8, 1899. By this time Galliffet was less sanguine about the outcome at Rennes. He wrote that, because of the morale of the army, it would be difficult to act if the decision were unanimous or near it, but he recognized that France was fatigued by the struggle and that there must be some kind of a settlement of the agitation "among the ministers, the Dreyfusards, and *abroad* [*l'étranger*. In the original this word is underlined. In the published version in Reinach's *Rennes* pp. 579–81, it is not in italics]."

43 For an example of how closely *Le Temps* and particularly this article of September 11 was observed, see *Le Journal de Genève* for September 12, 1899. The dispatch from Berne to Paris in M.A.E., *Affaire Dreyfus*, VI, Nos. 235–236, for this same day indicates that the article suggesting clemency had had its desired effect. See also the dispatch from Melbourne to Paris, M.A.E., *Affaire Dreyfus*, VII, No. 36, which shows that even the Australians got the hint.

44 Very quickly, however, Clemenceau and Jean Jaurès deplored the apparent closing of the heroic period of the Dreyfus Affair and wanted the unhappy victim to hold out for a declaration of his innocence, believing he had to suffer for France. Reinach says that his own appeals for a pardon as a means of calming opinion abroad finally touched Jaurès and Clemenceau (*Rennes*, p. 547). Even Clemenceau was deeply moved by the bitterness of the attacks on France in the British and German newspapers. See *L'Aurore*, September 14, 1899.

45 These manoeuvres, made difficult by legal objections, offended personalities, strained friendships, and led to broken promises; they are described in detail in Chapter V, "La grâce," in Reinach's *Rennes*.

46 See Abel Combarieu, *Sept ans à l'Elysée avec le Président Emile Loubet: De l'Affaire Dreyfus à la conférence d'Algeciras, 1899–1906* (Paris, 1932), p. 39. Combarieu was Loubet's secretary.

47 Reinach, *Rennes*, p. 549.

48 *Ibid.*, p. 560.

49 On September 13, 1899, Galliffet recommended a pardon to Waldeck-Rousseau because of his fears for Dreyfus' life and as a means of pacifying the nation. He also reminded Waldeck-Rousseau: "We must not forget that the Universal Exposition of 1900 ought to open the new century as an era of peace and labour." Bibliothèque national N.A.F. 24878 (Reinach papers), No. 205.

50 ". . . les passagères querelles n'ont altéré l'âme généreuse et douce de la France, pénétrée de sa mission de progrès et de paix." *Journal officiel de la république française*, XXXI, No. 255 (September 20, 1899), p. 6277.

51 "Il avait calculé qu'on verrait entre les deux faits une correlation étroite. La grâce de Dreyfus devait être la grâce de l'Exposition; menacée de mort par les amis du condamné de Rennes qui, à l'étranger, ont répondu au verdict en criant, Boycottons l'Exposition!" September 20, 1899.

52 *L'Exposition universelle 1900*, No. 128 (September 25, 1900).

53 "Nous tous, publicistes, nationalistes, scellons un marbre mortuaire sur l'Affaire. Qu'elle descende au caveau du traître pour ne plus apparaître dans nos discussions. Organisons le silence sur ce complot permanent de l'étranger." *Le Journal*, September 10, 1899.

54 See also his editorial, "Cela leur passera!" of September 15 and "La peur de l'armée et de la nation," September 17. *Le Petit Journal* had a circulation of 1,500,000. By contrast, *Le Figaro* printed about 80,000 daily. See Raymond Manevy, *La presse de la IIIe République* (Paris, 1955), p. 102.

55 And in a few years his circulation fell to 400,000. See Manevy, p. 102.

56 "Patriotes, offrez à la patrie le sacrifice de vos haines!" No. 19 (October 1, 1899), p. 668.

57 The series, "Notre enquête: La réconciliation nationale," appeared in seven instalments between October 19, 1899 and November 7, 1899.

58 "Engager tous les journalistes et publicistes à cesser d'étourdir et de troubler le public par des questions privées, et tourner les esprits vers les problèmes généraux dont la discussion a toujours fait l'honneur de la France." *Ibid.*, October 19, 1899.

59 "Pour obtenir l'apaisement que vous désirez, que nous désirons tous, je ne connais qu'un moyen: le silence. Ne parlons plus de l'Affaire, dont l'intérêt est d'ailleurs épuisé. La presse peut donner à cet égard le plus utile exemple. Quelle belle occasion aussi, pour notre diplomatie, de remporter une de ces victoires pacifiques et éclatantes qui, en satisfaisant l'orgueil d'un peuple, le guérissent d'un malaise passager!" *Ibid.*, October 23, 1899.

60 Zola, however, wrote (*Ibid.*, October 31, 1899), "Aux deux questions, je réponds: Par la bonté, par la vérité, par la justice."

61 *Ibid.*, November 3, 1899.

62 Clemenceau cursed the editor of *Le Temps* as an "expositioniste." *L'Aurore*, January 1, 1900.

63 Zola, in an open letter to the senators published in *L'Aurore*, May 29, 1900, said, "One dare not speak of the Affair during this armistice of the Exposition. But one can speak of the armistice freely." For an early attack on the policy of verbal evasions, see Félix Depardieu, "Trop d'euphemismes," *Le Siècle*, October 6, 1899.

64 See note 71 below.

65 Clemenceau's writings during the closing phases of the Dreyfus Affair were later assembled in a book called (significantly) *La honte* (Paris, 1903).

66 See "Inauguration," *La Libre Parole*, April 14, 1900. In the same paper the next day the columnist "Gyp" claimed in her article, "Entrrrrrrrez!!!," "Spain, the Boers, Monsieur Loubet, the Dreyfus Affair, Fashoda, and the Exposition are so intertwined that they shall never be disentangled in the future. It was for the Exposition, in order

to shy from complications that might compromise the Exposition, that we were cowardly at Fashoda, forgave Dreyfus, and shunned the Boers."

67 That Dreyfus was legally guilty was also the objection of Picquart, Zola, Reinach, and (naturally) Dreyfus.

68 A few weeks after Rennes "as by enchantment, the Dreyfus Affair disappeared from the diplomatic archives" (Baumont, p. 283). "The announcement of Dreyfus' pardon practically ended all pro-Dreyfus agitation in this country [U.S.A.]" (Halperin, p. 42). The German ambassador in Paris wrote to Berlin on December 4, 1899, "Like the ostrich who, upon noting danger, sticks his head in a tree or under the sand, so the French are sticking their political heads behind the Exposition." (Münster to Hohenlohe, *Die grosse Politik der europäischen Kabinette, 1871–1914*, Vol. 13, p. 342.) "The period that followed the pardon of Dreyfus was remarkable, to almost all the partisans of the Affair, for its sweet pacification." (Reinach, *La révision*, p. 1.)

69 This was suggested in *Le Matin* of September 17, 1899. See also "La détente," *Le Figaro*, September 21, 1899.

70 "On ne voit pas bien les interpellateurs professionnels de la Chambre réclamant du gouvernement la mise en train de la machine judiciaire au moment de l'Exposition, et la Chambre s'associant à leur manœuvre. Qui sait? Après l'Exposition personne peut-être ne voudra plus entendre parler de ces querelles pour des choses aussi inutiles et aussi lointaines." March 19, 1900.

71 ". . . nous avons nous-mêmes offert l'armistice pour toute la durée de cette grande fête du Travail et de la Paix qui est l'Exposition universelle. La parole une fois donnée, dans un intérêt patriotique, nous la tiendrons. Nous ne laisserons prescrire aucune de nos revendications; mais cette fête que la France offre au monde, non, nous ne la troublerons pas!" This speech was later published as "A Digne, Discours prononcé 24 avril 1900, au banquet de la Ligue française pour la défense des droits de l'homme et du citoyen," in *Les blés d'hiver* (Paris, 1901), pp. 230–6. For a similar contemporaneous statement by a passionate anti-Dreyfusard, see Ernest Judet, "La trêve de six mois," *Le Petit Journal*, April 13, 1900.

72 ". . . d'inviter le Gouvernement à s'opposer énergiquement à la reprise de l'affaire, de quelque côté qu'elle vienne." *Journal officiel*, Debates of the Chamber of Deputies, May 22, 1900.

73 The progress toward amnesty is covered well in Chapter I, "L'Amnestie" of Reinach's *La révision*, Reinach claims: "But so compelling were the moral objections which they [the militant Dreyfusists] represented, that it took Waldeck-Rousseau more than a year to pass the complete amnesty." *La révision*, p. 28.

74 *La vérité en marche* (Paris, 1901), p. 204.

75 See the indignant open letter of Georges Picquart to Waldeck-Rousseau in *Le Siècle*, November 14, 1900: "True appeasement can only be obtained by the regular and impartial march of justice. . . ." Zola's plea throughout the period of effacing the ugly traces of the Affair was also for justice. See parts of his speech of March 13, 1900, before a senatorial commission planning the amnesty. These were later published in Reinach's *Les blés d'hiver*, pp. 220 ff.

76 "Fatigué d'émotion, on escomptait le plaisir et le gain. Cette politique de l'Exposition, comme on l'appela, n'était pas très noble, mais ces sortes de réactions se

sont toujours produites au lendemain des grandes fièvres publiques et elles font partie de l'hygiène nécessaire au rétablissement de la santé." Reinach, *La révision*, p. 34.

77 Charles Seignobos, *L'Evolution de la IIIᵉ république* (Ernest Lavisse [ed.], *Histoire de la France contemporaine*, VIII) (Paris, 1922), p. 219.

78 François Goguel. *La politique des partis sous la IIIᵉ république* (Paris, 1946), p. 124.

79 "L'année 1900 allait être celle du retour au calme. Comme celle de 1878 après le 16 mai, comme celle de 1889 après le Boulangisme, l'Exposition universelle devait puissamment contribuer à l'apaisement des esprits." *Ibid.* Elsewhere Goguel has stated that in the later stages of the Dreyfus Affair the republic was in danger and the republicans knew it. See his *La vie politique et les partis en France* (Paris, n.d.), p. 37.

80 "La République s'amuse. Jamais on ne fut si gai dans les ministères. On festive, on se donne la comédie. Ce ne sont que trétaux. Des révolutionnaires découvrent qu'il y a dans l'ordre social des causes de joie, et ils en font part ingénument aux conservateurs . . . Des lampions partout, des éclats de cuivre, des danses. C'est la République qui s'amuse de mourir." *L'Aurore*, June 29, 1900.

Notes to Chapter Six

1 "Courrier de Paris," *L'Illustration*, September 29, 1900, p. 190.

2 *L'Exposition universelle 1900*, October 2, 1900, pp. 3.

3 Louis Joubert, "Fin de rêve, l'Exposition universelle de 1900," *Correspondant*, CCI, No. 4 (November 25, 1900), p. 779.

4 ". . . si les Américains et les Espagnols n'avaient pas dépensé leurs millions à s'entretuer, si les Anglais, au lieu d'envoyer cent cinquante mille hommes de troupe au Transvaal, les avaient gardés chez eux, si le roi d'Italie au lieu de tomber sous la balle de Bresci, était venu, comme il en avait intention, visiter l'Exposition et ouvrir la marche des souverains vers Paris, si les Chinois . . . si la peste . . . etc., etc. . . . [sic]" *L'Exposition universelle 1900*, September 10, 1900.

5 Charles Gide, "La liquidation de l'Exposition universelle," *Revue d'économie politique*, XV, No. 6 (June 1901), p. 674.

6 *Ibid.*

7 *Ibid.*

8 *Ibid.*

9 If one does not consider the subsidies totalling 25 million francs in 1889, the exposition's profit becomes a loss of 17 million francs. Similarly the exposition of 1878 lost 38 million, the one in 1867, 8 million and the exposition of 1855, 9 million francs. See Gide, "La liquidation," pp. 675-6. Though he opposed expositions (as Gide did not), the analysis of Joubert, "Fin de rêve," is very similar.

10 Gide, "La liquidation," p. 677.

11 *Ibid.*

12 See Georges Gérault, *Les expositions universelles envisagées au point de vue de leurs résultats économiques* (Paris, 1902).

13 "L'Exposition nous a malheureusement laissé une énorme quantité d'individus venus des quatre coins de la France et de l'Eroupe. Maintenant ils n'ont plus aucun moyen d'existence. Parmi ses parias, les uns ne sont que de pauvres miséreux, de pitoyables vagabonds; mais il y a les autres! Et les autres, le plus souvent, sont des bandits, des cambrioleurs, et des voleurs, ou—ce qui est pis encore—des souteneurs!" Quoted in *ibid.*, p. 15.

14 H. Georges Berger, *Les expositions universelles internationales (leur passé, leur rôle actuel, leur avenir)* (Paris, 1901), pp. 128ff.

15 This is the principal thesis of Gérault, *Les expositions universelles*. The argument was first and most vigorously stated in the pamphlet by the Ligue lorraine de décentralisation, *Pas d'Exposition en 1900!* (Nancy, 1895).

16 The best statement favouring French expositions is Adolphe Demy, *Essai historique sur les expositions universelles de Paris* (Paris, 1907).

17 See the extremely detailed analysis of attendance statistics in Paris, 1900, *Rapport général, Pièces annexes*, pp. 867–83.

18 Thus a critic of the administration was unjust when he objected that the so-called socialist Minister of Commerce permitted only one free day for the workers (November 7). By that time the low price of the *bons* made entry nearly free anyway. See Louis Joubert. "Fin de rêve," p. 775.

19 *Ausstellungsbriefe* (Berlin, 1909), p. 95.

20 H. Stuart Hughes, *Consciousness and Society* (New York, 1958), p. 34.

21 Patrick Geddes, "The Closing Exhibition—Paris 1900," *The Contemporary Review*, LXXVIII, No. 419 (November, 1900), pp. 656–7. See also his *Industrial Exhibitions and Modern Progress* (Edinburgh, 1887).

22 See his curious description and advocacy of Elisée Reclus's project for a "Great Globe—a literal temple of the Earth Mother . . . to have represented her image in true relief with an unparalleled magnitude and completeness . . . with a similarly vast and comprehensive pageant of world history." *Ibid.*, pp. 663–4.

23 *Ibid.*, pp. 654–5.

24 "In the grey political landscape of the Wilhelmian era . . . one figure alone caught the imagination of the younger scholars. Pastor Friedrich Naumann was . . . a personal force, a man of rectitude and social vision, he drew into his orbit men like Weber and Meinecke . . ." Hughes, *Consciousness and Society*, p. 48.

25 Naumann, *Ausstellungsbriefe*, p. 90.

26 *Ibid.*, p. 70.

27 "La belle féerie va s'évanouir. Il ne restera [que] l'admirable preuve de force que la France s'est donnée à elle-même, qu'elle a donnée au monde. L'Europe est unanime à saluer notre triomphe. Remercions tant d'ouvriers dévoués qui l'ont fait, depuis ceux qui en furent l'âme jusqu-aux plus humbles bras. . . . des étrangers, nos hôtes pour la première fois depuis vingt ans, il nous revenait ce sentiment de vie et de fierté que dut éprouver Lazare en remontant du tombeau." Eugène Melchior de

Vogüé, "A travers l'Exposition, IX, Derniers remarques," *Revue des Deux Mondes*, XCVI (November 1, 1889), p. 195.

28 Eugène Melchior de Vogüé, "La défunte Exposition," *Revue des Deux Mondes*, CLXII (November 15, 1900), p. 394.

29 ". . . exerce sa fantaisie sur les tissus et les bijoux, sur le meuble, la verrerie, la céramique; il cherche péniblement sa figure et ses lois." *Ibid.*, p. 395.

30 "Le bruit a couru qu'ils avaient offert de fournir à eux seuls toute la force et toute la lumière que réclamaient les services . . . de l'Exposition. Le contrat aurait été proposé; et, comme il y a des symbolistes jusque dans les affaires, ceux-ci auraient reculé devant le symbolisme formidable de ce simple énoncé: Paris recevant des mains allemandes sa force et sa lumière." *Ibid.*

31 *Ibid.*, p. 395. See also ***, "Note sur Japon," *La Revue de Paris*, VII, No. 8 (April 15, 1900), 886–90.

32 ". . . ses hôtes, dans son Exposition jubilaire de l'an 2000, un miroir colossal où ces étrangers ne verraient que la décadence de leurs amuseurs." De Vogüé, "La défunte Exposition," p. 399.

33 Henry Adams, *The Education of Henry Adams: An Autobiography* (Boston, 1918, printed privately 1906), p. 379.

34 Henry Adams, *The Selected Letters of Henry Adams*, ed. Newton Arvin (New York, 1951), November 7, 1900 to John Hay, p. 220.

35 Adams, *The Education of Henry Adams*, p. 380. Also see the whole Chapter XXV, "The Dynamo and the Virgin."

36 Adams, *The Selected Letters of Henry Adams*, p. 220.

37 "Nous avons offert à nos rivaux, Allemands, Anglais, Américains, une occasion unique de manifester leur écrasante supériorité industrielle et commerciale; à peine, sur ce terrain, pouvons-nous revendiquer un succès d'estime." M. Lair, "Après l'Exposition," *Reforme sociale*, XLI (February 1, 1901), p. 234.

38 *Ibid.*, p. 239.

39 "Au seuil d'un siècle. Cosmopolitisme et nationalisme," *Revue des Deux Mondes*, Period 5, I (February 1, 1901), p. 685.

40 De Vogüé, "La défunte Exposition," p. 399.

41 "Ainsi, l'éducation et l'enseignement se plaçaient en tête de la classification: c'est par là que l'homme entre dans la vie; c'est aussi la source de tous les progrès." See Paris 1900, *Rapport général*, I, pp. 56–7.

42 "Après vingt ou trente visites, on avait appris, sans d'ailleurs se l'expliquer, que, pour voir le Japon, il fallait aller successivement au Champ de Mars, à l'Esplanade des Invalides et au Trocadéro;—que la parfumerie confinait au 'fils et tissus,' l'hygiène à la guerre et l'optique au pianos,—que la Grèce était séparée de la Turquie par la Suède, l'Espagne, l'Angleterre, l'Allemagne et les Etats-Unis;—que l'Exposition rétrospective des anciennes corporations de charité se trouvait dans les galeries de l'Alimentation;— qu'il fallait chercher la manufacture de Sèvres parmi les sections étrangères;—que les peignes, les plumeaux et les brosses étaient classés dans les arts décoratifs;—que la baignoire de Marat se trouvait à l'assistance publique et que le

sabre porté par le Premier Consul à Marengo était au troisième étage du pavillon des Eaux et Forêts." Henri Houssaye quoted in Joubert, "Fin de rêve," pp. 777–8.

43 Adams, *Education of Henry Adams,* p. 381.

44 "Ces découvertes, en élargissant notre horizon, mettent aussi en évidence les étroites limites de notre sensibilité." M. Coste, "Impressions de l'Exposition universelle de 1900," *Revue Internationale de Sociologie* (December, 1900), p. 894.

Notes to Conclusion

1 Otto N. Witt, *Pariser Weltaustellungsbriefe* (Berlin, 1900), p. 1.

2 "Historique du Comité français des expositions à l'étranger," *Annuaire 1912–1913: Comité français des expositions,* p. 35.

3 Reprinted in Maurice Isaac, *Les expositions en France et dans le régime international* (Paris, 1928), p. 36.

4 "Historique du Comité français des expositions," p. 58.

5 Issac, *Les expositions,* p. 172.

6 The organizers of Montreal's "Expo '67" have planned a beautiful, educational, and relatively non-commercial world's fair. This noble spectacle is being lavishly subsidized and can be viewed as an affirmation to the world of Canada's economic and cultural vigour as well as a denial of her very real troubles in keeping her bilingual confederation together.

7 "The Closing Exhibition—Paris 1900," *The Contemporary Review,* LXXVIII, No. 419 (November 1900), p. 668.

8 See the excellent discussion in Eugen Weber, *The Nationalist Revival in France, 1905–1914* (Berkeley, 1959), p. 9ff.

9 Characteristically, French demographic worries became more widespread and more frantic after 1900. See the discussion in Chapter 2 and Joseph Spengler, *France Faces Depopulation* (Durham, 1938), pp. 122–4.

10 Quoted by Paul Morand from *L'Aurore, 1900 A.D.,* translated by Mrs. Romilly Fedden (New York, 1931), p. 64.

Index

ACADEMIES, art shows by, 4
Adams, Henry, 114, 117
Albert, Prince Consort of Great Britain, 8, 9
allegory at 1900, 73
aluminium, 13
Americans at 1900. See United States at 1900
anti-Semitism, 26, 159n27
Angkor Wat, 67
Annex at Vincennes in 1900, 34, 63, 81
antisepsis, 13
architecture at 1900: projects for, 45–47, 53; compared with Haussmann's in Paris, 62; surveyed, 71–78; foreign pavilions, 84; gifts to city of Paris, 107; Friedrich Naumann on, 112; mentioned, 57, 58, 63, 64
Argentina, relations with France, 96
Art Nouveau, definitions of, 155n41
Art Nouveau, present popularity of, 154n40
Art Nouveau at 1900: and Pont Alexandre III, 72; De Vogüé on, 113; surveyed, 74–78; mentioned, iv, 64
art at 1900: projects for, 45, 53; division of French and foreign displays, 64; surveyed, 70–78; aims compared with political aims of colonial exhibits, 73; mentioned, 63, 121
Assumptionists, 103
athletics at 1900, 69–70
attendance:
    at 1889, 109
    at 1900: total, iii, 109; projected 38–39; daily, 87; last day, 88
attractions:
    at 1889, 21
    at 1900: surveyed, 64–68; demolition of, 104; Friedrich Naumann on, 112; *Grande roue* and World War I, 152n11
Australia, relations with France, 95
Austria at 1900, 77
automobiles at 1900, 67, 86, 87
awards systems, i, 16

BANK OF FRANCE, gold holdings in 1900, 107
banquets in nineteenth century, 153n25
Banquet des maires. See Banquet of Mayors
Banquet of Mayors:
    at 1889, 22
    at 1900, 86–87, 107
Barrès, Maurice: opposition to 1900, 41–46 *passim*; and end of Dreyfus Affair, 98
Bauhaus, 77
Beaulieu, Paul Leroy. See Leroy-Beaulieu, Paul
Belgium, relations with France, 93; expositions after 1885, 119
Berlin 1834, 7
Bernhardt, Sarah, 65, 76, 152n5
Berthelot, Marcellin, 98
Bessemer process, 16
bicycles at 1900, 67
Bing, Samuel: at 1900, 75–76; at 1893, 146–47n32; mentioned 64, 77
Binet, René, 58, 74, 104
Bismarck, Otto von, 13
Boer War, 88, 89, 106
Bonaparte, Joseph Charles Paul. See Napoléon, Prince
Boucher, Henri, 49
Bouge, Jules, 44, 46, 47–48
Boulanger, General, 18
Boulanger episode: and weakness of republicanism, 18; recovery from, 24, 89, 103; mentioned, 26
Britain. See Great Britain
Brussels:
    1830, 7
    1958, ii, iii, 119
Bülow, Bernhard von, 159n35
businessmen and expositions, iii, 37
businessmen and 1900, 42, 106–7, 110

CALCUTTA 1883–84, 16
Cambon, Jules, 56
Cambon, Paul, 94
Canada, relations with France, 94, 95, 159n34
Caprivi, Count Georg-Leon, 31
Cassatt, Mary, 75
Catholics and Dreyfus Affair, 103

Carrière, Commandant, 97
Chapuis, Gustave, 102
Chéradame, André, 92, 93
Chicago 1893. *See* exposition and date
classification systems: and nineteenth century expositions, ii; at 1806, 5; at 1834, 6; at 1855, 11; at 1867, 116; at 1878, 14; at 1900, 115–16
Clemenceau, Georges: and Panama scandal, 25; as early Dreyfusist, 92; reaction to news from Rennes, 96; regrets consent to Dreyfus' pardon, 99–100; on end of Dreyfus Affair, 103, 160n44
closing ceremonies at 1900, 88
colonial exhibits: French pride in, 29; at 1849, 7; at 1889, 17, 22; at 1900, 66–67, 88, 153n13
Colonna, Eugène, 75
Comité français des expositions à l'étranger (C.F.E.E.), vi, 37–38, 118–19
"Commission des fêtes de l'exposition," 84–87
congresses, international: and nineteenth century expositions, ii; at 1878, 14; at 1889, 21; at 1893, 33; at 1900, 68–69, 111
Crane, Walter, 75
Creusot, 83
Crystal Palace Exhibition of 1851. *See* Exposition of 1851 (London)

DANCE AT 1900, 65–66
David, Jacques Louis, 5
decentralist opposition to 1900, 108. *See also* Lorraine Decentralization League
De Feure, Georges, 75, 76
Delcassé, Théophile, 90
demography:
French: surveyed, 27–28; historiography of, 145n7; and fears of Germany, 148n64; concern after 1900, 166n9; mentioned, 25
German, 28–29, 83, 148n64
demolitions before 1900, 45
demolitions after 1900, 104
Denmark, relations with France, 96

Deutschland, model of, 82
de Vogüé, Eugène Melchior, 112–14, 115
Dreyfus, Alfred, Chapter 5 *passim*, 105
Dreyfus, Mme Lucie, 96
Dreyfus Affair: *See* Chapter 5; mentioned, i. iii, 119
Drumont, Edouard, 96, 100
Dublin, 1853, 9–10
Dupuy, Charles, 90

ECLECTICISM AT 1900, 71–74, 154n35
Ecole des Beaux Arts at 1900, 53, 70, 72
economics and 1900, 107–108
Egypt, relations with France, 94
Eiffel, Gustave, 19–20, 23, 25
Eiffel Tower: first debate over, 18–20; as symbol at 1889, 22–23; opposition to 1n 1895–96, 47; painted for 1900, 66; after 1900, 143n32; mentioned, 54, 88, 112
elections:
of 1889, 24, 103
(municipal) of 1900, 103
Electricity:
at 1878, 14
at 1889, 21
at 1900: extended use of, 68; Germans and, 82, 112, 113, 114; mentioned, 111
engineering at 1900, 67–68, 111
England. *See* Great Britain
exhibitions. *See* Expositions
exhibition of. . . . *See* Expositions
Exposition
of the year VI (Paris), 4–5
of 1797 (Paris), 4
of 1798 (Paris), 4–5
of 1801 (Paris), 5
of 1804 (Paris), 5
of 1806 (Paris), 5
of 1819 (Paris), 6
of 1820 (Ghent), 7
of 1823 (Paris), 6
of 1824 (Tournai), 7
of 1825 (Haarlem), 7
of 1827 (Paris), 6
of 1830 (Brussels), 7
of 1834 (Paris), 6, 7
of 1834 (Berlin), 7

of 1839 (Paris), 6
of 1844 (Paris), 6
of 1849 (Paris), 7, 8–9
of 1851 (London): best remembered
world's fair, v; surveyed, 8–10; impact in nineteenth century, 16: architecture at, 72; spirit of in year 1900, 111; incentive to internationalism, 121
of 1853 (Dublin), 9–10
of 1853 (New York), 9
of 1854 (Munich), 10
of 1855 (Paris): surveyed, 10–12; as part of Napoleon III's policy, 14, 89; finances, 163n9; mentioned, 17, 40, 118
of 1862 (London), v, 16, 142n27
of 1867 (Paris): surveyed, 12–14; as part of Napoleon III's policy, 14, 89; Russia at, 78; finances, 15, 163n9; mentioned, 17, 40, 43, 49, 52, 118
of 1873 (Vienna), v, 16
of 1876 (Philadelphia), v, 16
of 1878 (Paris): surveyed, 14–16; and Franco-Prussian war, 41; and sixteenth of May crisis, 89, 103; architecture, 148n52; finances, 163n9; mentioned, 17, 18, 52, 145n8
of 1878–79 (Sydney), 16
of 1880–81 (Melbourne), 16
of 1883–84 (Calcutta), 16
of 1889 (Paris): as competitor of 1900, v; surveyed, 17–24; success of, 38; centenary of Revolution, 41; economic effects of, 42; delayed closing, 87; and Boulanger episode, 89, 103; Naumann on, 112; U.S. at, 150n9; finances, 163n9; mentioned, 25, 45, 47, 48, 52, 55, 45n8
of 1891 (Moscow), 16, 37
of 1893 (Chicago): importance in history of American Middle West, vi; surveyed, 33–34; and German policy towards expositions, 37, 82; impact on U.S. pavilion at 1900, 80; compared with 1900, 114; architecture, 146–47n32; mentioned, v, 31, 47
of 1897 (Brussels), 38, 54
of 1900 (projected, only, for Berlin), 29–33 *passim*, 146n22

of 1904 (St. Louis), 119
of 1937 (Paris), 119
of 1958 (Brussels), ii, iii, 119
of 1962 (Seattle), 119
of 1964–65 (New York), iii, 119
of 1967 (Montreal), 166n6
expositions, ancient, 3; mediaeval, 3

FAIRS, ANCIENT, 3; mediaeval, 3
Fashoda crisis of 1898, 89–90
Faure, Félix, 90
festivals at 1900, 84–87
Feure, Georges de, 75, 76
Finland at 1900, 77–78, 156n63
finances:
    at 1889, 17, 109
    at 1900: preparations, 38–39; subsidies, 44; Picard defends, 47; preliminary grants, 52; results, 106–108, 109
flower festival at 1900, 86
foreign participation, French proposals for in 1834, 7; in 1848, 7
foreign participation at 1900, 35–36, 48, 49
foreign trade, French, and 1900, 108
Fourth of July at 1900, 81
franc, compared with dollar, xiv
Franco-Prussian war, 14, 42
Freycinet, Charles, 50, 116
Fuller, Loie, 65, 74

GAILLARD, EUGÈNE, 75
Galerie des machines of 1889, 20–21, 54, 151n30
Gallé, Emile, 21, 75, 76
Gallifet, Marquis de, 90, 97, 160n42
Garnier, Charles, 46
Gautier, Henri: introduced, 51; mentioned, 54, 84, 87, 88, 91, 93
Geddes, Patrick, 111, 120
Germany, participation at 1900: compared with 1878 and 1889, 36; counters *Bier und Wurst* image, 66; technical supremacy, 68; "Jugendstil," 76–77; surveyed, 82–83; subsidies, 91, 118; tourists, 105; impact upon French, 112; Vogüé on, 113;

Adams on, 114; triumph, 121; mentioned, 56, 115
Germany, art schools, 77
  economics, 28–29
  watched by Italy and Japan, 145n15
  policy toward expositions, 37, 82, 156n68
  relations with France: calmness during preparations for 1900, 36; Alsace-Lorraine, 90; during Dreyfus Affair, 94–95; Roche on, 145n19; economics, 148n64; von Bülow on boycott movement, 159n35; mentioned, iv, 92
Ghent 1820, 7
Gide, Charles, 107
government subsidies and expositions, iii
Great Britain:
  at 1900, 56, 80, 88
  relations with France: pressure for boycott, 94–95; Fashoda crisis, 89–90; incidents at 1900, 105; *Times* (of London) and, 158n22; mentioned, 36, 92, 100
Grand Guignol at 1900, 65
Greece at 1900, 84
Greeley, Horace, 9
Grueby of Boston, 76
Guesde, Jules, 49
Guimard, Hector, 76
"Gyp," 161–162n66

HAARLEM 1825, 7
The Hague Peace Conferences, 121
Hamburg-America lines, 82
Haussmann, Georges Eugène, 14
Helios firm of Cologne, 82
Holland. *See* Netherlands
Hungary: at 1900, 77, relations with France, 95

IMPRESSIONISM, 27, 153n26
India, relations with France, 95
industrial displays at 1900, 67–68, 79, 118
industrial displays, early, 4
intellectuals: and 1900, 110–17, 121; French, at end of century, 27
international congresses. *See* Congresses
international exhibitions. *See* expositions

Italy at 1900, 84; relations with France, 94, 96

JAPAN: at 1867, 16
  at 1873, 16
  at 1878, 14
  at 1900: alarm at insufficient space, 56; Sadda Yakko, 65; industrial displays, 84, 113; taste, 121
  expositions after World War II, 119
Jaurès, Jean, 160n44
Java at 1900, 65
jewelry at 1900, 76, 79
Judet, Ernest, 98
"Jugendstil," 77, 83. *See also* Art Nouveau
juries:
  at 1851, 9
  at 1855, 11
  at 1900, 88, 111

KEYNESIAN ECONOMICS, and world's fairs, 108
Kruger, Paul, 87, 88, 105

"LABOUR," history of at 1867, 13
Lafayette, monument to, 81
Lalique, René, 75, 76
Langley, Samuel Pierpont, 114
Lavisse, Ernest, 98
Légion d'honneur, 6
Le Play, Albert, 49
Le Play, Frédéric: and classification system of 1855, 11; exposition of 1867, 12–14; opposes general expositions, 40; mentioned, vi, 48, 112, 118
Leroy-Beaulieu, Paul, 43
Ligue lorraine de décentralisation, 40, 41–51 *passim*, 109
London 1851. *See* Exposition and date
London 1862. *See* Exposition and date
Lorraine Decentralization League and opposition to 1900, 40, 41–51; *passim*, 109
Loubet, Emile: at opening ceremonies for 1900, 60, 61; at Banquet of Mayors at 1900, 86; assiduous fair goer, 87; chosen president, 90; promises to observe the decision at Rennes, 96;

pardons Dreyfus and tours exposition grounds, 97; insists on amnesty for Dreyfus, 100; and Comité français des expositions à l'étranger, 119; mentioned, 59, 81

McCormick Harvester Company, 81
Mackintosh, Charles Rennie, 75
MacMahon, Patrice de, 15–16
Maize Propaganda Association, 81
Massenet, Jules, 60
Medicine at 1900, 69
Melbourne 1880–81, 16
Méline, Jules, 40–41, 44, 48
Méline Tariff of 1892, 26–27
Mercier, General, 97
métro of Paris, 63, 76
Mexico at 1900, 84
Mezières, Alfred, 98
Millerand, Alexandre: at opening of 1900, 60; first socialist to enter European cabinet, 91; threatens resignation, 97; prevents strike in 1900, 107; and Comité français des expositions à l'étranger, 119; mentioned, 59, 100
mining technology at 1900, 67
Mirbeau, Octave, 43
Moltke, Helmut von, 13, 29
Monaco at 1900, 84
Montreal 1967, 166n6
Moscow 1891, 16
movies at 1900, 67
moving electric sidewalk at 1900, 63
Munich 1854, 10
Münster, Count, 32

Nancy and opposition to 1900, 40. See also Lorraine Decentralization League
Napoléon, Louis. See Napoléon III
Napoléon, Prince: made commissioner general of 1855, 10; disillusionment with large expositions, 11, 12, 13; mentioned, 40, 118
Napoléon III, 10, 14, 15
nationalism and exposition of 1900, 120–21
Naumann, Friedrich, 66, 110, 111–12

Netherlands, relations with France, 93–94
Neufchâteau, Francois de, 4–5
newspapers, French, and Dreyfus Affair, 96
New York 1964–65, iii, 119
New York 1853, 9
New Zealand, relations with France, 94
North German Lloyd Lines, 82
Norway, relations with France, 94

Opening ceremonies at 1900, 59–61
opposition to 1900, 39–51
Olympic Games of 1896 (Athens), 69
Olympic Games of 1900, iv, 69–70

Palais de l'Industrie of 1855: described, 10; debate in 1895–96 over, 46–49 *passim*; mentioned, 121
Panama scandal, 25–26, 92, 121
Pankok, Bernard, 83, 157n77
Paris exposition of. . . . See Exposition and date
Paxton, Joseph, 8, 20
Peck, Ferdinand, 55–56, 81
periodicity of French expositions, 17, 146n25
Persia at 1900, 105–106
Peru at 1900, 84
petroleum, 13
phenol, 13
Philadelphia 1876, v, 16
phonograph, 14
photography, 14
Picard, Alfred, commissioner general of 1900: career before 1900, 34; organizing for 1900, 35; relations with other commissioners general, 36–37; and attendance projections, 38–39; defends Government's project, 46–48, 51–54 *passim*; isolated from parliament, 52, firmness in opening 1900 on time, 59; and demands for exhibit space, 63; and classification system for 1900, 116; president of Conseil d'état, 118; and Comité français des expositions à l'étranger, 119; mentioned, 44

Picquart, Colonel Georges, 91, 96, 100
Pissarro, Camille, 75
plague, fears of for 1900, 57–58, 105
Poincaré, Raymond, 99
population. *See* demography
Porte de la Concorde at 1900, 58, 74, 104
Portugal, relations with France, 94, 96
Pre-Raphaelites, 11
Pre-Columbian art, 21
purchasing power, relative, of franc and dollar in 1900, vi

QUAI DES NATIONS. *See* Rue des Nations

"RASTIGNAC," 54, 55
railroad revenue:
  in 1888–89, 107
  in 1899–1900, 107
Reinach, Joseph: reaction to news from Rennes, 96; thought armistice temporary, 99; struggle against amnesties, 102; appeals for pardon for Dreyfus, 160n44
Rennes, trial of Dreyfus at, 93–98 *passim*
restaurants at 1900, 65–66, 106
Ribot, Alexandre, 32
Roche, Jules: on German economics, 29; Minister of Commerce, 31; and decree announcing 1900, 32; and classification scheme for 1900, 116
Rochefort, Henri de, 100
Rodin, Auguste, 71, 75, 154n27
Rookwood Potteries of Cincinnati, 76
Rosenburg of The Hague, 76
Rostand, Edmond, 67
Roujon, Henri, 70
Rousseau, René Waldeck-. *See* Waldeck-Rousseau, René
Royal Society of Arts (London), 4, 8
rubber tires, 14
Rue des Nations at 1900: U.S. demands for space, 55–56; before construction, 57; discussed, 78–84 *passim*; illustration pp. iv, v
Russia at 1900, 60, 77, 78–79
Russia, relations with France: Russian alliance, 49; during Dreyfus Affair, 90, 92; Tsar does not appear at 1900, 106; at opening ceremonies, 152n34

SAARINEN, EERO, 77
Saarinen, Eliel, 77–78
St. Gaudens, Augustus, 121
St. Louis 1904, 119
Saint-Saens, Camille, 60
Sandoz, Roger, 37, 38
Say, Léon, 116
Schneider et Cie., 83
science at 1900: surveyed, 67–68; Germany, 82; Geddes on, 111; and intellectuals, 117
seize mai, 1877, 15–16, 89, 103
Serbia at 1900, 84
Shah of Persia, 105–106
Simon, Jules, 12, 15
Seattle 1962, 119
socialism, French parliamentary, 26
socialists, French, debate over 1900, 49, 150n85, 150n86
socialists at 1900, 69
Sousa, John Phillip, 81
South Africa at 1900, 87–88, 105, 156n53
South American participation at 1889, 18, 21
space allocations at 1900, 55–56
Spain at 1900, 65, 84
Spanish-American war, 90, 106
sport at 1900, 69–70, 153n23
steam turbine at 1900, 67
strikes, 1898–1900, 104
Suez Canal, 23, 121
Sweden at 1900, 84, 105
Sweden, relations with France, 94
Switzerland, relations with France, 94
Sydney 1878–79, 16

TECHNOLOGY AT 1900: discussed, 111, 112; compared with 1889, 113
Tiffany, Louis Comfort, 75, 76
Toulouse-Lautrec, Henri de, 75
Tournai 1824, 7
Trans-Siberian railroad, 79
Trocadéro Palace, 14
Turkey at 1900, 84
Turkey, relations with France, 96
typewriters, 14

UNITED STATES at 1900: disappointment at allotted space, 55; furor over projected Sunday opening, 58, 151n21;

athletes, 69–70, 153n21, 153n23; surveyed, 80–82; industrial superiority, 115; and mechanical ingenuity, 121, space compared with 1889, 150n9; language trouble, 151n13
United States, relations with France: and Spanish-American war, 90; and boycott movement, 94, 95, 100, 159n29
universal expositions. *See* expositions

VALÉRY, PAUL, 28–29
Velde, Henry van de, 75, 77
Victoria and Albert Museum, 9
Vienna 1873, v, 16
Vincennes, annex at in 1900, 34, 63, 81
Vogüé, Eugène Melchior de. *See* de Vogüé, Eugène Melchior

Wagon-Lits Cook, 79
Waldeck-Rousseau, René: forms ministry June 22, 1899, 90; suggests "cooling-off" period after Rennes, 97; works

for amnesty, 100; and Assumptionists, 103
William I of Prussia, 13
William II of Germany, 36, 91, 94
wine festival at 1900, 86
wireless telegraphy at 1900, 113, 117
workers, free day for at 1900, 164n18
"World's Columbian Exposition" 1893 (Chicago). *See* Exposition and date
world's fair. *See* expositions

X-RAYS AT 1900, 67, 117

YAKKO, SADDA, 65, 152n6

ZOLA, EMILE: and hypocrisy of 1900 because of Dreyfus Affair, 100, 102; open letter of Nov. 14, 1900, 162n75; publishes "J'accuse", 92; on pardon of Dreyfus, 161n60
Zollverein exposition (Berlin) 1834, 7
Zorn, Anders, 75

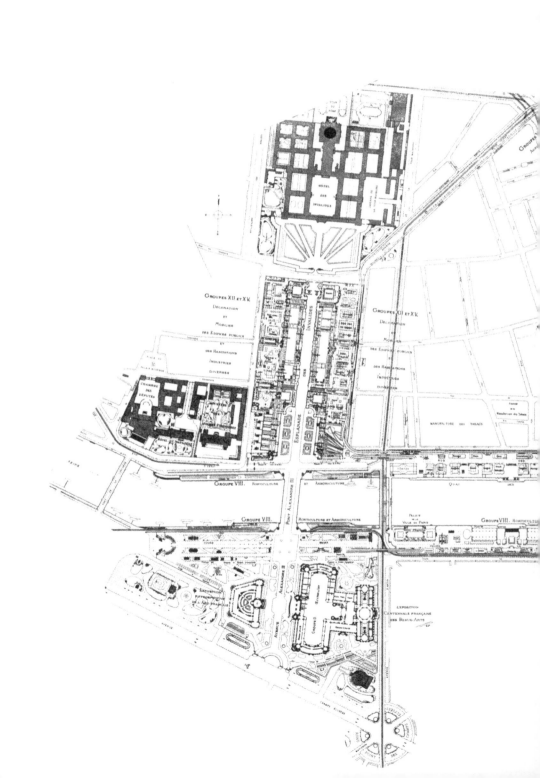

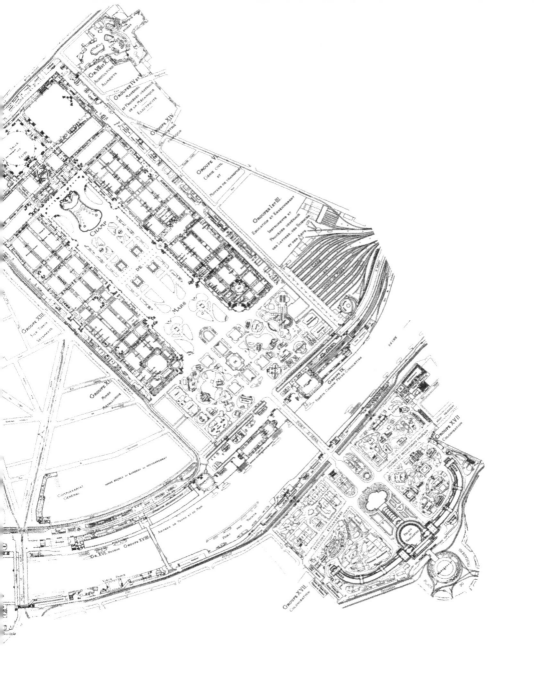